PRAISE FOR *AMERICAN SW.*

"If you want to understand the white power movement in the United States, you must read *American Swastika*. Pete Simi and Robert Futrell draw on their own observations and interviews as well as the work of previous researchers to produce a compelling, well-researched, and comprehensive examination of white power activism. They skillfully tackle the difficult issue of explaining why this movement has persisted in one form or another for so long."—**Betty A. Dobratz**, Iowa State University, coauthor of *White Power, White Pride*

"As liberal activists have pointed out, the Obama presidency has not signaled a new era of racial harmony or quelled racial animosity in America. [The authors] here demonstrate that white supremacy, racial hatred, and white solidarity are still alive and well. Through their revealing and disturbing ethnographic accounts of the activities of white supremacist groups, referred to as the Aryans, the authors argue that white supremacist ideas, identity, and pride are cultivated and disseminated through Aryan 'free spaces.' Aryan homes, parties, white power music, and the Internet create places in which they can reaffirm white power ideology and instill white racial pride in themselves and their families, including their children."—*Library Journal*

"[A] fascinating read. . . . [Pete Simi's] walk on the wild side not only enriched the sociological insights of the book, but inspired vivid, frightening narratives from his time spent walking with some of this country's most fanatically racist people."—*Omaha World-Herald*

VIOLENCE PREVENTION AND POLICY SERIES

This Rowman & Littlefield series publishes new books in the multidisciplinary study of violence. Books are designed to support scientifically based violence prevention programs and widely applicable violence prevention policy. Key topics are juvenile and/or adult community reentry programs, community-based addiction and violence programs, prison violence reduction programs with application in community settings, and school culture and climate studies with recommendations for organizational approaches to school-violence reduction. Studies may combine quantitative and qualitative methods, may be multidisciplinary, or may feature European research if it has a multinational application. The series publishes highly accessible books that offer violence prevention policy as the outcome of scientifically based research, designed for college undergraduates and graduates, community agency leaders, school and community decision makers, and senior government policy makers.

SERIES EDITOR:

Mark S. Fleisher, Director, The Dr. Semi J. and Ruth W. Begun Center for Violence Research Prevention and Education, Case Western Reserve University, 10900 Euclid Avenue, Cleveland, OH 44106-7164 USA, 216-368-2329 or msf10@po.cwru.edu

EDITORIAL BOARD MEMBERS

Devon D. Brewer, Alcohol and Drug Abuse Institute, Seattle and Departments of Anthropology, Psychology & Sociology, University of Washington
Barbara Cromer, M.D., Professor of Pediatrics; Director, Center for Adolescent Health, School of Medicine, Case Western Reserve University, Cleveland OH
G. David Curry, Professor of Criminology and Criminal Justice, U of Missouri-St. Louis
Scott H. Decker, Curators Professor of Criminology and Criminal Justice, University of Missouri-St. Louis
Frieder Dunkel, Ernst-Mintz-Arndt-Universitat Greifswald, Germany
Finn-Aage Esbensen, Chair and E. Desmond Lee Professor of Youth Crime & Violence, Department of Criminology and Criminal Justice, University of Missouri-St. Louis
C. Ronald Huff, School of Social Ecology and Professor, Department of Criminology, Law & Society, University of California, Irvine
James Jacobs, New York University School of Law
Cheryl Lee Maxson, Department of Criminology, Law & Society, University of California, Irvine
James F. Short Jr., Social & Economic Sciences Research Center, Washington State University
Mark I. Singer, Professor of Social Work, Case Western Reserve University, Cleveland OH
Frank van Gemert, RegioPlan Groep (Research Institute), Amsterdam, The Netherlands
Michael L. Walker, Executive Director, Partnership for a Safer Cleveland, OH
Stanley Wasserman, Professor of Psychology, Statistics, and Sociology, and Beckman Institute's Human Perception and Performance, University of Illinois
Neil A. Weiner, Center for the Study of Youth Policy, University of Pennsylvania

BOOKS IN THE SERIES

Gang Cop: The Words and Ways of Officer Paco Domingo, by Malcolm Klein
Measuring Prison Performance: Government Privatization and Accountability, by Gerald G. Gaes, Scott D. Camp, Julianne B. Nelson, and William G. Saylor
European Street Gangs and Troublesome Youth Groups, edited by Scott H. Decker and Frank M. Weerman
Violence and Mental Health in Everyday Life: Prevention and Intervention Strategies for Children and Adolescents, by Daniel J. Flannery
Studying Youth Gangs, edited by James F. Short Jr. and Lorine A. Hughes
Family Abuse and Violence: A Social Problems Perspective, by JoAnn Miller and Dean D. Knudsen
Reducing Youth Gang Violence: The Little Village Gang Project in Chicago, by Irving A. Spergel
American Swastika: Inside the White Power Movement's Hidden Spaces of Hate, by Pete Simi and Robert Futrell

American Swastika

Inside the White Power Movement's Hidden Spaces of Hate

Pete Simi and Robert Futrell

ROWMAN & LITTLEFIELD PUBLISHERS, INC.
Lanham • Boulder • New York • Toronto • Plymouth, UK

Published by Rowman & Littlefield Publishers, Inc.
A wholly owned subsidary of The Rowman & Littlefield Publishing Group, Inc.
4501 Forbes Boulevard, Suite 200, Lanham, Maryland 20706
http://www.rowmanlittlefield.com

Estover Road, Plymouth PL6 7PY, United Kingdom

British Library Cataloguing in Publication Information Available

Library of Congress Cataloging-in-Publication Data

The hardback edition of this book was previously cataloged by the Library of Congress
as follows:

Simi, Pete.
   American swastika : inside the white power movement's hidden spaces of hate / Pete
Simi and Robert Futrell.
      p.   cm.— (Violence prevention and policy)
   Includes bibliographical references and index.
   1. White supremacy movements—United States.   2. Hate groups—United States.
3. Racism—United States.   4. Terrorism—United States.   5. United   States—Race
relations.   I. Futrell, Robert.   II. Title.
E184.A1S599   2010
305.800973—dc22   2009034863

   ISBN: 978-1-4422-0208-5 (cloth : alk. paper)
   ISBN: 978-1-4422-0209-2 (pbk. : alk. paper)
   ISBN: 978-1-4422-0210-8 (electronic)

♾ ™The paper used in this publication meets the minimum requirements of American
National Standard for Information Sciences—Permanence of Paper for Printed Library
Materials, ANSI/NISO Z39.48-1992.

Printed in the United States of America

Contents

Preface to the Paperback Edition

Right-wing activism is on the rise. This activism goes beyond conventional conservative Republican politics to include loose collections of people identifying themselves as militia members, sovereign citizens, anti-immigration activists, white power racists, Patriots, Tea Partiers, Oath Keepers, and Birthers, to name a few. These radicals share a deep distrust in the government and imagine that a shadowy cabal of elites are robbing Americans of their freedom. Their conspiratorial anxieties are rooted in populist worries about racial and ethnic change, immigration, soaring public debt, bank bailouts, a depressed economy, and concerns that left-leaning Barack Obama is using his presidency to turn America into a socialist regime.

The signs of a right-wing rebellion are everywhere. Southern Poverty Law Center analyst Mark Potok observes that,

> Armed men have come to President Obama's speeches bearing signs suggesting that the "tree of liberty" needs to be "watered" with "the blood of tyrants." The Conservative Political Action Conference held this February was cosponsored by groups like the John Birch Society, which believes President Eisenhower was a Communist agent, and Oath Keepers, a Patriot outfit formed last year that suggests, in thinly veiled language, that the government has secret plans to declare martial law and intern patriotic Americans in concentration camps. Politicians pandering to the anti-government right in 37 states have introduced "Tenth Amendment Resolutions," based on the constitutional provision keeping all powers not explicitly given to the federal government with the states. And, at the "A Well Regulated Militia" website, a recent discussion of how to build "clandestine safe houses" to stay clear of the federal government included a conversation about how mass murderers like Timothy McVeigh and Olympics bomber Eric Rudolph were supposedly betrayed at such houses.[1]

Popular media hosts, such as Glen Beck, Ann Coulter, and Rush Limbaugh, broadcast right-wing anger by television and radio to millions of Americans. The largest and most visible ranks of the uprising, the Tea Parties, are peppered with racists, bigots, and nativists. While Tea Party leaders and many members disavow racism in their ranks, racial extremists see the Tea Parties as prime recruiting opportunities and "vehicles to cross over into mainstream American politics."[2] At the National Tea Party Convention, keynote speaker Tom Tancredo, former Colorado Congressman with ties to various white power groups including the Council of Conservative Citizens, VDARE.com, and League of the South, opined that voter literacy tests once used in the racially-segregated South should be reinstituted to prevent outcomes like the election of Barack Obama. Tea Party–endorsed politicians like Sharron Angle, Nevada's Republican candidate for the U.S. Senate, pander to the antigovernment right by openly suggesting armed revolution as a solution to the nation's woes.[3]

The rhetoric of violence runs deep through right-wing politics and extremists are beginning to seize the moment and act on these radical ideas. During the past year, "lone wolf" terrorists have killed at least ten people in incidents that range from the neo-Nazi James von Brunn's attempted massacre at the Holocaust Museum in Washington, D.C., to Scott Roeder's shooting and killing of a Kansas doctor known for performing late-term abortions, to alleged neo-Nazi Richard Poplawski who was arrested for shooting and killing three Pittsburgh police officers in part because he feared losing his gun rights, to Joe Stack, the anti-tax activist who hoped to ignite a war against the federal government by flying his twin airplane into an IRS building in Austin, Texas, killing one person and himself. Other extremists are taking up arms in highly volatile contexts, such as J. T. Ready's U.S. Border Patrol, a recently organized armed border patrol in Arizona with links to the white supremacist National Socialist Movement.[4]

Authorities have also uncovered some violent plots before extremist conspirators have put them into action. Federal authorities indicted members of the Hutaree Militia, a neo-Nazi militia group reportedly stockpiling weapons and bomb-making materials in preparation for attacks on local, state, and federal law enforcement agencies that, according to court documents, "would then serve as a catalyst for a more widespread uprising against the government."[5] The raid on the Hutaree turned up neo-Nazi paraphernalia, including writings by Adolf Hitler and an audio copy of "The Turner Diaries," the white supremacist tome that inspired Timothy McVeigh's 1995 antigovernment bombing of the Alfred P. Murrah Federal Building in Oklahoma City. Members of the Connecticut White Wolves, a neo-Nazi group with a long history of criminal behavior, were recently charged with trafficking weapons to raise funds and further their radical ideology.

Barack Obama has also been directly targeted during this surge of extremism. Neo-Nazis and antigovernment activists have been arrested and charged in plots to assassinate the nation's first black president.[6] One case, which highlights a disturbing trend of extremist members infiltrating the U.S. military, involved Kody Brittingham, a white supremacist and one-time lance corporal in the Marine Corps, who recently received a twenty-year prison sentence for making assassination threats against President Obama during his election campaign.[7] Federal agents also broke up a planned neo-Nazi murder spree to shoot Barack Obama and eighty-eight other blacks and decapitate another fourteen. The numbers eighty-eight and fourteen are symbolic references to Adolf Hitler and the 14 Words mantra popular among white power members.[8]

The emergence of neo-Nazi and paramilitary activism has taken many people by surprise. Commentators give little explanation about where the resurgence of right-wing radicalism is coming from. Media reports recall the vibrant militia movement of the 1990s, but note that it fell apart in the aftermath of the Oklahoma City bombing. This is only part of the story. While many militia members withdrew their participation after that infamous event, the most extreme elements persisted in white power networks that have grown under the radar of most Americans. Their members are now beginning to surface.

The right-wing resurgence is not all that surprising to those of us who have been tracking extremism. For *American Swastika*, we researched white power extremism for more than a decade, interviewing leaders and rank-and-file activists and watching them nurture their violent, paranoid, racist, anti-Semitic, and antigovernment fantasies. During that time we watched white power extremists sustain a potent culture of hatred in seemingly benign settings such as homes, backyard parties, Bible study meetings, bars, music festivals, and on the Internet. We call these settings "Aryan free spaces" because they afford racial extremists opportunities to openly express their radical ideas with likeminded comrades. For the past ten years, extremism and hatred have simmered in Aryan free spaces.

Now the Southern Poverty Law Center estimates that hate groups are at record levels with almost one thousand spread across the U.S. political landscape. "Anti-immigrant vigilante groups soared by nearly 80 percent, adding some 136 new groups during 2009. And . . . so-called 'Patriot' groups—militias and other organizations that see the federal government as part of a plot to impose 'one-world government' on liberty-loving Americans—came roaring back after years out of the limelight."[9]

When extremist ideology endures, so does the potential for extremist action. Our collective ignorance of how the radical right persists is risky. Written off by many observers for the past decade as politically innocuous whackos, they have thrived by concealing their extremism in public while nurturing it in private. Neo-Nazi and paramilitary militia radicals wield potent ideas about violence, dispossession, and hate. We should not be surprised if more of them lash out violently because the inspiration for their violence is anchored in the extremist culture that has been percolating for years. *American Swastika* explains where white power radicals, the most extreme elements of the right-wing surge, sustain their culture of hate.

Acknowledgments

We would like to thank the National Science Foundation; the National Institute of Justice (2006-IJ-CX-0027); the University of Nevada, Las Vegas; and the University of Nebraska, Omaha, for their generous financial support for this project. Although these institutions do not necessarily agree with the opinions expressed in this book, we appreciate their willingness to encourage and assist our research.

We also thank a number of law enforcement agencies who offered invaluable insights into our case through conversations and data on white power activism. These are: Anaheim, CA, Police Department; Costa Mesa, CA, Police Department; Fullerton, CA, Police Department; Huntington Beach, CA, Police Department; La Habra, CA, Police Department; Las Vegas, NV, Metro Police Department; and Orange County, CA, Parole and Probation.

As with any complex project, we owe a lot of gratitude to our colleagues for their camaraderie, advice, and helpful feedback on our research and arguments. This book is much stronger because of your efforts.

Our editors have been invaluable. Mark Fleisher's hard-hitting critiques forced us to clarify our argument and improve our prose. Although we may never fully meet his high standards, we are grateful for his prods and insights. Sarah Stanton and Julia Loy at Rowman & Littlefield also deserve great thanks for their professionalism, enthusiasm, and patience with us.

We thank our friends and families. We are grateful for your love, care, wisdom, and understanding. We could not have completed this book without your support.

Lastly, without the access that our Aryan contacts provided us, we could not have written this book.

1

Hidden Spaces of Aryan Hate

RaHoWa!
(rä-ho-wä, Racial Holy War) Expression of white power solidarity

In the 2008 presidential election, more than 69 million people elected Barack Obama, a forty-seven-year-old son of a white American mother and black Kenyan father, as the forty-fourth president of the United States. President Obama's election symbolizes a crowning achievement in the nation's push toward freedom and integration sought by heroes of equality such as Nobel laureate Martin Luther King Jr.

America's constitutional freedoms also allow people the liberty to speak hatred. "We have to kill the niggers," says Troy, a Southern California neo-Nazi skinhead. "We should just start digging a hole and bulldozing 'em all in! The Jews and spics too! We can't rest till they're all dead 'cause they won't till we are." Troy and others like him believe that the white race is on the verge of extinction and that a conspiracy of Jews who play puppet master to African Americans, Hispanics, and white-race traitors are to blame. For neo-Nazis like Troy, blacks with power represent a travesty. President Obama's election symbolizes how far a white nation has succumbed to the suicidal stupidity of integration. Troy believes that racial and ethnic integration represents no less than white racial genocide.

Troy and his comrades are embedded in a potent culture of racial and anti-Semitic hatred, paranoia, and conspiracy that continues to ferment in American society. They call themselves Aryans, white power, and racial separatists. We know them commonly as white supremacists and neo-Nazis. These racist groups promote the white power movement (WPM), which is based on the ideology that the white race is genetically and culturally superior to all nonwhite races and deserves to rule over them.

Aryans[1] claim that both their genetic lineage and cultural heritage is under attack by race-mixing and intercultural exchange. They draw inspiration and symbols from Hitler and Nazi Germany, Pagan ritualism, Nordic warrior myths, and the Judeo-Christian Bible, which they interpret from a radical, racialist point of view.[2] Members of this subculture imagine that African Americans, Jews, Hispanics, homosexuals, and other nonbelievers are out to destroy them. Aryans are driven by a deep hatred of these groups, but also by pride, camaraderie, and the solidarity they feel toward fellow believers.

Aryans believe they are prosecuting a war to combat the extinction of the white race. Advocates of white power ideology proclaim themselves as race warriors fighting a shadowy cabal of powerful Jewish families they call ZOG, or Zionist Occupied Government, that directs America's culture industry, business, and government with the intent of eradicating the white race. Aryans have committed some of the most violent acts of homegrown terror and hate crime in the history of modern America, brutalizing and killing their racial enemies and those they suspect of supporting them.[3] Many Aryans still plot against their enemies, and they hope to one day awaken the sleeping masses of whites, fight a race war, and retake their rightful position of power.

EXPLAINING ARYAN PERSISTENCE

How is such radical hatred able to persist in modern America? *American Swastika* seeks to provide an answer to this question. We build our explanation from firsthand ethnographic accounts of Aryans' lives. Our goal is to provide a sober explanation of Aryan persistence and inform strategies to counter the threats posed by Aryans and white power ideology. Our discussion exposes how Aryans cling to their extremism even as they are enmeshed in a wider society that vilifies their radical beliefs. Where radical beliefs endure, violent radical action may follow. One factor in the endurance of these beliefs is the role of the hidden social contexts where Aryans gather to privately cultivate racial hatred. We call these contexts Aryan free spaces.

Aryan Free Spaces

Aryan free spaces are settings where white power members meet with one another, openly express their extremist beliefs, and coordinate their activities. The term *free space* is a metaphor social scientists use to describe settings where marginalized groups feel some degree of freedom to express oppositional identities and beliefs that challenge mainstream ideas.[4] Free spaces provide relatively powerless groups opportunities to safely articulate the aggression and hostility they feel toward the powerful.

Free space can be created in real-world physical spaces, such as a corner table in a busy restaurant where political activists quietly discuss plans for a guerilla demonstration, or in small, private, at-home meetings behind locked doors. Free space can also be created for larger gatherings such as backwoods survivalist camps organized on private lands. Likewise, activists may find sanctuary in virtual spaces on the Internet, where they log in to chat rooms, read political writings, listen to movement music, or watch videos that promote their cause. Whether large or small, physical or virtual, the common denominator of free spaces is that participants use them to nurture oppositional identities that challenge prevailing social arrangements and cultural norms.

American Swastika describes how Aryans use free spaces to overcome feelings of isolation and alienation by connecting with other Aryans and immersing themselves in white power culture. Aryan free spaces offer members solidarity, affection, and support for their crude fantasies of a utopian, militant, racially exclusive, all-white world.

Aryan free spaces may take the form of ordinary and benign settings and activities, but the content of the talk, rituals, and symbolism is anchored in white power ideology. For instance, most Aryan homes do not stand out as dens of hatred to neighbors or casual passersby. Outwardly, they tend to blend into their neighborhoods, apartment buildings, and communities. Inside, however, swastikas decorate the walls, white power literature lines the bookshelves, family pictures are full of Aryan symbolism, and mealtime prayers stress white power visions. Aryan homes are refuges from the mainstream world where members escape into a context defined by their white power beliefs.

The groups that meet in Aryan free spaces can vary greatly in size. Small Aryan cadres of a dozen or less may gather under the auspices of informal gatherings such as backyard barbeques, Bible study meetings, weekend campouts, or hiking excursions. Up to 500 Aryans may gather at the bar shows, concerts, and festivals that make up the white power music scene. Thousands of Aryans from around the world meet online through racist websites that promote white power culture. In some private Aryan communities, like Elohim City, Oklahoma, white power advocates are physically walled off from the outside world in order to live their image of a pure Aryan lifestyle.

Stigma, Concealment, and Aryan Survival

Aryans straddle the worlds of white power ideology and the mainstream culture. Aryans detest the mainstream culture as the mainstream detests them. They are abhorred and stigmatized at work, school, and in their neighborhoods where their self-conceived enemies surround them.

Sources of Aryan Stigma

A stigma is a mark of infamy and disgrace.[5] Perhaps the most significant source of Aryan stigma derives from their reverence for Adolf Hitler and Nazi Germany as a model nation-state. Aryan advocacy of racial separatism and white supremacy also valorizes the most bigoted aspects of the Southern Confederacy. White power ideology claims that whites' biological superiority is reflected in their political and cultural superiority as well. Aryans see the mainstream masses who oppose white supremacy as deluded by ZOG conspirators into supporting white genocide. They fantasize about exposing ZOG to the masses of whites and empowering Aryan ideologues.

These Aryan fantasies contradict several trends in modern American society. Since the late 1950s, integrationist policies and multicultural ethics have isolated racial extremists in America and increased the public stigma attached to white power culture and its adherents.[6] Public opinion data indicates strong opposition to overt Aryan extremism in the United States.[7] And fantasies of white genocide and an impending race war have little significance in the lives of most American citizens.[8]

Popular media, government, and human rights organizations all vilify Aryans and white power culture. News accounts of white power activity typically lampoon Aryans as ignorant buffoons and fringe whackos.[9] Government attempts to combat white power groups have been ongoing since the 1960s, when the FBI began the Operation White Hate Group Program.[10] Most recently, human rights organizations, such as the Southern Poverty Law Center, Simon Wiesenthal Center, and the Anti-Defamation League, have challenged white power groups through successful lawsuits against White Aryan Resistance, Aryan Nations, and Imperial Klans of America.[11]

Aryans Hide among Us

Aryans are intensely aware of the stigma attached to their beliefs and the risks of publicly communicating their ideas.[12] Exposure would likely mean loss of employment and possibly the vandalizing and picketing of their homes.[13] Most of the Aryans interviewed for *American Swastika* report such concerns about being shunned, or even surveilled and arrested, if they were to openly voice their extremist beliefs.[14]

In order to avoid constant confrontations they cannot win, Aryans camouflage their identities in public. In our midst, they blend into ordinary life and often pass by us without our recognition. These are not, as popular images have us believe, strident, hostile fanatics who stand out from the crowd and are always ready to fight.[15] In most everyday settings, Aryans are invisible.

To be sure, hate does not always keep a low profile. Racist skinheads (skins) get into brawls with blacks and Hispanics. Klansmen beat racial enemies and white race traitors. Neo-Nazis may go on gay-bashing walkabouts. National Socialists stage intermittent marches and rallies to promote white power. And there will be the spontaneous confrontations that occur on subways, in bars, and on the street. White power groups have also spawned organized crime, murders, and bombings.

But for all the vitriol and valorizing of violence in white power ideology, overt confrontations and organized violence are relatively rare events.[16] James Scott notes that hiding hostility is a rational tactic of marginalized, powerless groups.[17] Only fools fight openly when the deck is so stacked against them. Aryan resistance is a much more prosaic struggle to withstand or counteract the forces they oppose.

While Aryans project an image that hides much about their extremism, they do not see their secrecy as a lack of commitment to white power ideas or acquiescence to anti-Aryan mainstream culture. Rather, they see concealment itself as a form of activism. Concealment is essential for Aryan survival, both for individuals and for the movement. Many white power leaders now explicitly advocate that Aryans limit their public displays of allegiance. When members go to jobs where they work alongside African Americans, attend schools with Jews, live in neighborhoods with Latinos, buy groceries from gays, and ride trains with white race traitors, there should be no hint of hatred for these groups. In these contexts, Aryans play down their extremist identity.[18] They see members "who use overtly racist symbols in public or who adopt an exaggerated racist style as movement novices."[19] By strategically concealing their extremism from outsiders, savvy Aryans prepare themselves for future opportunities to instigate and fight the race war they believe is drawing near.[20]

Aryans use their free spaces to escape from the mainstream and openly celebrate their mutual bigotry and hatred. In these hidden cultural worlds they are able to build the emotional connections that reinforce individual and collective white power identity.[21] Aryans' use of free spaces helps them overcome isolation, despair, and hopelessness, which might otherwise sap their devotion to white power culture.

Hatred and Violence Thrives in Free Spaces

Aryans are not unique in their use of free spaces to sustain a radical worldview. By definition, extremists operate on the margins of society and face repression from those in power. They try to avoid repression by hiding their radical beliefs, blending into the crowd with an appearance of normality. Extremist groups—from al Qaeda in the Middle East or Jemaah Islamiyah in Indonesia to environmental extremists, right-to-life radicals, and racial extremists in the United States—create places of refuge where they meet, find comfort with like-minded comrades, and plot to advance their cause.[22] For such marginalized groups, "the sheer maintenance of a cultural community of activists is the outer limit of what is possible" under some circumstances.[23]

Free spaces shed light on how Aryanism persists and where potential sources of hate violence remain in America. Aryans' low-profile activities typically do not produce the sort of headline-grabbing events that bring attention to their extremism. But we should not confuse a low-profile with a weak and innocuous form of radicalism. Their efforts reproduce a radical cultural milieu filled with ideas about hate and violence. Ideas of violence precede acts of violence, and Aryan free spaces create the contexts for nourishing such ideas. Thus, the potential for radical action persists. Violent Aryan terror remains a constant threat to tolerance and integration in America.

STUDYING ARYAN PERSISTENCE

Gaining access to Aryan free spaces was not easy. Our approach was time-consuming, labor-intensive, and emotionally draining, as we tried to overcome our gut feelings of shock, revulsion, rage, and sadness at the things we saw and heard. Our research goal was to understand Aryans on their own terms in their natural settings. This required listening to them with the discipline to temper our reactions to what our subjects said. It meant repeatedly reading over Aryans' views about the world and taking those views seriously. It was necessary to exclude our own moral and ethical values and assumptions in order to understand and interpret the meaning of Aryans' point of view.

We conducted fieldwork with white power activists and groups between 1996 and 2006. We used a multimethod approach,[24] including interviews, participant observation, and content analysis of white power movement websites and related Aryan literature. Interviews included one- to three-hour, face-to-face and telephone interviews with eighty-nine Aryan activists. Seventeen respondents were group leaders and seventy-two were rank-and-file members. Ninety-four follow-up interviews with primary contacts led to 183 total interviews.[25] Snowball and purposive sampling strategies produced contacts with a wide range of white power networks.[26] Specific organizations represented in the sample include: White Aryan Resistance, Aryan Nations, Hammerskin Nation, National Alliance, and branches of the Ku Klux Klan.

Of the eighty-nine interviewees, sixty-five were male and twenty-four were female. Their ages ranged from eighteen to seventy-eight years. Our informants represent a broad cross section of socioeconomic status found in the movement.[27] The majority described either their current or childhood socioeconomic status as middle class. We confirmed that a sizeable minority worked in mid- to upper-level professional occupations, such as attorney, college instructor, X-ray technician, and so on. Most informants had a high school diploma or the equivalent and a quarter of all informants attended some college.[28]

Our participant observation includes Christian Identity adherents in the southwest and northwest, and a variety of Aryans in Southern California. We made twenty-three house visits with groups in Arizona, Nevada, and Utah. These visits lasted from one to three days and gave us access to a variety of social gatherings, such as parties, Bible study sessions, hikes, and campouts. Additionally, we made four separate three- to five-day visits to the Aryan Nations' former headquarter in Hayden Lake, Idaho, to observe and interview participants at Aryan Nations World Congresses and informal gatherings that Aryans organized outside the official congress proceedings.

Our fieldwork in Southern California included observations of social gatherings and twenty-two stints in activists' homes ranging from two days to five weeks. Our extended involvement in these settings allowed for, among other things, insight into how these Aryans express their racist identity. Our firsthand data are rare among research on Aryan activism.[29]

We organized our data around six primary themes: (1) early childhood experiences (for example, political socialization in the family); (2) educational experiences and peer group socialization; (3) entry into the white power movement; (4) level and type of movement participation; (5) ideological orientation; and (6) identity-maintenance strategies. Our qualitative coding techniques[30] helped us to identify and extract relevant information across our data set.

In the book's chapters, we intersperse analysis with extended descriptive, firsthand observational and interview data. Our observations and interview data give readers insight into the raw experience of being in the settings and the energy and emotion Aryans express as they bond with one another.

Some of the stories described or language used throughout the book may be offensive to readers; it was offensive to us. But omitting it would only serve to soften the positions of the people quoted. We have kept some of the language in to illustrate the intensity of Aryans' feelings. In some instances, we have paraphrased, while in other instances we have let the record speak for itself.

We have disguised names and certain details of our observations to protect the confidentiality of our research subjects. While we present our themes in a systematic and organized way, we do not intend to depict a homogeneous picture of Aryans and their experiences. Our goal is to render an accurate and insightful representation of the enduring culture and organization of contemporary white power activism and the hidden social contexts where hate endures.

PLAN OF THE BOOK

American Swastika provides intricate descriptions of Aryan free spaces to explain how white power ideas are sustained and reproduced. Before turning to those free spaces, chapter 2 discusses the various branches of the white power movement, their specific ideological beliefs, and the common doctrines among the branches that bind diverse Aryans together.

Chapters 3 and 4 focus on Aryan free spaces where small, local cadres of Aryans meet. Chapter 3 describes Aryan homes as free spaces where parents socialize their children into their white power visions. Aryans also use their homes to stage a range of small, informal gatherings, Bible study groups, and ritual parties. Chapter 4 highlights parties, skinhead crashpads, and other Aryan meeting places where activists model their culture of hatred and recruit new members to the cause.

In Chapter 5, we focus on white power music as an organizing resource that draws together Aryans in a range of activities such as concerts, festivals, music websites, streaming radio, fan magazines, and chatrooms. The movement's music scene engages both seasoned activists and new members in activities that promote Aryan style and politics.

Chapter 6 turns to white power activists' use of the Internet to promote their politics. Aryans utilize cyberspace to create strong virtual links between organizations that members use to quickly transmit information about the movement. Aryans also use cyberspace for online social networking and as a gateway to connect in real-world settings.

Chapter 7 describes private white power communities. These Aryan settlements are devoutly racist. They create a pure white space that symbolizes the white supremacist world they seek. The communities house worship centers and white power archives stocked with Aryan literature and movement paraphernalia. The settlements also support paramilitary training and have been the seedbed for the most notorious acts of extremist violence.

White power families, parties, crashpads, music shows, cyberspace, and private communities are the free spaces where Aryan hatred survives. We conclude *American Swastika* by discussing what Aryan persistence means for the future of racial and anti-Semitic hatred and violence in America.

2

Contemporary Aryan Hate

What is the character of Aryan organization and ideology? Observers of white power activity offer two distinct answers to this question. One answer suggests that Aryans are an irrational and disorganized subculture rife with internal conflict.[1] For instance, Mattias Gardell says, "The level of discord, mutual enmity, organizational fragmentation, and ideological division characterizing the world of white racism [is] far too high to be able to speak of a white racist movement in any meaningful way."[2] From this point of view, it appears that ideological schisms threaten to divide Aryans into politically innocuous and fragmented factions. Yet Gardell also affirms, "If there is not a 'movement,' there is still a 'something' that all or most of the different networks, channels of communication, organizations, activists, and tendencies may be seen as parts of."[3] An emphasis on the disorganized aspects of Aryanism obscures its strategic and structured dimensions.

We advocate a second perspective that sees racist activism as "a social movement, a 'family' of overlapping groups organized to spread racist and anti-Semitic ideas and terrorist tactics."[4] To be sure, most Aryan activity does not closely resemble the standard depiction of social movements with traditional, centralized organizations that mobilize insurgents to action. Aryan organization is anchored in fluid, transitory, and informal "submerged networks" that periodically coalesce in Aryan free spaces.[5] But Aryan free spaces require deliberate, calculated organization and sustained commitments among participants to persist. Aryan free spaces are *movement spaces* where white power advocates congregate to reinforce their dedication to the cause and draw others into the ranks of Aryan activism.[6]

The Aryans who connect in free spaces manifest white power ideology in four distinct branches: the Ku Klux Klan, Christian Identity and neo-Pagan racists, neo-Nazis, and racist skinheads. We discuss each of these branches below in some detail, specifying their history and core ideological principles. The ideological and stylistic differences across the branches can be a source of discord and power struggle. But Aryans from across these branches also embrace basic doctrines that transcend their ideological differences and create points of general agreement. We conclude by describing each Aryan branch, their common doctrines, and the solidarity Aryans build with these beliefs.

KU KLUX KLAN

The Ku Klux Klan (KKK) has persisted through several eras of change in America's political climate. A small cadre of young Confederate veterans organized the first Klan group in Pulaski, Tennessee, in 1866. Ku Klux refers to the Greek word *kuklos*, meaning circle or band. Original Klan members conceived of the group as a fraternal order where Confederates could continue to meet after the Civil War.

Klan members quickly developed a doctrine based on the defense of white supremacy in the era of Reconstruction. The KKK's ranks swelled in 1868, and the organization grew more political as Southern whites reacted against black civil rights policies. The Klan expanded from outposts in half a dozen Tennessee counties to multiple groups in nearly every Southern state. Klan activity became violent, and numerous members were implicated in whippings, beatings, and murders of Southern blacks. Klan groups assassinated black Republican politicians and murdered voters during the 1868 election. Allen Trelease estimates that more than 1,000 racial murders occurred in Louisiana alone.[7]

This wave of Klan violence was the impetus for the federal government's adoption of the Civil Rights Act of 1871, then known as the Ku Klux Klan Act. In response, Klan officials formally disbanded to avoid federal sanctions, although many local groups continued to meet regularly.

The KKK reemerged in 1915 when Alabama native William J. Simmons founded the Second Era Klan in Stone Mountain, Georgia. Simmons implored all white Americans to join "The World's Greatest Secret, Social, Patriotic, Fraternal, Beneficiary Order." Simmons emphasized a doctrine of "100% Pure Americanism" to preserve the racial purity of white Anglo-Saxon Protestant Americans. White mobs targeted African American communities across the United States and anti-Semitism flourished as the KKK cast Jews and other "mongrel" groups as "outsiders" who threatened white America's racial integrity.[8]

KKK membership reportedly reached between 2 and 5 million people nationwide by 1925. Such high numbers reflected the extent to which early-twentieth-century Americans accepted the Klan's explicit racist and anti-Semitic views. The KKK also gained political strength and became one of the largest and most powerful political organizations in U.S. history.

Klan-sponsored candidates won U.S. Senate races in Alabama, Colorado, Georgia, Indiana, Oklahoma, and Texas, and in 1924 a Klan-endorsed candidate won the Kansas governorship. Klan membership crossed class lines and included influential Americans, such as Supreme Court Justice Hugo Black and presidents Harry Truman (who resigned after attending one meeting) and Warren Harding. By the late 1920s, however, membership numbers began plummeting as various scandals, including stories of indiscriminate terrorism and brutality, tarnished the Klan's self-righteous image. By the 1930s, the Klan was active in limited areas, such as Florida, where membership topped 30,000.

Klan activism reemerged again in response to civil rights protests in the 1950s and 1960s. Klan members carried out arson and numerous bombings and assassinations, including the murder of three civil rights workers in Philadelphia, Mississippi, in 1964, which became the topic of the motion picture *Mississippi Burning* (1988). Federal authorities responded with Operation White Hate Group, infiltrated Klan organizations, and arrested and prosecuted many leading members in Alabama, Mississippi, and other Southern states.[9]

Government pressure led to a precipitous drop in KKK official membership numbers during the 1970s and 1980s. By the late 1980s most KKK groups were fragmented and in dire financial straits. By 1995, about 60 splintered Klan groups remained in the United States and membership had declined to well below 10,000.[10] However, KKK numbers rose again a decade later. The Southern Poverty Law Center estimates that 143 Klan chapters were active in 2008.[11]

Immigration fears and economic concerns, along with a "new racist discourse"[12] of white victimization and loss of white cultural heritage, have combined to rejuvenate the modern KKK. The Anti-Defamation League asserts that Klan participation has grown over the past decade in several areas where the Klan has not been strong for many years, such as Iowa, as well as traditional Klan strongholds, such as Florida, Louisiana, and Indiana.[13] The largest and most active Klan groups today are the Empire Knights of the Ku Klux Klan, active in eighteen states in the South, Northeast, and Western United States; the Church of the National Knights of the Ku Klux Klan, headquartered in Indiana with chapters in twenty states; and Brotherhood of Klans, with fifteen state chapters.[14]

Today's Klan members are active in the white power scene, organizing events such as Nordic Fest, which draws several hundred Aryans to the heavily guarded, gated compound of the Imperial Klans of America. These events have driven the "Nazification" of the Klan. KKK networks increasingly overlap with neo-Nazi racists, and Klan members are integrating neo-Nazi symbolism and rituals into long-standing KKK traditions. The German swastika has become a familiar symbol at KKK-sponsored gatherings along with the German Iron Cross emblazoned on traditional Klan robes and hoods.

The Klan's greatest impact on the white power movement may be its historic legacy. The Ku Klux Klan has now persisted for more than 140 years. Radical groups in addition to the KKK have emerged in the landscape of racist extremism. The Klan remains a symbol of perseverance alongside these groups and continues to inspire Aryan vigilantism and devotion to white power. We turn next to discuss Christian Identity and neo-Pagan racists, neo-Nazis, and racist skinheads.

CHRISTIAN IDENTITY AND NEO-PAGANISM

Christian Identity and neo-Paganism make up a branch of Aryan extremists anchored in religion and mythology. Christian Identity is a movement that espouses a theological justification for white superiority through interpretations of the Judeo-Christian Bible. Neo-Pagans combine pre-Christian pagan myths with Aryan racist and anti-Semitic ideals.

Christian Identity

Christian Identity believers define nonwhites as evil incarnate and promote racial violence as acts ordained by God. They see blacks, Latinos, Asians, and other nonwhites as lower-order subspecies of "pre-Adamic mudpeople" and, therefore, not fully human.[15] These beliefs are rooted in British Israelism, a nineteenth-century English theology that posits the true Israelites were Anglo-Saxons. Christian Identity adds to this interpretation the notion that Jews are descended from Satan and resulted from Eve's copulation with the serpent. Identity believers imagine they are warriors in a righteous battle against the Jewish conspiracy to eradicate the white race.[16]

Historically, the most prominent Christian Identity group has been Aryan Nations/Church of Jesus Christ Christian, founded by Richard Butler in 1974. Under Butler's leadership, Aryan Nations grew to include chapters in twenty-six states with multiple chapters in Louisiana, New Jersey, and Ohio. Butler hosted a number of annual gatherings on his compound in Hayden Lake, Idaho. The most notorious were the Aryan Nations World Congresses, which brought together members from other white power branches.

Aryan Nations was bankrupted in 2000 when the Southern Poverty Law Center (SPLC) won a $6.3 million lawsuit against Butler. The Aryan Nations compound was transferred to the plantiffs in 2001 and the group splintered following Butler's death in 2004. Now three separate Aryan Nations organizations claim to be the rightful heirs to Butler's legacy. August Kreis leads one faction, currently in Lexington, South Carolina. Kreis is well known among Aryans for advocating an alliance between Islamic jihad and the white power struggle. Jonathon Williams leads the second Aryan Nations faction based in Lincoln, Alabama. Williams holds annual Aryan Nations gatherings that bring WPM activists together from across the country. Both factions are struggling to match the resources, membership, and notoriety Aryan Nations enjoyed under Butler's leadership. In 2009, Jerald O'Brien emerged to lead a third Aryan Nations faction claiming rightful inheritance of Butler's legacy. Located in Coeur d'Alene, Idaho, members have leafleted the Coeur d'Alene area announcing the return of Aryan Nations to Idaho.

Christian Identity also persists in many small, independent cells of believers. Christian Identity members meet in Aryan free spaces such as small Bible study groups, independent churches, and cultural heritage organizations linked by a range of websites devoted to the cause.

Neo-Paganism

Racist neo-Pagans celebrate the ancient pre-Christian, proto-Germanic spiritual traditions of Odinism and its Icelandic cousin, Asatru. Odinism and Asatru share a social Darwinist philosophy that defines the survival of pure whites as a goal to be achieved at all costs.[17]

Racist neo-Pagans draw upon Norse mythology to emphasize the mystical and heroic nature of European folk heritage. Neo-Pagans construct racial consciousness and solidarity around the worship of Odin, the chief Norse god of wisdom; Thor, the Norse god of strength; and Freyja, the Norse goddess of fertility and love.[18]

Racist neo-Pagans see these gods as pure white deities that stand apart from the bastardized spirituality of mainstream Christianity. They also tend to "biologize spirituality" through the belief that their white gods and goddesses are "encoded in the DNA of their descendants."[19] Gardell explains, "Blood is thought to carry memories of the ancient past, and divinities are believed to be genetically engraved upon or reverberate from deep down within the abyss of the collective subconscious or 'folk soul'" of true Aryans.[20]

As they are interspersed throughout the larger Aryan networks of the neo-Nazi and skinhead faithful, neo-Pagans have spread their motifs to other factions of the white power movement. Thus, Aryan websites, racist literature, white power musicians, and racist music lyrics feature "muscular heathens, pagan gods and goddesses, runes and symbols, magic, and esoteric themes in abundance."[21] The warrior imagery appeals to Aryans across all branches because warrior imagery symbolizes the righteous, combatant ideal with which many contemporary Aryans identify. Not all Aryans are devout followers of Pagan rituals and spiritual beliefs, but neo-Paganism provides modern-day Aryans with a collection of symbols, images, and ideals that amplify white power ideology.

NEO-NAZIS

Neo-Nazi networks persist through parties, crashpads, the white power music scene, and the Internet. Neo-Nazis embrace traditional Nazi symbolism, such as the swastika; describe themselves as National Socialists; revere Adolf Hitler and the Third Reich; and promote eugenics to ensure the existence of a pure white race.[22] George Lincoln Rockwell formed one of the earliest versions of neo-Nazis in 1958 with the American Nazi Party (ANP). The ANP popularized Holocaust denial among the American racist right and encouraged followers to join forces with Christian Identity churches.[23]

The National Alliance, White Aryan Resistance, and the National Socialist Movement (NSM) have been three of the most influential sources of American neo-Nazism.[24] William Pierce founded the National Alliance in 1974 after he became involved with Rockwell and the American Nazi Party during the 1960s. In 1978, Pierce, a former physics professor, authored the *Turner Diaries*, which depicts a racist guerrilla war and a truck bombing of a federal building. Timothy McVeigh reportedly used the *Turner Diaries* as an inspirational blueprint for the 1995 bombing of the Alfred P. Murrah Building in Oklahoma City.[25]

Pierce established the National Alliance headquarters in 1985 on his 346-acre farm in Mill Point, West Virginia. He and a small cadre of members used the headquarters to publish white power books and other propaganda, operate the white power music company Resistance Records, and organize Internet activities. In 2001, the Alliance claimed thirty-five groups in thirty different states. Pierce's death in 2002 dealt a severe blow to the group, resulting in a substantial drop in the number of Alliance units and members. Recent evidence points to a shift in the National Alliance from a relatively large membership organization toward a small, loosely organized clique of white supremacists with long histories of violence and other criminal offending.[26]

Since Pierce's death, several groups have splintered from the National Alliance. One of the most prominent neo-Nazi groups is Billy Roper's White Revolution. Roper, a former high school history teacher with a master's degree in anthropology, founded White Revolution in 2002. White Revolution draws upon Nazi-era ideals of *volk*[27] to celebrate an ideal of Aryan racial kinship. Roper is noted for his efforts to pull together factions from across the movement for rallies, music shows, and other Aryan gatherings. White Revolution has an extensive Web presence and active chapters in sixteen states.

Tom Metzger's White Aryan Resistance (WAR) is a popular multimedia clearinghouse for neo-Nazi ideology. Metzger founded WAR in the 1980s after traveling a circuitous route through several white power branches. Metzger began his career in right-wing extremism during the 1960s and joined the John Birch Society. He quickly left the organization dissatisfied with their unwillingness to openly advocate anti-Semitism. In 1975, Metzger joined David Duke's Knights of the Ku Klux Klan and ascended to the rank of grand dragon, the KKK's highest-ranking state officer in California. Eventually Metzger and Duke parted ways and after an unsuccessful Congressional bid in 1980, Metzger founded the White American Political Association, which he eventually renamed the White Aryan

Resistance. WAR has been in the forefront of the white power movement's Internet presence and aggressively recruits younger generations to the cause.[28]

The National Socialist Movement formed in 1974 as an off-shoot of the American Nazi Party, but remained on the periphery of U.S. neo-Nazi groups until the mid-1990s when Jeff Schoep took over NSM leadership. Schoep has stepped into the vacuum created by William Pierce's death to recruit new members into the NSM. The fifty-six NSM groups in the United States periodically sponsor public rallies against illegal immigration and gay marriage. The NSM also sponsors an armed border watch unit that patrols the U.S./Mexican border in Southern California.[29]

RACIST SKINHEADS

Racist skinheads are the youngest branch of the white power movement. They derive from a distinct youth subculture, and since the late 1980s racist skinheads have synthesized neo-Nazi ideals and symbolism. Racist skinheads persist in loosely organized gangs and activist networks that congregate in skinhead crashpads and white power music gatherings. The largest organized groups, such as the Hammerskin Nation, produce white power concerts and festivals and have active cells around the world and an extensive Web presence.

Racist skinhead groups formed in the United States during the late 1970s as a response to increased economic pressures, Latino and Asian immigration, and the growth of minority street gangs. The early U.S. racist skinheads in the 1970s and 1980s drew inspiration from disaffected British skinheads associated with the extreme right-wing National Front and the British National Party.[30] Prior to the mid-1980s, skinhead racism was limited mainly to intermittent local conflicts with nonwhites and minority street gangs. In the late 1980s, however, WAR leader Tom Metzger, along with Aryan Nations' Richard Butler and other white power groups, began vigorously recruiting skinheads into the cause of global Aryan activism.

Racist skinheads organize themselves in a variety of ways.[31] There are racist skinhead gangs with state-level affiliations, such as the West Virginia Skinheads; county affiliations, such as Orange County Skins; and city affiliations, such as the Las Vegas Skins.[32]

The two most prominent American skinhead groups are Hammerskin Nation and Volkfront. The Hammerskins claim six regional chapters in the United States—Northwest Hammers, Midland Hammers, Confederate Hammers, Western Hammers, Northern Hammers, and Eastern Hammers—and official chapters in twelve other countries.[33]

Hammerskins hosted dozens of white power music shows in 2008, along with Aryan barbeques, mixed martial arts viewing parties, and a "Fuhrer's Birthday Party" to commemorate Adolf Hitler's birthday. In December 2008, more than

100 Aryans from five states attended a "Martyrs Day" party in Florida to commemorate the Silent Brotherhood founder Robert Mathews, an Aryan terrorist
who was killed in a 1984 shoot-out with federal authorities in Whidbey Island,
Washington. Martyrs Day was cosponsored by the Confederate Hammerskins,
Volksfront, and the American Front, and featured a keynote address by Richard
Kemp, an imprisoned member of the Silent Brotherhood, who phoned in from
federal prison.

Volksfront is one of the fastest growing and most active racist skinhead groups.
Founded in an Oregon state penitentiary by Randal Lee Krager and Richard
Arden in 1994, Volksfront calls itself "The Independent Voice of the White
Working Class" and claims chapters in sixteen states and eight countries.[34] Volksfront members are closely linked with Hammerskins and Blood & Honour, and
Aryans from across the movement's branches attend its annual music festivals
and participate in their Web forums. One of Volksfront's main goals is to create
an all-white private community, and the group has reportedly purchased land for
this purpose in Oregon, Washington, and Missouri.[35] Volksfront uses their Missouri property to host an Aryan summit and music festival called Althing, dedicated to Samuel Weaver, martyred son of Christian Identity adherent Randy
Weaver who was killed by federal authorities in an Idaho standoff in 1992.

Our sorting of Aryan branches overstates the lines of distinction among these
networks, which in reality are much more blurred and porous. The white power
movement encompasses contradictory realities. Some Aryans hold hard-line
stances against other believers, which creates the basis for schisms.[36] However,
many Aryans collaborate across ideological lines to sustain the Aryan cause.
Aryans of all stripes move back and forth across racist networks that meet in
Aryan free spaces and uphold some basic white power doctrines on which all
Aryans agree.

ARYAN DOCTRINE AND COLLECTIVE IDENTITY

Aryans sustain a sense of solidarity anchored in fundamental aims and ideological doctrines shared across the different white power branches.[37] Their free
spaces nourish and reinforce a sense of group unity around these doctrines and
certain elemental beliefs about what it means to be an Aryan.

First and foremost, Aryans across all branches believe that they possess a
unique ancestry that links them literally as racial brothers and sisters. That is,
Aryans imagine that they are all connected by an innate biogenetic superiority.
This presumed racial superiority is used to justify their belief in Aryan cultural
superiority. Aryan doctrine claims that race mixing and intercultural exchange
threaten their superior genetic and cultural lineage. In this way, Aryans see themselves as victims of a society that not only fails to acknowledge the natural superiority of whites but also suppresses and destroys all things Aryan.[38] This view

is summed up in the Aryan mantra known as the "14 Words": *We must secure the existence of our people and a future for white children.*

Aryans idealize traditional male-dominant families in which women are meant for domesticity, particularly for rearing white children who will become the early risers of the racial revolution. Aryans desire a racially exclusive world where nonwhites and other subhumans are vanquished, segregated, or at least subordinated to Aryan authority.

These beliefs are amplified by the emotions that accompany them. While it is easy to imagine that hate is the sole emotion underlying Aryan solidarity, it is only part of the picture. Expressions of intense hatred, anger, frustration, and outrage toward racial others do permeate Aryan networks. These "reactive emotions"[39] are prominent in the relationships that galvanize white power members against their enemies. But Aryans also express a range of "vitalizing"[40] and "reciprocal"[41] feelings of pride, pleasure, solidarity, loyalty, solicitude, affection, gratification, and love directed toward one another. These sorts of convictions are the "glue of solidarity."[42] They transcend ideological and stylistic differences among Aryan branches and help link members around the common goal of white power.

★

Constructing solidarity is a major accomplishment for members of such an extreme and marginalized ideology as white power. Aryan free spaces are the primary contexts where white power members fashion a sense of unity around core beliefs and the emotions they arouse.

We now turn to discuss *how* Aryans build solidarity in their free spaces. We begin with the family as the most intimate of Aryan free spaces. Aryan families are the clearest and most direct representation of white racial kinship. The family home is meant to be a pure white space offering escape from mainstream society. Aryan parents use this space to envelope their children in white power hate culture, to socialize new recruits for the movement.

3

Aryan Hate in the Home

We all know the movement begins with the family. If you can't save your family, then what's the point? Keeping your families pure and raising your kids among your kin is what we fight for.

—Darren, SWAS member[1]

Aryan homes are the most private, guarded, and valued of the white power movement's free spaces. Homes offer Aryans control over what they say and do, and they are the spaces where Aryans can close the doors and draw the blinds to hide their subversive acts from those who oppose them.[2] Aryan parents use the home as a place to raise their children as tomorrow's warriors who will defend the white race against genocide.

I stood in the doorway to Erik and Andi's living room and watched the scene unfold. Four Aryan mothers sat around the room chatting about their children. Two toddlers played on a blanket in the middle of the floor. Andi busied herself with the birthday cake in the kitchen behind me. It all seemed rather unremarkable, except for the white power themes that dominated the occasion.

Seven Aryan families had gathered to celebrate Erik and Andi's son Hunter's birthday. Erik and Andi named Hunter for the fictional killer of Jews and interracial couples in the infamous white power fantasy novel *Hunter*. This was only Hunter's fourth birthday, but he and his friends already appeared to embrace an Aryan attitude.

I stepped quickly out of the doorway as two young boys, Turner and William, came stomping through in their black Doc Marten boots, arms raised in salute, repeatedly shouting, "White power!" Turner wore a white power music T-shirt, while William wore a red T-shirt emblazoned with "88," the Aryan code for "Heil Hitler."[3]

The parents watched Turner and William's display. As Turner passed his mother, she patted his head, looked at the others, smiled, and said proudly: "He's already racially aware."

Throughout the afternoon, Hunter and friends played tag and hide and seek, and wrestled in the yard. As the children prepared to play hide and seek, Erik helped them decide who was "it": "Eeny, meeny, miny, moe. Catch a nigger by the toe. . . ."

The most shocking white power symbol was Hunter's birthday cake. Erik called the kids and parents into the dining room, and then Andi walked out of the kitchen carrying a red-and-white birthday cake in the shape of a swastika. A lit candle topped each arm of the swastika. The group sang the happy birthday song followed by a *"Sieg heil"* chant and Nazi salutes.

I lingered at the edge of the group, watching in amazement as Aryans transformed one of the most common family rituals into a deeply racist experience.

Aryan parents normalize racist extremism among their children by making white power culture central to family life. They fill their homes with racist and anti-Semitic symbols and name their children after icons of the movement. They use white supremacist stories to teach hatred and homeschool to immerse their children in Aryan ideology.

But homes are not completely free. The degree to which Aryans can explicitly fashion their homes and family life to normalize extreme racism varies, in part, by where they live. While some isolated rural families live very private lives that allow them to openly display their extremist beliefs, most Aryans reside in urban and suburban settings surrounded by those they hate. Prying neighbors and land-lords pose the risk of exposure and confrontations. It is therefore important for Aryans to balance their desire for white power purity and expression in the home with the need to conceal their extremism from outsiders.

In this chapter, we focus on white power parents' socialization styles.[4] Social-ization refers to the process by which humans learn the norms, values, and ideals of a culture and community. Socialization strategies can vary among members of the same culture. We discuss three distinct Aryan family types—hard-core, newly respectable, and communitarian—to describe how Aryans use the home as a free space.[5]

Seth and Jessie are a hard-core family that mirrors popular stereotypes of extremely dysfunctional, raucous, violent, and impoverished Aryans with criminal histories. Kate and Todd represent a newly respectable family, maintaining a façade of mainstream normality that masks their home's racist and anti-Semitic hate culture. Darren and Mindy raise their family as part of a rural communitarian network of Aryans who meet regularly, share resources, and collaborate to raise their children in a private setting saturated with Aryan idealism.

Although Aryan family styles differ, the common factor across Aryan families is that they use their homes as free spaces where Aryan culture survives through child socialization and family rituals. Aryans agree that rearing white children is a righteous task essential for strengthening the movement.

SETH AND JESSIE'S HARD-CORE HOME LIFE

Seth and his wife, Jessie, are staunchly committed racist skinheads. Seth is thirty-four years old, and his short and stocky build, shaved head, goatee, and tattoos create an intimidating public persona. He earned his veteran skinhead status during his nearly two decades with the group White Aryan Resistance, or WAR Skins, and later as a Hammerskin. Seth grew up in what he describes as a "pretty typical everyday family" and calls his father a "traditional conservative who was racist but never put race as the most important factor."[6]

When Seth was a teenager, he met racist skinheads at punk music concerts. Despite the tensions that carousing with racists caused with his father, Seth talks fondly of his recruitment into white power groups, getting inked with racist tattoos, and playing in racist bands.

Jessie, a year older than Seth, is tall and slender with dark red hair. She has a volatile personality shaped by a life on the streets as a member of the white power criminal gang Nazi Lowriders and two stints in prison for drug dealing. Her life has been steeped in racism. Her father, a successful attorney, taught Jessie about racial hatred as a young child. He advocated pseudo-scientific theories of racial supremacy and trained Jessie to believe in a natural order of white dominance. Although Jessie came from an affluent family, after dropping out of school in her teens, she turned to street life and befriended skinhead gang members.

Seth and Jessie live in an ordinary-looking three-bedroom apartment in a small working-class city in Southern California with Jessie's three young children from two earlier marriages, Ronnie (age five), Sven (four), and Ethan (three).[7] Seth's daughter, Amber (twelve), from his first marriage, regularly visits them. Jessie is jobless and stays at home with the kids. The family struggles to get by on Seth's job as a credit collection agent.

Seth and Jessie both talk passionately of their deep commitment to Aryanism and saving the white race from genocide. They claim their main goal in life is to raise their children as young white power warriors. Seth has been active in the Southern California white power music scene for more than a decade, playing in a number of bands and organizing white power concerts. Despite their low

Figure 3.1   Young Aryan girl salutes with her family at a neo-Nazi gathering in Valley Forge, Pennsylvania, on September 12, 2004. Her "88" shirt symbolizes an Aryan code for Heil Hitler. "H" is the eighth letter of the alphabet; 88 = HH = Heil Hitler.

Photo by William Thomas Cain/© Getty Images

income, he takes leave from work several times a year to play with his band at Aryan festivals around the United States and Europe.

Seth and Jessie's home is a far cry from Seth's classic skinhead crashpad where he lived prior to their marriage. The crashpad was constantly filled with Seth's skinhead friends and Aryan musicians. Walls were covered with signs of the movement, including white power music posters, a Hitler portrait, and a swastika flag displayed in the living room. White power books, pamphlets, and CDs littered the tables and floors.

The white power symbolism throughout Seth's old crashpad is like the accessory items in other Aryan family homes we had seen. Religious Aryans fill their homes with the Christian cross along with spiritual movement messages. Neo-Nazi, Christian Identity, and Klan families display statuettes and paintings of Hitler, swastika flags, and images of Nazi Germany, along with Confederate flags and wall hangings to mark their local group affiliation. Iconic Nordic imagery appears commonly in homes across Aryan branches.

Seth and Jessie avoid openly brazen signs of Aryanism in their home. They fear exposure to their Hispanic neighbors, who vastly outnumber whites in their complex, and the apartment manager, who sometimes enters unannounced. They hide the most obvious signs of their beliefs, but they are not happy about these constraints. Seth says they are just biding their time in the apartment as they save money for a house where they can be free to "live as we please."[8]

Seth and Jessie express their Aryan beliefs in some inconspicuous ways. Seth wears T-shirts, many emblazoned with the insignia of his favorite white power bands. To the uninitiated, Aryan band logos can be difficult to decipher as white power symbolism, but to the Aryans like Seth who wear them, band logos are very meaningful symbols of resistance.

Jewelry is a staple in the wardrobes of activist parents and children. The first time we met Jessie, a necklace of tiny swastikas dangled loosely around her neck. She later showed us Waffen-SS lightning-bolt earrings and a Celtic ring with "HH" and "88" stamped around it.

This is not to say, however, that Aryan clothing is always subtle in its meaning. We observed Aryans whose around-the-house clothing choices displayed images that are impossible to misconstrue: Nazi soldiers, swastikas, and hooded Klansmen, as well as messages such as "Supreme White Power." Kathy, a Southwest Aryan Separatist, wearing a "Hitler World Tour" T-shirt as she cooked breakfast one morning, explained: "At work I can't wear a shirt like this. So I feel pretty good around here to be able to put it on and be myself. I like that a lot."[9]

Around their apartment, Seth and Jessie typically dress their two oldest boys to mimic their father's skinhead uniform of Doc Marten boots, jeans, and T-shirt. Their youngest son sometimes sports infant bodysuits covered with swastikas and German iron crosses. Their children also play dress up in Nazi uniforms and wear more covert clothing styles that include ordinary jersey shirts that bear the numbers "14" to represent the "14 Words" mantra, "88" for "Heil Hitler," and

"18," which is code for the first and eighth letters of the alphabet, A and H, Adolf Hitler's initials.

While Seth and Jessie's home décor did not scream "white power," they did create displays infused with Aryan themes. Like many families, Seth and Jessie displayed family photographs around their home. After Jessie pointed at a photo of her oldest son, Ronnie, giving a *Sieg heil* salute, we realized that in several pictures their children wore movement clothing and were surrounded by racist symbols.

Raising "Little Hitler"

Seth and Jessie's hard-core parenting style encourages an acidly racist and anti-Semitic culture among their children. We found their tactics painful to watch. Seth and Jessie were under supervision by Child Protective Services. Jessie was on parole. Their oldest son, Ronnie, was undergoing psychiatric therapy. Jessie was particularly vicious at times, cursing, yelling, and hitting the kids at the slightest provocation.[10] The violence carried over into constant fights among their three young boys. Seth and Jessie paid little attention to these fights, except when they encouraged the battles so their boys would, according to Seth, "learn self-defense." The effects of racist socialization in this hard-core environment were clearly visible on Ronnie, whom Seth and Jessie's friends nicknamed "Little Hitler."

Ronnie was born while Jessie was incarcerated and spent the first three years of his life living with his biological father, Lars, an active Nazi Lowrider. Lars and his friends reportedly forced Ronnie to drink malt liquor and abused him physically, sexually, and psychologically. When Ronnie was three years old, Lars was convicted of murder and sentenced to life in prison. Ronnie lived with Lars's parents until Jessie was released from prison.

Ronnie had just turned five years old when we met him. Psychologists had recently diagnosed him with several mental health problems including attachment disorder and oppositional defiance disorder. Ronnie is physically aggressive. He constantly fights with his brothers and his peers, and he killed a small bird and tried to kill a kitten with his bare hands. Ronnie is also sexually aggressive and brags about "sticking his ding-a-ling in girls' mouths."

Seth and Jessie are adamant about turning Ronnie into a neo-Nazi. Seth and Jessie have taught him movement slogans such as *Sieg heil*, which he frequently yells at his parents and anyone else around him. When Seth puts Aryan music on the stereo, Ronnie dances excitedly around their living room singing the lyrics. Ronnie has learned to call himself a skinhead and to label all dark-skinned people he sees as niggers and muds. He watches a lot of television, mostly violent cartoons and movies. Seth and Jessie tell Ronnie to mimic the violence in the shows as practice for fighting their racial enemies. When watching television, Seth and

Jessie point out the "darkies," "faggots," and "Jewbags" to remind Ronnie about his racial enemies.

Like other Aryan families we studied, Seth and Jessie use birthday celebrations as ritual initiations for their children to embrace white power culture. For Ronnie's fifth birthday, Seth and Jessie presented him with a cake decorated with swastikas and iron crosses. Aryan parents often use phrases like "14 Words" or "white power" along with figurines of robed Klansmen or Nazi guards on their children's birthday cakes. During the parties, parents and friends racialize the happy birthday song by substituting the child's name with phrases like "young Aryan" and "white warrior" and infuse entire celebrations with *Sieg heil* salutes and choruses of "White power!" and "Rahowa!"

Parents also infuse gift-giving at birthdays and holidays with racial themes. Seth and Jessie transformed a G.I. Joe action figure into "G.I. Nazi" complete with swastika arm bands and SS emblazoned on the doll's forehead. As they gave the doll to Ronnie, Seth and Jessie explained to him that G.I. Nazi will help save the white race. Other parents gave blond, blue-eyed Barbie dolls they called "Aryan girls" to their young daughters. We also saw gifts of clothing with racist symbols, Aryan comics, white power coloring books, neo-Nazi video games, Aryan music, and SS knives among other weapons.

Seth and Jessie also commemorate Aryan holidays, such as the birthdays of Hitler and his deputy, Rudolph Hess. They use these celebrations to help Ronnie imagine an Aryan legacy that extends beyond his own family. Seth and Jessie also join with other Aryan families to memorialize the death of Ian Stuart Donaldson, the "godfather" of white power rock music. Similar ritual commemorations occur in Christian Identity families. We witnessed families praying for martyred Aryans such as Gordon Kahl, a tax evader and founder of a Texas Posse Comitatus cell, and Silent Brotherhood founder Robert Mathews, who led a terrorist cell in murder, counterfeiting, and armed robberies.

Aryan parents control their children's environment in these ways to expose them to role models and experiences that affirm the attitudes and aspirations they think are best for their children. This socialization style is no different in families of other cultural backgrounds, except that Aryans emphasize violent, racist white power fantasies that must be kept hidden from outsiders.

The home is one of the places where Aryans are able to sustain their racist visions in the most unrestricted manner. Seth and Jessie's hard-core Aryan home life reflects a style we also saw with other skinhead families. But Aryan families are varied. The next type of family racializes the home in more subtle ways.

THE NEWLY RESPECTABLE: TODD AND KATE

Todd is thirty-two years old, short and slender. Tattoos of Aryan warriors, Celtic crosses, and swastikas cover his chest, stomach, and back. Todd's parents divorced when he was twelve years old, and he spent much of his youth on the streets of Los Angeles.

> My mom was all fucked up and there was nobody else to take care of me and my brothers, so my aunt took us. They were pretty racist. . . . She would say, "I don't want you hanging out with niggers. I don't want you hanging out with beaners." [She] dated the grand dragon of the local KKK. They were adamant about [extreme racism].[11]

In his early teens, Todd followed his older brother Jason into the notorious Southern California Aryan criminal gang Public Enemy Number One (PEN1). Todd spent fourteen years with PEN1, committed to the group's hard-core racism, which couples a "mercenary and criminal nature"[12] with white power ideology.

At thirty, Todd began to distance himself from PEN1's hard-core lifestyle of drugs, crime, and gangbanging. He felt burned out from his hard-driving lifestyle and wanted to settle down with his new wife, Kate. He did not completely exit white power activism, however. He is a regular in the Southern California white power music scene, often visits his friends' crashpads, attends Aryan house parties, and keeps in close contact with PEN1 leaders.

Todd's wife, Kate, is thirty years old and a veteran Orange County Skin. In high school, she rebelled from her middle-class upbringing by befriending a group of local racist skinheads. Kate said, "I made some bad choices when I was young, doing drugs and helping skinhead friends break into some homes."[13] She was arrested for one burglary, served three months in jail, then "cleaned up her life" after her release.

Kate met Todd at a white power concert when she was twenty-five. Todd and Kate dated and married three years later. Like Todd, Kate remains committed to the white power movement. She closely follows the movement through Aryan websites, but each year limits her face-to-face contact to just a few white power music shows or parties.

Todd and Kate's attitude about raising their Aryan family reflects the new respectability ideal advocated by White Aryan Resistance leader, Tom Metzger. Metzger and other prominent Aryans encourage activists to strategically hide their Aryanism in order to blend into the mainstream. The rationale is that clandestine Aryans are not easy to detect and can therefore infiltrate the social system; rise to positions of wealth, power, and respectability; give resources back to the movement; and become role models for future Aryans. This strategy encourages racist skinheads to grow out their hair, cover their tattoos, stay out of trouble, earn college degrees, find good jobs, and raise children in a stable environment filled with potent Aryan idealism.

Judging only by outward appearance, Todd and Kate live a rather ordinary, solidly middle-class way of life. Todd works full-time as a welder; Kate as a paralegal. They have two young boys, Teddy and Alex, whom they see as their fore-most responsibility. Their freshly painted, well-landscaped house looks no different from others in their attractive middle-class neighborhood. Signs of the white power movement are hard to find inside the home as well. Todd stashes his swastika flag and other racist paraphernalia in a closet, hides his Aryan tattoos, and lowers the volume when he plays white power music. Yet their home is an Aryan enclave.

Todd and Kate hope to shield their kids from the street life they experienced. They reject the hustling, gangbanging, and drugs of their youth, but not their commitment to white power ideology. They are still devoted racists and steadfast in their plans to raise Aryan children. They imagine their boys attending college, taking professional jobs, and rising to influential positions where they can change society with their white power vision.

Like most Aryan parents we studied, Kate and Todd talk of strikingly familiar parental worries. We listened as they spoke about many of the same anxieties as other doting parents, such as their children's health and nutrition and what they learn in school. They fret about Teddy and Alex's future, but these worries are sifted through the filter of white power ideology.

When Teddy and Alex are sick, Todd and Kate worry about the care they will receive from doctors and nurses who might be secret agents of ZOG. They also worry that their children might be brainwashed in public school by ZOG-controlled teachers. ZOG could turn them against white power ideals and control their future.

Todd and Kate expose Teddy and Alex to home-based white power culture in several ways. They pepper their talk with matter-of-fact statements about "niggers," "spics," "Jew-dogs," and "muds." They clothe their boys with covert Aryan symbols, such as football jerseys numbered "88." Todd and Kate read their sons bedtime stories about Aryan heroes, give toys that purportedly reflect their Aryan values, and emphasize Aryan superiority. Todd tells Teddy and Alex about the white power music shows he attends, describes in detail the meaning of song lyrics, and emphasizes that they are among the enlightened few engaged in a struggle against ZOG. If Teddy and Alex embrace Aryan ideals, Todd and Kate are convinced that they will be among the chosen few who are prepared for the race war that will come.

Todd and Kate teach their children more than Aryan hatred. They also empha-size love, camaraderie, and kinship among Aryans. Kate says: "I'm raising our kids so they understand that racialism isn't just about hate and violence. I want them to only have white friends and understand their white heritage. I plan to teach them to be proud of their ancestors and to love their whiteness."

Todd and Kate stress racial kinship with other Aryans. As Randall Collins says, these sentiments are the "the 'glue' of solidarity" that really binds all peo-ple to one another.[14] Kate and Todd hope that by nurturing these same feelings in their young children, they will imagine themselves as part of a larger Aryan family.

Soft-Sell Socialization

Todd and Kate also use an indirect socialization strategy to teach their children white power ideas. Quietly persuasive, soft-sell tactics favor a subtler tone that serves to normalize Aryan beliefs. Such methods reflect the hard reality that Aryans cannot totally exorcise mainstream influences from their children's lives.

Todd and Kate direct their kids' mainstream exposure toward experiences that are consistent with Aryan ideals. They surround their kids with white people and white culture, hoping to make nonwhites seem odd and undesirable social contacts. This tactic is relatively easy for them now, since the boys do not yet attend school, but the difficulty will increase as they grow up and become exposed to a greater number of outside influences.

This strategy is a popular topic of conversation in many Aryan circles. We listened as a group of Aryan parents at a party related how they limited their children's contact with nonwhites. Ryan, a Colorado Skin, said: "I surround them with white culture, friends, and family. . . . We don't discuss race much, but my kids only attend birthday parties and play groups with white children. They have white parents, white children, and white friends and that's what they know."[15]

Other Aryans emphasize their Eurocentric cultural heritage to subtly accentuate white culture without pushing young children too early to confront explicit and extreme styles of racial hatred. Brandy, a Christian Identity mother, explained:

> I just teach them about their Irish heritage. I teach them to be loyal to their kin. I don't want my children to ruin their lives by hating everything like I've seen happen. My six-year-old goes to school, and I volunteer for class parties and field trips. I just allow my kids to have their own ideas and I do my best to instill white pride in them. I think this works a lot better than force feeding them.[16]

Television, films, and other media are a major thorn in the side of Aryan parents, so they closely monitor what children watch. Beth, a Christian Identity disciple, ended one of her daughter's favorite shows when a black character was shown. "She used to watch *Clifford the Big Red Dog* all the time, but then we saw an episode where he had a black friend and we said no more. *Little Mermaid*'s not too bad, but it's got some multicultural crap too."[17]

Aryan parents that we studied did not totally ban popular media from the home, but, like Beth, they screened the content of television shows and movies for how many nonwhite characters would be shown, whether nonwhites were villains or heroes, and if plot lines promoted race-mixing or homosexuality. Michelle, a Colorado Skin, blocks channels, such as Nickelodeon, Cartoon Network, and PBS, to ensure that her daughters are not inadvertently exposed to culturally diverse shows. "The media is so antiwhite, so we have to use what we can to our advantage. We use white books and movies that have the right message. We block the cable channels that have antiwhite kid shows."[18]

Some Aryan parents allow their children to watch shows with ethnically diverse casts and then use those shows to teach their kids about racial doctrine. Seth and Jessie used movie characters to teach their son Ronnie about racial enemies. In one instance, Ronnie asked, "Mommy, is that guy [the Rock's character in the movie *Scorpion King*] on our side or is he one of our enemies?" Jessie replied, "Honey it's hard to tell, but he's not white. Those other guys are on our side [pointing at two, clearly white, protagonists]."

Soft-sell socialization strategies attempt to address the dichotomy between Aryans' desire for a purified white-only existence and the reality that such racial purity is almost impossible to achieve. Like other newly respectable Aryan families, Kate and Todd try to bring their children along gradually, decreasing the confusion youngsters may feel as they are taught extremist values that conflict so starkly with the mainstream norms that also surround them. They try to cloak their radical beliefs in the appearance of mainstream normality while simultaneously rejecting mainstream anti-Aryan ideas. But living a veiled resistance inevitably creates dissonance and a double bind.

Todd and Kate worry about their kids being co-opted by mainstream culture and drifting away from white power ideals. Their worries reflect those of some hard-core white power members who criticize the new respectability strategy for creating soft, uncommitted Aryans. But, if Todd and Kate were to be more open about their Aryanism they would run the risk of jeopardizing their middle-class success, leading to the downward mobility so common among Aryan activists.[19] They fear that exposing their true identities would bring critical scrutiny and stigma, possible job loss, and disruptions to their home life and to many of the relationships they use to mask their Aryan beliefs.

Hiding under the veil of normality may not create the kind of powerful socialization experiences that white power parents hope will ensure their children become Aryan warriors. But public exposure of parents' racial extremism might well weaken the movement's goal of gaining a foothold in mainstream society. The power of Aryan free spaces is that they allow Aryans to retreat into contexts that challenge multicultural ideology and experiences. Newly respectable families adopt mainstream appearances while mixing explicit and implicit racialized messages in their homes. Communitarian families, to which we now turn, are not as encumbered, although, as with all Aryans, there are also limits to their expression of hate in the home.

DARREN AND MINDY'S COMMUNITARIAN FAMILY LIFE

Darren and Mindy are parents in a communitarian white power network in rural Nevada. They both grew up near Reno, Nevada, and describe their parents as "patriots but not white power." Raised as Mormons in the Church of Jesus Christ of Latter Day Saints (LDS), Darren and Mindy also experienced socialization into a narrow worldview. They now reject the LDS Church for straying from white supremacist beliefs.

Mindy is twenty-six years old and traces her white power extremism to high school confrontations with blacks and Polynesian girls. These confrontations drove her toward white groups, where she took up with skinheads and immersed herself in white power ideology. Darren, twenty-nine, turned to Aryanism in high school. "I felt there was a lot of racial bullshit in school. I got tired of all these niggers walking around doing whatever they wanted and the skinheads weren't having any of that shit. We stood up to people and kicked ass."[20]

Darren and Mindy married soon after high school and, fearing a race war, joined a small communitarian white power group, the Southwest Aryan Separatists (SWAS) to avoid the major cities, where the racial fighting would begin.[21] Darren learned from his Aryan friends about the rural hotbed for racism where SWAS was located. The dozen families that made up SWAS welcomed them. SWAS families live within twenty miles of one another and meet regularly for events, such as weekly dinners, Bible study meetings, homeschooling, camping, and birthday celebrations.

After several years renting a home, Darren and Mindy bought twelve acres with another Aryan couple, Erik and Andi. During our fieldwork both families were building a solar-powered home, growing their own food, and stockpiling weapons and supplies in preparation for the government collapse and racial battles they anticipated. Darren and Mindy talk enthusiastically about the freedom they experience living with other Aryans in a communitarian style. Darren wants to "just live off the land, live by the scripture, raise my family, raise my crops."[22] They see their secluded homestead as a fortress to defend against ZOG. "I want to see 'em coming. I know eventually they will. When they do we'll be ready."[23]

When we met them, Darren and Mindy were living in a mobile home parked on their land. They spent much of their free time in the afternoons and weekends working on their new home and a barn. Darren erected a Confederate flag outside their trailer and decorated the inside with a portrait of Hitler and a Klan painting in the living room. White power children's books, movement pamphlets, and other paraphernalia were scattered throughout their home.

Cultural Isolation

SWAS parents like Darren and Mindy romanticize the idea of total societal withdrawal to create a pure Aryan lifestyle for their children. They go to great lengths to try to ensure a purified existence, free from anti-Aryan society, by carving out private family spaces where they can be submerged in white power culture.

Such social-geographic isolation is an extreme measure, which is relatively uncommon among WPM families, who often reside in urban and suburban areas. But SWAS members see a purification effect in their seclusion. Withdrawal shields the family from mainstream authorities and anti-Aryan culture, they say, and helps nurture the survivalist skills and sensibilities required for the inevitable race war.

Daily life at Darren and Mindy's reflects a pastoral ideal. They are transforming their land into a sustainable homestead. Their kids play carefree in the woods that cover their property, participate in chores, and help to build their solar home. The SWAS families in the area trade hosting duties for gatherings such as bonfire parties, birthday celebrations, and Bible study meetings. They also trade labor, such as carpentry, gardening, and babysitting, within the SWAS network.

Mindy and Darren's isolation means that their children are not directly exposed to much mainstream culture as compared to families like Seth and Jessie who live in urban areas surrounded by what they define as mainstream filth. Yet Mindy and Darren's socialization style is still fueled by the fantasy vision of a coming race war, which all SWAS families are gearing up to survive. Mindy and Darren encourage their children to explore the woods as a way to become familiar with the land they will protect with their lives from "niggers, ZOG, and the bad, evil government." They work together as a family on their building projects, as well as hunting, fishing, and other survivalist skills, to ready themselves for the apocalyptic race war. Bill, a SWAS parent, explained: "Our youth are going to be responsible for securing our race. Everything we do, it's not just for fun, it's very serious and he needs to know what he's up against."[24]

SWAS children are ensconced in their closed society and know little about the outside world. Their lives are dominated by the specter of race war and survival. But it is hard to predict whether exposure to inevitable outside non-Aryan influences will reshape their intense childhood Aryan socialization experiences.

Gender Lessons

SWAS kids learn that Aryan men and women in the movement have distinct roles. Like most Aryan families, Darren and Mindy idealize the patriarchal structure in which men are esteemed protectors of family and race, and women are relegated to the subordinate, albeit vital, roles of motherhood and homemaker.

Aryan ideology prescribes that men must be warrior combatants. In their role as fathers, men are expected to prepare themselves and their family for the enduring racial struggle. SWAS men like Darren fancy themselves as outdoorsmen. They camp, hike, and hunt to hone their survivalist skills, and they stockpile weapons, food, and water. SWAS men lead backcountry outings as survivalist training missions to prepare families against ZOG attacks.

Families are the core Aryan fighting unit. Homes are their defensive refuge in the race war. SWAS boys quickly learn their roles in this mythic battle. Darren explicitly models the dominant male role for his sons, repeatedly reminding them of their responsibility to family and race. He prepares them to fight to the death to repel ZOG. "All my kids, you know, we're shooting it out; we're staying. My boys, they say, 'Dad, we're going to hold our guns and shoot back, and if you and Mom get killed we're gonna shoot it out.'"[25]

Urban neo-Nazi men also play out warrior fantasies in their gangbanging and bar fights. But frequent fighting is a young man's game. Older veteran skinheads like Todd and Seth typically stay out of brawls they once instigated. Todd and Seth own weapons, however, and practice combat at shooting ranges.

The main role of SWAS women is to procreate. Women encourage one another to have children for the movement and talk to their own young girls about the responsibility to have Aryan babies when they are grown. The women's prodding of one another comes with the tacit assumption that the Aryan community of women will support one another by trading child care, dinners, hand-me-down clothes, and domestic help. The mutual support moderates the expense of rearing children, making it possible to have more than they could otherwise afford alone.

White power ideology defines procreation as Aryan women's main contribution to the racial struggle. Mindy explained: "I love having white babies! I love the fact that I can contribute in that way, helping my people by helping produce the next generation. When you look in your white baby's eyes you can see the world you're creating."[26]

Kathy, a fellow Southwest Aryan Separatist, proudly showed us her newest child and spoke of the honor of motherhood. "Look at him [her newborn son], he's so special. He's white and that just makes it even more special. That's what's so amazing, knowing that I'm helping save my race. It's an honor to raise white babies."[27]

In their role as movement mothers, women do more than procreate and raise their own little Aryans. For example, Mindy and other SWAS women operated an outreach program called Operation White Care to send care packages to Aryans in the U.S. military stationed in the Middle East.[28]

Mothers in hard-core and newly respectable Aryan families also connect with one another for support and camaraderie. Jessie takes her kids to the beach with other skinhead families and trades hand-me-down clothes and toys. Kate is an Aryan soccer mom, carting her kids along with two others from Aryan families to soccer games on their all-white teams. While these activities may look like typical family activities, each mother ensures that their children's experiences are situated in a context where racial extremism bubbles just below the surface.[29]

Aryan Names

SWAS racial socialization begins at birth with the choice of baby names drawn directly from Aryan symbolism. Darren and Mindy's eight-year-old daughter is named Liberty, symbolizing white power commitment to freedom from ZOG and patriotism to America, which they envision as a pure white nation. Forrest, their five-year-old son, is named for the first Ku Klux Klan imperial wizard, Nathaniel Bedford Forrest. As mentioned earlier, Erik and Andi named their son Hunter after the fictional character in William Pierce's infamous white power fantasy novel, *Hunter*, who guns down interracial couples and Jews to cleanse America and save the future of white civilization.[30] Their daughter's name, Ariana, derives from the word Aryan.

Aryan parents use these names to link children to a racist tradition, which they expect will help instill in their children a racialized identity. White power parents commonly look to Nordic mythology or to German culture, which they associate with the Nazis, for names that symbolize their beliefs. We did not meet anyone named Adolf, but parents do use less notorious German names.[31] Randy, a SoCal Skin and friend of Seth and Jessie's, told us, "I'll probably name my child Dieter if I have a son. That would be in honor of my grandfather, who was SS, and because it's a good German name and that'll help my son stay in touch with his roots."[32]

Parents reinforce the significance of names with stories and admonitions about their meaning. Cal, a SoCal Skin, said, "Aryan names won't start a revolution or anything, but names are like a lot of other things; it's what they symbolize that's important. [Names] tell you something about what's in a person's heart. It's kind of like the '14 Words'; they may just be words, but they're also a lot more than that."[33] Baxter, a father of four and veteran neo-Pagan believer, agreed. "The name is very important; it defines the spirit of a newborn, and parents should think carefully about their decision of what to name their child. Think of anyone you know. Their name represents everything about that person."[34]

White power parents choose names explicitly to instill their children with racial extremism. The act of naming a child with some meaningful referent is not unique to Aryans. Parents of all cultures do it. But unless those Aryan names reflect the most infamous historical figures, like Hitler, they are not likely to be noticed. To the uninitiated, the meaning of Hunter, Forrest, Ariana, and other common white power names is not clear, which helps children pass in main-stream settings. For those in the know, however, such names may represent a significant, lifelong symbolic attachment to the white power movement. Parents' goal is to convert the Aryan-named child into a person committed to a white power identity.

Homeschooling Hate

Aryan homeschooling systematically transmits white power culture to kids. Mindy homeschools her children, focusing on the fundamentals of reading, writing, and math, but her makeshift curriculum is saturated with Aryan themes. History and social studies lessons concentrate on European cultures and Western civilization while vilifying Asian, Middle Eastern, and African cultures. Her lessons are historical accounts of Nordic nations, Anglo-British experiences, and Nazi Germany. Mindy uses these narratives to emphasize white accomplishments that convey Aryan superiority. She says homeschooling gives her the chance to transmit Aryan truth.

SWAS and other Aryan communitarian networks divide teaching responsibility across parents to ease each family's burden and draw on complementary skills of the parents. The mothers who teach come together to plan lessons, organize supplies, and discuss teaching strategies to insure that all SWAS children receive well-rounded white power instruction. Carrie, a SWAS mother with two boys, said, "We completely control the environment where they're raised, and this means we can exclude nonwhites from their childhood, which is excluding them from their worldview."[35]

Another SWAS mother, Brenda, reflected on the purity of homeschooling. "Homeschool is the best. You provide the information; they live it. Homeschool allows me to know that my children will get the truth and not all this liberal propaganda."[36]

Homeschooling is not limited to communitarian families like SWAS. Aryan parents worry about their children's education, and many see homeschooling as a way to control their children's political indoctrination. Homeschooling gives parents the direct and systematic power to racialize the content of their child's learning and to keep their children out of the public school system, which Aryans see as a brainwashing tool to perpetuate lies about race mixing and to force-feed students with liberal Jewish propaganda.

The white power website, Stormfront.org, declares:

> Education is a key component to our survival, however, the conventional idea of education is not sufficient, because of the liberal, Jewish bias that is imposed on most learning materials. . . . For our children to be properly educated we must have places to teach them the accomplishments of white Europeans and the importance of staying true to one's race. If we don't take the time to show them the way, they will be brainwashed by ignorant liberal teachers . . . that encourage race mixing and degeneracy.[37]

Aryan parents also fear for their children's safety in public schools, imagining schools as playgrounds for nonwhite gangs who have declared open season on white students, bullying, beating, and murdering them as school officials sit idly by. Homeschooling resolves the problems of public school and guarantees that Aryan children will remain immersed in racist culture. Melanie, a SoCal Skin, summed up the attitude of the Aryan homeschoolers we studied:

> We need to educate our children. They're being indoctrinated into a society that has no morals, no responsibility. To survive, we need to teach our children that there's more to life than the garbage they're feeding us. Our kids shouldn't be afraid to walk

the streets and schools without being preyed upon; they should be able to enjoy being white kids. I've worked hard to be a mother and a teacher.[38]

White power lessons saturate children with ideals that stress biological and cultural attachment to their Aryan racial kin. Cal, a SoCal Skin with a three-year-old son, uses themes of white heritage and cultural preservation to justify his child's racist education. "My son is homeschooled. I teach him to be proud of his people . . . that he's part of the race that created civilization. I just want to make sure he inherits what is rightfully his and what our forefathers fought so hard to pass on."[39]

Similarly, Janine, a SoCal Skin and mother of three, homeschools her children to stress sacred cultural knowledge that public school would deny them. "European culture is fading; our tradition is being stripped away so we have to do something to fight the assault. I think with the public schools just promoting filth and hypocrisy, I can't imagine sending my kids there, so I teach them here."[40]

Despite its appeal, however, homeschooling remains an unattainable luxury for most Aryan parents. With a few exceptions, the families we studied sent their children to public schools. Homeschooling requires a support network that is absent for many Aryans. Seth and Jessie want to homeschool but do not know other Aryans near them who homeschool and do not feel prepared to do it alone. Thus, Seth and Jessie's socialization prepares their kids to stand up and fight the "niggers and spics" who, they imagine, will threaten Ronnie and his brothers in public schools.

Aryans like Kate and Todd take a different approach to school. They acknowledge the virtues of homeschool, but they both work and do not have the time to spare. They moved to their neighborhood precisely so their children could attend a predominantly white public school. They view public school as a place where their kids will learn to exist as Aryans in settings that champion anti-Aryan attitudes. They also talk about public school as an essential experience for their children prior to college. College, they believe, will guarantee their children the credentials for getting a good job in a mainstream setting.

In accord with the newly respectable creed that a poor Aryan is an ineffective one, Kate and Todd plan for their kids to blend into the mainstream and secretly contribute to the Aryan cause. Their choice of public schools adds risk and exposes their children to precisely the type of social influences that hinder extreme racism and blind hatred. Yet Kate and Todd believe that they can saturate their children's experiences in the home with enough Aryanism to combat the normalizing tendencies of the public school experience and harden their children against mainstream, anti-Aryan culture.

★

Aryan families—hard-core, newly respectable, and communitarian—live diverse styles while sharing a fundamental commitment to white power. Debates rage inside the white power movement over which style is most effective for the move-ment's survival. Hard-core parents and activists claim that newly respectable families have sold out and do little more than play act as Aryans. Likewise, hard-core Aryans see many communitarian groups, especially those ensconced in rural hideaways, as shirking from the front lines of the racial struggle occurring in urban zones. Aryans committed to the newly respectable strategy dismiss hard-core families as rogues of the movement who lend little to the ultimate goal of preparing to take the reins of political and social power. Newly respectable fami-lies offer another route into Aryanism that does not require self-denial of soci-ety's fruits. All Aryan families imagine that it is only a matter of time before whites will take over society.

What white power adherents all agree on is the importance of the family to anchor and sustain the white power movement. Aryan homes provide a private setting where white power members trace in-group/out-group boundaries and attempt to create the next generation of believers. Their weaving of white power ideological messages into the mundane routines of daily life reduces the psycho-logical distance between everyday life and virulent racist hate.

Homes are white power sanctuaries that affect both children and parents. By nourishing their children on Aryan ideas, parents hope to create budding little soldiers committed to carrying on the fight against ZOG for white supremacy. But the devotion to raising Aryan children also gives white power parents a strong sense of purpose and direction that sustains their own commitment to the cause. White power parents identify an intense responsibility to use their children to keep alive the racist and anti-Semitic ideology of violence and hate that anchors the white power movement.

Racial socialization in the free space of homes is part of Aryans' constant struggle against ZOG and multicultural ideals. Aryan resistance in the home makes no headlines, but each seemingly inconsequential act helps sustain white power ideas in the family and makes possible the persistence of the white power movement. We now turn to another Aryan free space—informal gatherings—that intersect closely with homes and provide an added layer of socialization and sup-port for the cause.

4

Hate Parties

To have people over, get the bonfire going, the more people come around the more they want to be here. We're building the community we desire.

—Darren, SWAS member[1]

Bonfire parties, house parties, backyard barbeques, Bible study meetings, bars, and campouts all serve as gathering places where Aryans nurture white power identity. They use these contexts to display their ideals and commitments through their talk, dress, and ritualism. At first glance it may be difficult to see the overtly political nature of these gatherings. Their form mirrors very ordinary social events. But a closer look reveals these occasions as clearly political movement activity.

It all seemed so familiar. Thirty or so people in a field, under the stars, warming themselves by a bonfire, drinking beer and carousing, as music blared from a car stereo nearby. I couldn't count the number of times I had attended a party like this in high school and college. But this party was also very different. I stared across the flames at five boisterous guys telling a string of jokes about "muds" and "kikes." Every few seconds the flickering fire illuminated their shaved heads, swastika tattoos, and clothes emblazoned with symbols of hate.

The distorted guitar and thumping bass drum of the music suddenly became louder, bringing me out of my trance. Rich, a burly, heavily tattooed, nineteen-year-old skinhead, shouted, "Hey I just put on some

Skrewdriver! Are there any Jews out there? Ha ha!" He gave a Nazi salute toward the blasting stereo. Others followed his lead and responded to his question with "Fuck no!" A few seconds later the song began—"Nigger! Nigger! Out! Out!"—and a couple nearby started singing along, arm in arm. Soon, the entire group joined in a chorus of *"Sieg heil!"* and "White power!" and a collective energy moved across the gathering. I was impressed by their camaraderie and scared by their message.

I knew only a few people at the party. My invitation had come from Darren and Mindy, the Southwest Aryan Separatist (SWAS) couple that I had made contact with a few months earlier. They had twelve acres in the high Nevada desert and had mentioned to me that they regularly hosted these parties. I asked if I could attend, not knowing quite what to expect other than it would be a party for racists.

Most of the partygoers were either young male skinheads or SWAS families. Some families had brought their teenage children, who mingled with a few other teens from the county high school. When the *Sieg heil* salutes stopped and the crescendo of chants died down, I turned to one of the shaved-headed teenagers standing nearby, introduced myself, and after some idle small talk, I asked, "So how did you hook up with these guys?" He replied, "I met a couple 'em at a music show down in Quincy about a year ago and they've been kind of looking out for me since."

"Oh yeah? Like how?" I asked.

"Well just teaching me about being a skinhead and letting me read some of the books, giving me tapes and CDs to play."

As we talked, one of his friends joined the conversation. Cindy was fifteen, and although she knew of SWAS, she said she wasn't a member. She came to the party to "just hang out and have fun."

After a while, Darren introduced me to Russ, a twenty-something construction worker who was new to SWAS. Russ told me that, like many other SWAS adherents, he had grown up in a strict, conservative family that held some racist views, but he had decided that he was more radical. He wasted no time putting me on the spot

"You seem like you're really trying to take all this in," he said in a tone I took as suspicion. He went on, "I can tell you're not sure about all of this. I can tell you're trying to hide certain things."

He was right, of course, and I admitted it. "You're right, I guess. I'm just trying to learn as much as possible."

He seemed satisfied, for the moment, and he quickly turned our conversation toward the intricacies of Christian Identity beliefs. I just listened.

Aryans need these informal gatherings to sustain a shared identity against the anti-Aryan world.[2] Cal, a SoCal Skin, explained the importance of intimate, informal gatherings for sustaining the movement: "When you live in a world like we do, you have to find places where you don't have to hold back on being racist;

where other people feel and act the same way you do. The parties are definitely part of it. You get a chance to come together in a small setting where it's easier to know people and build friendships."[3]

Aryans build their friendships by sharing personal stories about how they became Aryans, the injustices they face, and how they persevere. Their talk evokes feelings of pride and pleasure about being an Aryan, and hope about the movement's future. By congregating with other like-minded activists, Aryans cultivate and sustain an oppositional racial consciousness.

GETTING BACK TO "GOD'S WHITE WILDERNESS"

Like most Aryan gatherings, Darren and Mindy's bonfire parties were much more than an excuse to drink beer and carouse. SWAS members talk of the spirituality of their experience. On their land far outside of town, under the stars and beside the primal warmth of the fire, they feel that they are communing with nature, or more specifically, "white nature." They invest nature with feelings of deep racial purity.[4] They revel in the feeling of "getting away" to places where they can stand under the stars before God's sublime universe and imagine that the universe was made solely for whites.

SWAS members, Southern California neo-Nazis, and Pacific Northwest Aryans that we observed incorporate a get-back-to-white-nature ethos into outings like hikes and campouts. They use excursions to places like the Sierra Nevada Mountains to amplify feelings of autonomy, transcendence, and faith in white power.

Bill, a SWAS founder, said: "The hikes we do up here have a religious significance. The hikes get us back in nature. They get us back into that spirit of living and being close to the land."[5]

On a group hike with six other Aryans, James, a twenty-three-year-old SWAS member, stopped at the edge of a cliff, gazed out over the canyon, and declared to the group:

> It's when you come here and stop and look around, that's when you realize your racial destiny and heritage. This is what we struggle for, the right to maintain this kind of purity. You know, the way things are going, thanks to the multicultural third-world invasion, if it continues, there won't be places like this for much longer. I'd sacrifice my life to keep that from happening.[6]

SWAS members spoke of their fantasy to take over the Sierras and turn it into the pure white space they feel it is meant to be. Gazing skyward at a majestic limestone monolith, Erik, a SWAS veteran, talked reverentially of hanging a gigantic Nazi banner across the cliff face. He said, "We want to reclaim this for the true people of Israel."[7] When we asked Darren directly about the meaning of the wilderness experiences, he said: "We consider the hikes and campouts like a kind of racial and religious retreat. We look at them as much more than just having fun on the side of a mountain. These are our opportunities to come together. It's a time for us to be together."[8]

Pacific Northwestern Aryans also invest their region with racialized religious meanings. Gus, a Christian Identity believer, said he feels physically and ideologically protected from the "polluted" mainstream. "This part of the country is still white and we're trying to keep it this way. You come up here and you thank God there are still a few places like this."[9] Gus and his Aryan Nations comrades construe their wilderness excursions as racial bonding that helps them remain committed to white power ideals despite living in the culturally diverse society they despise.

Aryan Bible Study

SWAS members make the spiritual meanings of their outings even more explicit by studying scripture in what they believe is God's white nature. Darren and Mindy alternate between Bible study hikes and Bible study gatherings in their home. Darren explained: "We have Bible study classes once a week or whenever I can get people together. You know, we meet at someone's house or go hiking and study the scripture."[10]

Bible study meetings help members elaborate and refine white power spirituality and ritualistically commit to their cause. The movement's most religious branches organize home-based Bible study gatherings that typically begin with a racially themed prayer followed by study of biblical passages. Members interpret passages as evidence of God's favor for Aryans. Some groups chant white power religious slogans as part of initiation rites and commitment ceremonies, where members pledge themselves to God and the movement.

Many meetings we saw were planned weekly affairs with regular times and days. These gatherings draw from five to twenty members to explore biblical insights that inform their racist ideals. Members of Christian Identity sects, like SWAS and Aryan Nations, along with adherents to Odinism and Asatru, use these gatherings to reject the watered-down Christian rhetoric they see dominating other religious settings.

Sessions organized by small, independent movement churches may attract up to fifty members at a time, and congregations may include several hundred members. Prior to the demise of his Aryan Nations compound in 2001, Richard Butler held weekly prayer services and Bible study classes for twenty to thirty local Aryans. Sarah, a veteran Aryan Nations member and mother of three, recalled the gratitude she felt about the congregation's support:

> We're blessed that we can actually worship together the way Yahweh intended us to. We have the freedom to raise our hand [as she salutes Nazi-style], to give thanks to our Lord, to show our Lord that we continue to respect the laws of racial separation

that are prescribed in the Bible, and that one day in the future this will be the law of the land.[11]

Most Aryan religious gatherings occur at homes, where members are assured privacy and control. As we saw in chapter 3, the home is an important site for white power gatherings of all kinds. The most common type of white power gathering at homes is the house party.

HOUSE PARTIES AND CRASHPADS

The following ethnographic narrative offers a glimpse into a typical neo-Nazi house party.

It was a warm summer night in Orange County, California, just the kind of idyllic, top-down, "wind blowing through your hair" night mythologized in countless songs and stories about Southern California. I was driving Seth home after an Aryan house party we'd been to that night. We had just dropped off his friend Paul at his apartment and began heading across town to Seth's crashpad when he turned to me and said, "We only wish you were one of us. I mean it's cool what you're doing trying to get it from our perspective, but we want you to be one of us. We've never given anyone access like this."

Trying to deflect this clear invitation, I replied, "Didn't you guys take the people from American History X all around?"

"Yeah but not like this," Seth said. "We never took them to parties and over to people's houses for get-togethers."

I felt strangely flattered, but wondered about the cost for this unprecedented access. I quickly got my answer.

After a pause, Seth's tone changed. This was a quirk of his that I was becoming accustomed to. He turned and said, "Just keep in mind if it turns out you're a cop, I'll personally hunt you down and slit your fucking throat, after I kill your family."

Strangely, death threats were also something I was becoming accustomed to. I told him, as I always had, that I was a sociologist, not a cop, and then tried to convince myself that he was just posturing as part of his skinhead bravado, even as I knew that some Aryans were not content with aggressive words alone. Seth's threat capped a long and interesting night.

The party in Costa Mesa had been filled with Aryans. I'd seen plenty of small Aryan parties where about a dozen white power friends hung out, drank beer, and commiserated about race problems. But this was the first large white power house party I'd been able to get into.

My guides were Aryan Front Skins. I knew Seth the best. He'd always been the most open to me, inviting me to meet his family and offering to introduce me around to his Aryan friends. Seth's band mates Paul and Jay were friendly to me the few times I'd met them before, but I was not nearly as familiar with them.

We got to the party early because Seth, Paul, and Jay were performing and wanted to set up their equipment before others arrived. They called their band Hate Train. They were using the party for rehearsal before they began a run of bar shows in the local white power music scene.

We pulled into the driveway of a modest, single-story, ranch-style stucco house with a single-car garage. It was on a corner lot, which was a little bigger than most others in the neighborhood. The backyard was not walled off. Only a small picket fence separated it from the sidewalk.

Paul knocked and the front door swung open. Donny, beer in hand, welcomed us in with a big smile. He looked to be in his mid-thirties and his style seemed more rockabilly than neo-Nazi. His medium-length brown hair was slicked back from his muttonchop sideburns. I learned later that Donny was a punk rocker as an adolescent and eventually turned to Nazism in his rebellion against some of the left-wing elements in the punk scene. In his spare time he promoted white power music and ran a Web-based company that trafficked in hate rock. He also worked full-time as a manager at a telephone company where he concealed his Nazi beliefs so he could, as he called it, "infiltrate the system."

From the outside there was nothing to mark the place as a white power haven. The décor inside was a different story, however. As I scanned the rooms, it was clear that this was a headquarters for white power activism. National Alliance and Klan leaflets were piled on the kitchen table. Photos of Don posing with skinheads and other Aryans at music shows hung on walls around the house. Don covered his refrigerator with Aryan photos and promotional posters for white power music shows. One prominent display showed Don and WAR leader Tom Metzger shaking hands and embracing. There were also many photos of young, pretty female activists dressed in revealing clothes marked with Aryan symbols.

Other Aryans trickled in, and within an hour, more than fifty people packed the house. Most of them looked to be in their late twenties or early thirties, although a few were clearly teenagers. Two-thirds of the attendees were male. They wore jeans or cargo shorts and T-shirts. Swastika, SS, and German iron cross tattoos on their arms clearly marked many of them as devoted Nazis. The women dressed in jeans and T-shirts.

Hate Train began to play songs about white unity and the racial struggle. Most of the lyrics were difficult to make out, as the loud, distorted guitar and heavy drums overshadowed their vocals. Some words were clear however—"nigger," "white power," and "Aryan pride."

Partygoers packed the living room where the band played. Only a couple of feet separated the front row of people from Seth and his bandmates. People stood shoulder to shoulder, making the room claustrophobic. No one seemed to mind, though. Skinheads sang along to the choruses, gave *Sieg heil* salutes, and periodically chanted "White power! White power!" at almost deafening levels.

Hate Train played nonstop for about an hour. As the set wore on, some men became more animated, clasping hands and shoulders and bouncing to the beat. Those who could not fit into the room craned their necks from the kitchen and bedroom hall to see the band and the crowd.

I was anxious in a room so tightly packed with Aryans. The band members were my "protection" should someone question my presence. But no one hassled me, since only those in the know had been invited. I presumed that others thought I was one of them, but I could not shake my worries that word might spread of an outsider in their midst.

While standing there, my mind flashed back to the story Paul had told me earlier in the day about the newspaper reporter who was invited to a Hammerskin party in Texas but by the end of the night found that he was no longer welcome. A group of Hammers took him from the house, nearly beat him to death, and left him in a drainage ditch. I took that as a warning and felt on edge during the night, like the moment I caught the eye of a skinhead whom I did not know. Dressed in full-on skinhead garb and already close to drunk, he just stared at me while leaning over to one of his friends, mouthing the words, "That's the guy who wants to study us."

Hate Train finished their set and I had my guides back. I listened to conversations about ZOG, the global Jewish conspiracy, the "mud problem," and small victories for the movement. The party felt like a private mini-rally as they lamented the injustices they faced.

I watched closely as two veteran Hammerskins from Florida started a conversation with a group of young skinheads. Quickly, Ray, a tanned, muscular skinhead with racist tattoos on both arms, turned his attention toward the two youngest skinheads. He motioned them toward the corner, drew them closer and in a deep guttural voice intoned, "We are the warriors! That's our God-given racially determined destiny. We have to remain strong. We have to keep healthy. That's why I love hanging out with my brothers because that's what this does; it keeps me proud, it keeps me strong."

The youngsters listened intently and nodded in approval.

Whites Only!

House parties like Don's are the most common occasions for small groups of Aryans. They occur at private homes, where entrée is often tightly controlled. The parties give activists a chance to connect with one another by displaying their allegiances, telling stories, and participating in Aryan rituals. They flaunt their beliefs by way of T-shirts, pullovers, and jackets marked with insignias of hate bands, white power group names, and Aryan codes. They uncover their tattoos, putting them on full display, and openly greet one another with Aryan gestures. The house itself is decorated for the event with swastikas, Confederate flags, and other movement symbols.

In these "whites only" environments, hosts closely scrutinize who enters the home to keep out nosy neighbors, police, and antiracists. At small gatherings that do not draw much attention, keeping the space free of outsiders is a simple task. But the scene changes at larger parties where unknown people show up and entry is more difficult to control. Hosts and their friends take turns watching the door to ensure they know who is coming in and going out. They closely scrutinize strangers for Aryan tattoos, clothing, or other indicators of being true to the cause. If they do not conform, hosts and friends confront and interrogate them about their background and affiliations, forcing them out of the party if they fail the test.

As celebrations grow and become more raucous, however, attention to who comes and goes can wane, so eventually almost anyone can enter. When entry opens up, a mood of defiance seems to build. The message for non-Aryans is: "C'mon on in and see who we are. We dare you. If you don't agree, fuck off."

Confrontations are especially likely when strangers enter whom Aryans suspect of having traces of African, Latino, Asian, or other nonwhite ancestry. In one instance, a drunken Indonesian neighbor wandered into an Aryan backyard barbeque that had been hopping for several hours. He quickly drew attention from several partygoers, and Smitty, a veteran skinhead just released from his second stint in prison, sauntered over and began questioning him: "Who the fuck are you and what the fuck are you doing here? Do you know where you are? This is a fucking white power party! White-fucking-power! Get the fuck out, you fucking mud!"

Staring blankly and appearing confused, the neighbor stood his ground. Smitty drew closer and readied for an attack until another partygoer intervened, telling the neighbor that, for his own good, he needed to "get the fuck out." The command hit home and the neighbor quickly left.

The party's normal pace resumed, albeit with a new focus for conversations. The night's theme became the "drunk Indian who almost got beat down," which provided a jumping-off point for commentary about various aspects of Aryan superiority and power, along with mock fighting moves to mimic what violence might have been done to the neighbor had he stayed. The confrontation was a display of Aryan bravado that set the boundary for the "pure white" space.

Symbolic Tales, Myths, and Meanings in House Parties

Aryans use house parties to swap stories about who they are and what they want. The settings are filled with a cacophony of Aryan voices spinning tales about what it means to be Aryan, the injustices they face, how they became enlightened to the cause, and of small victories against ZOG. Their talk amplifies solidarity and purpose among veterans and introduces initiates to the Aryan culture of hate.[12]

The Meaning of Aryan

White power members talk incessantly about what it means to be Aryan. In particular, they imagine themselves as aware of aspects of the world that non-Aryans do not see. This enlightened worldview illuminates the secret cabal of ZOG, pure whiteness, signs of a coming race war, and a fine-tuned reading of anti-Aryan themes in popular media and politics. During a Southern California house party, Dylan stood at the center of six Aryans, regaling them with his disbelief of whites "not down with the cause."

> What baffles me is how so many white people can't see what's going on before them, or worse, they don't care. I don't see how anybody in their right mind could look at blond, blue-eyed woman with a Negro, with mulatto children and look upon that and see that's not wrong.[13]

Aryan race myths require leaps of faith that can only be sustained in a context where others constantly nourish them. Aryans talk about the need for collective support to sustain their views. Paul, a SoCal Skin, declared to several other Aryans at a small party in his apartment:

> We really need people to stand up right now. The only way to get through this is by leaning on the others in your race who see through all this bullshit. We are the only ones who know. Without that moral support, we could never make it, we'd never last as a people, and our culture really would die off.[14]

These informal discussions play a central part in both defining and sustaining Aryan extremism.

Aryans tend to idealize themselves as a special group with hard and fast boundaries that define insiders versus outsiders. But some conversations in parties and other Aryan free spaces highlight how members work to clarify the essence of being an Aryan. For instance, at a bonfire party we watched as confusion brewed among a group of SWAS members over marriage and race mixing. Russ claimed that he "might be willing to marry an Indian or Mexican, but not a black, that's just wrong."

Visibly disturbed, Mindy replied, "That's disgusting, they're spics, how can you say that?"

"I only meant maybe," he responded.

The others launched into a vigorous debate to negotiate and clarify the boundaries of Aryan relationships along strictly white racial lines. This conversation not only clarified group norms about Aryan relations and marriage, but also pressured Russ to acknowledge his momentary lapse of reason and draw him back into the fold.

Injustice Tales

Aryans define themselves by the alleged injustices they face. Their conversations about Aryan identity invariably lead into morality and injustice tales that highlight just how the deck is stacked against whites. Aryan injustice talk revolves mostly around worries about the preservation and advancement of the Aryan race.[15] They lament to one another about the slow death of white culture and Aryan superiority. They attribute their problems to broad conspiracies against the white race.[16]

Aryans see ZOG clandestinely distorting whites' "true and righteous racial claims" while promoting "sick values to contaminate the Aryan mind by controlling television, media, music, art, fashion, religion, science, and education."[17] An Orange County Skin explained to his comrades during a backyard party: "In today's world it's a crime to be a white heterosexual male. Through the government and through the media, we're always getting the short end of the stick and getting screwed."[18]

A WAR Skin replied by pointing out the injustice he saw in the uneven treatment of races that want to express their racial pride: "How come a black guy can call another black guy a nigger and I can't? How come a guy with brown pride is cultural and white pride is racist? How come we need affirmative action, if everybody is equal? Why do we have to stack the deck for nonwhites?"

Aryans are particularly quick to talk with new recruits at parties about such injustices. We watched as veterans told tale after tale of dramatic conversion experiences that took them from "racial naïveté to racist enlightenment."[19] Many of these tales highlight schoolyard fights with African Americans and Hispanics as the catalyst that turned them into racial extremists.[20]

At an Idaho house party, Matt, an Aryan Nations veteran, told seven young skinheads gathered around him that his moment of racial consciousness came when "I was stabbed during the 1980s during the racial uproar [over desegregation]." He crouched into a fighting stance and slashed through the air as if holding a knife. "Goddamn niggers! Sliced me across the stomach! Look here." He lifted his shirt to reveal a dark, eight-inch scar across his abdomen. "That just showed me their mentality," he hissed. "Why should I have to live with these animals who'd rather see me dead? It don't make sense." Then, he paused for effect, looking each young skinhead in the eye. "That's when I knew."[21]

We watched similar scenes repeated in house parties in Southern California. These groups were the most active recruiters we saw. They organized most of their house parties with the clear intention of identifying "freshcuts," a skinhead term for young new recruits, and bringing them into the fold.

Most recruitment parties are overtly Aryan. Veterans show off their racist tattoos, white power clothing, and other signs of affiliation to impress the uninitiated. But not all recruitment parties are so straightforward. Racist skinheads also hold incognito recruitment parties by inviting audience members at local punk and metal concerts to an after-show party. Racist skinheads strategically play down their extremism at these parties to soften the shock to newcomers. They purposely tone down the racist décor in the house and feel out partygoers to determine their receptivity to white power ideas. If veterans sense that enough of the partiers might be receptive, they begin to expose their ideology by uncovering their tattoos, playing Aryan music, and talking with partiers about white power beliefs.

Veterans use toned-down versions of their injustice tales to introduce their ideology to neophytes. Eschewing hardcore words like *nigger*, veterans convey injustices against whites that led them into activism. Jack, an Orange County Skin, told his conversion tale to three punk rockers in a corner at one recruitment party: "I was barely fifteen years old and all the white kids were being harassed. You know how it is with all the black music, rap music, break dancing, and everybody wants to be Negro. The white kids were ashamed of their heritage." He went on, with an air of disbelief, "They were ashamed to be white! Like you, I just rejected all that. I became the opposite of all these other misled white kids. They were cowering. They had no spines. It was my way of rebelling against the liberals."[22]

Fortifying Tales

Aryans have relatively few grand tales of success. The race war has not happened and they remain relatively powerless. So members talk about small victories that foreshadow greater future triumphs. Their fortifying tales convey ideas about Aryan destiny and the righteousness of the racial struggle to sustain members' belief in the movement.[23] Stories of small victories help them to persist against the odds.

A common skinhead fortifying tale revolves around the idealized image of the Aryan warrior. Aryans tell stories of battle that, while they may be embellishments or outright lies, dramatize Aryan courage, strength, honor, and fearlessness in the face of their enemies. Ross, a SoCal Skin, related a superhuman feat to a group gathered at an after-concert party:

> So we want to get in this party and the guy is saying "you can't come in." My brother punches him and all of sudden you see this crowd of fuckin' niggers coming from the party, and they know we're skinheads, and my brother is standing in the doorway. Every hit was a knockout, and I'm not fuckin' exaggerating. My brother

had a pile of fifteen or twenty niggers in front of him. Finally he turns around and says, "Get in the car. Let's go." That's my brother, he's a super skinhead.[24]

This talk of small victories often concerns defensive tactics used to keep white neighborhoods "clean and safe" from racial enemies. We listened to conversations about defending Aryan turf from African American and Hispanic "intrusions." During a house party in Anaheim, California, Angie recounted a recent incident in her neighborhood when she noticed an African American woman looking at a house for sale near her own home: "I was looking out my front window and noticed this black chick walking around the neighbor's house that's for sale. So I walked out and told her the house was no longer available. No way I'm letting some nigger move in next to us."

Her fellow Aryans praised her and told several similar stories. Of course, people who do not identify with extremist hate also may voice racist statements. In Aryan circles, however, these statements carry the weight of intense hatred and violent ideals. The group agreed that it was next to impossible to "keep neighborhoods white," but anytime Aryans can stem the tide, they feel they win a small victory against ZOG and racial genocide.

Aryans also find small victories when old acquaintances affirm a member's racist convictions. Roger, a WAR activist, talked of frequent run-ins with former high school friends who seemed to acknowledge Aryan principles:

Oh yeah, I run into people I went to high school with. At the time they didn't agree with me and then all these years later I run into them and they say, "Hey, all those things you were saying, you were right you know. You hit the nail right on the head." That's real encouraging, you know?[25]

This alleged proof of the righteousness of hate gives Aryans like Roger confidence to keep fighting in the face of disbelievers. These fortifying myths and other morality tales are a form of Aryan ritualism that reproduces white power culture.[26]

Crashpads

Young neo-Nazi and racist skinhead crashpads have the look and feel of nonstop house parties. These Aryan free spaces resemble frat houses for young racists, where white power culture draws nascent Aryans deeper into extreme hate.[27] Young skinheads organize crashpads in houses, mobile homes, and apartments. These spaces shelter comrades and provide opportunities to carouse with others who believe in the cause.

Our brief story of Damon's house offers a glimpse into a typical skinhead crashpad.

Seth asked me to drive him to "a friend's house," but he didn't tell me why. I was leaving that afternoon, but had some time and agreed to take him. I had only known Seth for a few weeks, but it was clear to me that he was holding something back about where we were going.

We drove across Riverside and twenty minutes later turned into a dilapidated neighborhood. After a couple more turns, Seth said, "Right there," motioning for me to pull over and park in front of a ramshackle two-story house with chipped and faded yellow paint, a large front porch, and an old Ford truck in the driveway.

We got out, and as we were closing our car doors, Seth looked across and, in a grave voice, said, "Look, you don't wanna mess with this guy. He'll cut your fuckin' head off if he thinks you're causing trouble. Just don't ask any questions. But if you do start talking with him or any others in there make sure they know what you're doing. You don't want them thinking you're trying to hide something."

The "guy" was Damon, an ex-con and a badass Aryan Front skinhead. He was six feet tall, bald and stocky. His tank-top showed off his muscular body fully sleeved—covered neck to wrists—with racist tattoos. Seth told me later that he had gotten many of the tattoos in prison while serving a five-year sentence for attacking three Latinos in a city park.

I followed Seth through the front door. He greeted Damon in the middle of the living room and Seth told me to wait while they both walked into the kitchen. I scanned the living room. A swastika banner and Confederate flag hung on opposite walls. The house smelled like a dirty ashtray. The floor was littered with fast-food wrappers. The couch was ripped and had cigarette burns all over it. The rickety wooden coffee table in front of the couch was covered with rows of beer cans, bottles, and white power CDs.

Seth and Damon were standing in the kitchen where I could see dirty dishes overflowing the sink. I overheard Seth say, "No, he's not a cop, you don't need to worry about that."

Damon stayed silent, stared at me, and nodded his head slightly. He seemed willing to tolerate me on Seth's word, but nothing more. I was uncomfortable but decided to walk into the kitchen. Seth told me to wait while they went down into Damon's basement to talk more.

A woman who looked to be in her middle thirties sat at the kitchen table looking down at a small pile of white powder. She picked up the straw, looked up at me, and asked in a tired, hoarse voice, "Do you want some?" I thanked her for the offer but declined. She didn't seem to mind and quickly returned her attention to the powder on the table in front of her.

She looked like the stereotypical tweaker. Tangled, unwashed hair; acne-covered skin; and an edginess that reminded me of a hyperactive child. Just beyond the kitchen window a beat-up swing set and a few other toys were scattered about. My stomach churned as I contemplated the idea of raising children in this environment.

As I shuffled back into the living room, Seth came out, motioned to the door and said, "Let's go." He never told me what he and Damon were up to.

On the drive back, Seth described Damon's house as a place where skins "partied and crashed all the time." He had seen at least twenty people living there at times, sleeping on the couches and floors. Many of them were new to Southern California and needed a place to crash temporarily "until they got their bearings." Damon hosted white power bands in town for gigs and had house concerts for local bands.

Seth took me to Damon's crashpad four more times over the next two years. Each visit was for a party. Two of the gatherings were relatively low-key affairs with about twenty skins. The other two parties were rowdy blowouts with more than fifty Aryans packing the house and spilling out into the yard. At both parties I had expected the police to show up for noise and nuisance complaints. They never came, and I wondered if neighbors were simply too intimidated to call.

At each party, duffle bags and backpacks with sleeping bags were strewn throughout the house, a clear sign that some of the partyers had been traveling and were probably new to the scene. Alcohol and drugs flowed freely, and white power music blared from the stereo in the living room. The skinheads talked about the Southern California hate music scene, gang battles, and ZOG.

The ritualism was always the most fascinating part of these parties. At each party eight or nine skinheads formed a circle in the living room, arms clasped around each other's necks, and stomped and chanted in unison to hate rock. At times, it felt as if the floors would cave in. An Aryan Front tattoo artist set up shop in the kitchen and inked several members as part of their initiation into the group.

Damon and his comrades used his crashpad as a key recruitment space. At each party seven or eight teens shuffled around, appearing unsure of their place in the group. The veteran skinheads called them freshcuts, and throughout the night chatted them up about what they thought of the scene, what they knew about the white cause, and if they were "down with white power." Damon's friends had already identified these youngsters as recruitable, although I wasn't quite sure how they did this. Seth said they wouldn't have been brought to Damon's if they weren't already associated with other Aryans.[28]

Most of the regulars I met at Damon's crashpad were male skinheads. For them, Damon's place was not just a hangout, but one of the few places they could meet with other extremists like them.

In the five years of field observations and interviews to follow we learned that Damon's crashpad was just one of many across the country where skinheads stay. Crashpads are filled with Aryan symbolism, racist books, hate music fanzines, and political pamphlets. White power banners and slogans cover the walls. The most extreme crashpads also decorate the exterior of the home with Nazi banners and graffiti-style writing boasting Aryan slogans.

Weapons and race war are consistent topics of crashpad conversations. We watched members pass around for inspection guns, knives, and brass knuckles as they discussed urban survival strategies and the coming race war. Crashpads are also used as staging areas for leafleting racist literature, public protests, and "city walks," in which skinheads cruise urban areas looking for confrontations with racial enemies.[29]

Crashpads vary in permanence. Skinheads seem to have an attitude of planned obsolescence toward their hangouts, typically treating them with reckless abandon. Most crashpads are in disrepair, and the walls, ceilings, and floors are typically strewn with crude Aryan graffiti.

Aryan gang crashpads like those created by PEN1 are temporary spaces where people congregate for days or weeks until either they are compelled to leave by property owners or police or new opportunities arise elsewhere.[30] PEN1's members move weekly between motels and dilapidated apartments around Los Angeles, Orange, Riverside, and San Bernardino counties. They take over these locations, transforming them into crashpads as they party, graffiti the space, and organize their criminal operations. They then leave them demolished. Ace, a PEN1 skinhead, said: "We never really claim territory, you know, we just think that wherever we are is our territory. That's how PEN1's always been. Why claim specific territory? We don't need to say this street or block is ours. It's all ours."[31] This attitude reflects the idealized notion of Aryan supremacy, which gives them natural dominion.

Veteran skinheads with some financial success will sometimes open their homes as crashpads for younger Aryans. Clay, a founding member of the Southern California skinhead gang Aryan Reich Skins, moved to Phoenix, Arizona. There he started a mortgage company and purchased a new two-story home in an affluent Phoenix suburb. He immediately offered the home to young skinhead recruits as a space to live and be immersed in white power culture.

Unlike most Aryan crashpads we saw, where ten or twenty racist skinheads cycled in and out every few weeks, the scene at Clay's was stable. Few skinheads moved in and out, partly because Clay wanted to keep a low profile among his neighbors and saw his home as an informal halfway house where skinheads could congregate, find some stability, and make a new start with school and jobs. He expected them to follow his example and give money and time back to the Aryan cause.

Most crashpads are semipermanent spaces somewhere between Clay's secret house and PEN1's temporary motel rooms. Crashpads carry reputations in skinhead circles as gathering places where Aryans can find camaraderie among other members.

Skinhead crashpads also are sites of ritualism. We now describe dramatic performances and tattooing ceremonies, which Aryans use to build strength and solidarity

ARYAN RITUALISM

Aryan rituals are collective acts that arouse emotions and intensify solidarity by marking the boundaries between white power advocates and their enemies.[32] Aryans' storytelling itself is ritualistic, invoking common themes time after time. But Aryans also elaborate their tales with performances and ceremonies that reproduce group solidarity and commitment.[33]

Performing White Power

Ritual performances occur routinely at Aryan parties. Some are as simple as semi-spontaneous gestures by members who arrive at parties and give animated *Sieg heil* salutes or shout Aryan mottos to the group, who respond in kind. At other gatherings, however, time was set aside for more elaborate performances, including organized group shouts of *Sieg heil*, pledges, and commitment ceremonies that amplify Aryan values.

Darren and Mindy staged performances at their regular bonfire parties. They were particularly fond of burning effigies of blacks and Jews. Darren called this "nigger lynching." The first time he said, "We're going to lynch a nigger tonight," it was not clear that he wasn't talking about a real person. The lynching was symbolic, but nonetheless, it heightened solidarity among the partyers.

> Partyers began arriving at six. As the first car drove up, Darren said, "I'll be back in a minute," and he turned and strode to the barn. He emerged a half hour later, walked to the keg, poured a beer, and said with a smile to the group gathered around, "Wait till you see what I made for the party!"
>
> Two hours later about thirty Aryans gathered around the bonfire. Darren nudged his friend Erik and they both turned and walked to the barn. Darren soon came out carrying a large wooden cross, with Erik behind him carrying in his arms what looked like a scarecrow. As they approached, it was clear that this was the "nigger" they planned to lynch.
>
> The effigy was covered with black cloth to mimic dark skin, and dressed in a blue baseball cap turned to the side, an old Michael Jackson T-shirt, and blue jeans.
>
> Darren and Erik positioned the cross on the edge of the fire pit and

pounded it into the ground with a sledge hammer. The crowd of more than thirty adults and their children began to gather in a circle around the cross. Darren secured the effigy in place on the cross and added wood to the fire. After a few minutes, flames licked the bottom of the cross and it started to burn.

The effigy caught fire, and the entire group began chanting in unison, "Rahowa! Rahowa! Rahowa!" Children chanted, imitating their parents. Older kids gave Nazi salutes to one another. A woman standing next to me knelt down beside her young daughter and said, "Honey, that cross celebrates our ancestors. The niggers and spics want to take that away from us."

"Let's go nigger hunting!" shouted a young skinhead whose fist was thrust toward the sky.

Fortunately, his plan was met with disdain. Several SWAS parents told him to cool down. I wondered if a younger, less family-oriented crowd may have taken to his idea more enthusiastically.

The chants of "Rahowa" faded when a new mantra emerged: "Burn, nigger, burn! Burn, nigger, burn!"

Darren stepped in front of the fire, facing the crowd, silhouetted by an orange glow, face shrouded in shadows. "I want to thank all of you for coming out tonight. Our little Buckwheat," he said solemnly, pointing to the effigy as the group laughed, "is to remind us that we're in a fight." His voice got louder as he continued, "This is guerilla war, and we need to start thinking in those terms. They call it hate, hate crime, whatever. It's self-defense! You're defending yourself, your family, your country, and your culture!"

The fire continued to burn. The cross and effigy were soon reduced to ashes.

After Darren's speech, the group was clearly more energized. They talked excitedly of the movement, ZOG, Illuminati, the black menace, illegal immigrants, and other Aryan threats.

Ritual occasions illuminate how a person becomes an Aryan. This ritual created a palpable group feeling of camaraderie and affection, emphasized love among Aryans, and translated hatred and violence as righteous self-defense. Such emotional messages help us imagine the compelling force among people who surrender themselves to the group. Aryan rituals are powerful tools to encourage commitment to the cause and camaraderie with white racial kin.

Sieg Heil

Group chants of *Sieg heil* are a ritual performance Aryans use to intensify members' esprit de corps. At bonfire parties, house parties, and barbeques, we

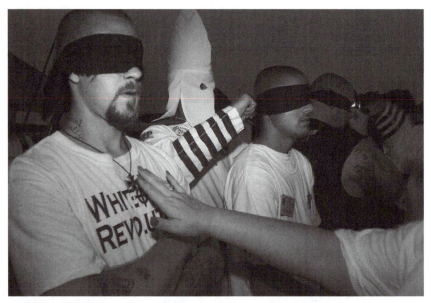

Figure 4.1   Several members of White Revolution are blindfolded before their commitment ceremony as part of their initiation into the Aryan Knights of the Ku Klux Klan. August 16, 2003, Colt, Arkansas.

Photo by David S. Holloway/© Getty Images

watched the ominous scene of ten, twenty, and sometimes dozens more skinheads and neo-Nazis as they chanted in unison and thrust their arms upward, with each *Sieg heil* shouted louder than the last.

Aryans usually combined the chants with backslaps and bear hugs, which heightened the intensity of the collective experience. Skinheads also broke into mock fights, and circling group members clasped hands and stepped in unison to the chant and music.

Dramas

Choreographed dramas are Aryans' most striking ritual performances. These are usually violent, like Darren's mock lynching, complete with props, such as a hangman's noose and effigies of blacks or Jews hanging from trees or doorways. We recorded stories and saw photos of mock beheadings, where Aryans dressed as hooded executioners with double-edged axes and swords symbolically behead other Aryans painted in blackface and dressed in "ethnic" clothing with afro wigs.

Aryans sometimes blend these performances with commitment ceremonies.

New recruits are formally initiated into the movement by performing part of the mock execution themselves while veterans prompt them to declare their commitment to "the Aryan way."

Tattoos

Aryans view tattooing rituals as one of the most important ways to demonstrate their commitment to the cause. They cover themselves with swastika tattoos, German iron crosses, Confederate flags, portraits of Hitler, German soldiers, crossed hammers, and white power slogans. Slogans may be ones that have broad unifying themes across the movement, such as "White Power," "White Pride," "SKIN," "Proud to Be White," and "SWP," for Supreme White Power, or may be ones that signify allegiance to specific groups like Orange County Skins, WAR Skins, or Hammerskin Nation.

Tattoos are the clearest symbol of an Aryan's devotion. Randy, an Orange County Skin, said that a swastika or other obvious Aryan tattoo "basically says you're down for the cause. If you have a swastika on, you're letting it all hang out. You're saying 'I'm gonna fight and be down for the cause so much that I'm willing to take that risk to show everybody white power.'"[34] Like many Aryans, Randy's racist tattoos cover his back, chest, and upper arms.

Sleeves, or tattoos that cover arms from neck to wrist, denote members who are the most deeply committed. They are willing to overtly display their allegiance to the Aryan cause. Aryans may take this a step further by tattooing their entire body, including their face, with race-related insignia.

Tattoos show commitment that goes beyond mere rhetoric. We asked Hank, a SoCal Skin whose arms are sleeved with hate insignia, why tattoos are so revered in the movement. "Well," he said, "they're about displaying your racial pride, making sure there's no doubt. As you get more and more, it's a way of reinforcing who you are and drawing that line a little harder each time."[35]

Similarly, Cory, a Hammerskin, said: "Why do we want [tattoos]? We want to tell a story, to establish who we are, and what we've done or will do. We want people to know we're down for our race and down for the cause."[36]

Darren talks of a deepening devotion he feels with every new tattoo. Pointing to a German iron cross on his forearm, he said, "This was my first tattoo. I've had seven since that one and with each one you feel a little more committed. You know you're never going back."

Aryans use tattooing as a bonding ritual. At several parties, we watched racist skinheads get inked in the company of other skinheads as parts of initiation and hazing ceremonies. Just after the tattoo is complete, other skinheads slap the tender tattooed area while chanting racist slogans or singing hate songs. The tattooing ritual signifies rugged masculinity and unity with other skinheads. At times, tattooing becomes extreme. Anthony, a longtime SoCal Skin, described the ritualistic violence that can be sparked by the commitment rituals surrounding tattooing:

> We were at a party at an apartment and a couple of guys at the party were American Alliance, and they wanted this guy Chucky to become part of 'em, but he had to like earn his bolt [lightning bolt tattoo] before they would let him in. Everybody there was drunk. Chucky was drunk, so he goes down to the street corner to look for somebody that he can assault to earn his bolt to get in. He comes back with a bloody knife and he's all sweaty and says, "Hey I just stabbed these spics," and of course the party goes crazy. Chucky gets carried off to some other place and they are so pleased with him, they take a staple and an ink pen and that is how he got his first lightning bolt.[37]

The extreme version of this commitment ritual involves an initiate who commits murder to earn a particularly significant tattoo. In November 1995, four Nazi Lowriders beat to death a homeless African American man to earn their lightning bolts. They were later arrested and convicted of murder.[38]

White power tattooing is neither a one-time ritual for most Aryans nor is it for initiates only. Veterans often add repeatedly to their tattoos. Successive tattoos are a physical symbol of their identification with extremist hate and social distance from the mainstream. Fellow Aryans typically etch the tattoos, and their art is their most significant contribution to the movement. Nick, an L.A. County Skin and tattoo artist, explains the pride and service to the movement he feels when inking fellow skins:

> I'm most proud about the work I do on other skins. I get to see young ones who are getting their first one and will always remember that one, but I also get to give my brothers who've been out here for years their fifteenth or whatever tattoo. Either way, I'm doing my little bit to help the movement where I can.[39]

Like many groups whose membership is highly restrictive, Aryans anchor their commitment symbolically through visual symbols.[40] Tattooing rituals help Aryans take on signs of their racial loyalty, consciousness, and self-completion as devoted to the cause. It is the intense collective experience that establishes much of the meaning the tattoos have for Aryans who get them.

★

The combination of veterans with new recruits at Aryan parties and gatherings gives younger Aryans a chance to interact with more seasoned extremists, who model Aryan style and attitude, share stories, and involve recruits in rituals to draw them into the movement. These informal Aryan gatherings are political to their core.[41] They offer Aryans a racist milieu crucial to the survival of extremist hatred. Aryan gatherings are also seedbeds for recruitment. A 2006 National Institute of Justice study on right-wing terrorist recruitment indicates about 75 percent of right-wing extremists who have planned or participated in terrorist activity were recruited in homes and crashpads.

Another component of Aryan gatherings is the strategic use of music. In the next chapter, we shift our attention to Aryan music concerts and festivals. The extensive network of white power bands, music companies, Web-based music sites, and music shows offer Aryans spaces to meet and nourish hate culture.

5

The White Power Music Scene

I listen to white power music and I have that feeling of being involved with something as a whole. It's something where I can sit at home alone and even though I know the whole world is against me I can pop in a CD and listen to it.

—Mike, Midwest Aryan[1]

Music is integrated into the white power movement.[2] Aryans use music to convey ideas about their righteous struggles, focus movement activities, and unite racists in Aryan free spaces, which range from house parties to bar shows and festivals to the hate rock websites. In these free spaces, Aryan members display their style and share attitudes and emotions that bind them as racial extremists.

Hate rock performers and listeners think of Aryan music as a form of activism. White power music helps performers and listeners stay committed to their cause by reminding them why they fight for Aryan supremacy. The crowds that gather for bar shows and concerts participate in collective rituals that help anchor them to an ethos of hate.

We begin this chapter with a discussion of the Aryan band Hate Train and its rise to prominence in the white power music scene. We then focus on other white power bands, their music, and the bar concerts and festivals where Aryans gather to hear white power music and nourish their commitments to the movement. Finally, we discuss the Aryan recording companies who promote and sustain the white power music scene.

HATE TRAIN'S RISE

Hate Train's rapid rise in the white power music scene began in the winter of 1998. The band had been playing a series of house parties to prepare for their first public gig in a tiny dive bar on the outskirts of Anaheim, California.

They expected a few dozen local Aryan friends to watch them play their first show. This public performance raised the ante for them. Playing private house parties felt safe, but if word about the show got out to the wrong crowd, namely antiracist groups and the police, there was no telling what would happen.

The show was a coming-out party for Hate Train's singer, Hank. He had never been so publicly open about his racism. As a relative newcomer to the movement, Hank was anxious about performing publicly. Antiracists frequently picketed Aryan shows. Police also sometimes raided concerts, arresting audience and band members alike. He was nervous.

Seth, Hate Train's drummer, was anxious for different reasons. He could not wait to perform. A veteran racist skinhead, Seth had long ties to the hate music scene. During the 1980s, he worked closely with White Aryan Resistance (WAR) leader Tom Metzger to use music to draw skinheads and punks into white nationalist politics. Seth organized house shows and bar concerts, then joined his first white power band, Aryan Rage, in 1991. The band broke up two years later, and ever since then, Seth had been trying to form another group.

Seth recruited Hank after hearing him play at a punk show in L.A. Hank recalled:

> I met Seth at one of my old band's shows. We [Hank's band] were punk but mainstream. I was already white power in my views, but kept pretty quiet about it. After this one show Seth came up to me and introduced himself, and said he liked our set. He bought me a beer and we sat down and started talking. He told me he was thinking of starting a new band but needed a singer. I liked what I heard and we decided to form Hate Train not long after that. I told my old band, "Hey I'm going to start playing music for our people." They haven't talked to me since.[3]

That was six months before Hate Train's first public gig. In that time Hank fully embraced white power culture and Aryan activists embraced him. The camaraderie and support he's received from his fellow Aryans surprised him. His new friends made up for the old friends he lost when he joined the movement.

> Being new and all and not knowing anyone really at first I wasn't sure how it was going to turn out. I got started pretty late in life, but it hasn't seemed to make a difference. People are like, "Way to go! We're glad you're with us," and it feels good knowing I'm actually doing something for my race.[4]

Hate Train's guitarist, Lance, dressed more like a skateboarder than a white power skinhead. At his day job as a marketing analyst for a large public relations firm he played down any visible racist leanings even more. He slicked back his hair in a fashionable rockabilly style and covered the racist tattoos inked on his shoulders, back, and chest with a dress shirt and tie. Lance, like Seth, also had a long history as an Aryan. He ran with two skinhead gangs in his early teens. But as many of his gang friends succumbed to drugs or were arrested, he shifted course toward college.

Lance also began to read more about White Aryan Resistance and attend Aryan music shows in Southern California. He jumped at Seth's invitation to join the band. Hate Train and the white power music scene provide the perfect anchor for his activism. As he explained, "I'm now part of an international movement of nationalists. We're all fighting to end the reign of the International Jew and the domination he has over our race's destiny."

For their first-ever show, Hate Train was booked with another Aryan band and two nonracist punk bands. The night went off without a hitch. No protesters arrived, and no police interrupted. Some thirty Aryans mixed with a few regulars who seemed curious and slightly amused at the racist skinheads. Second in the music lineup, Hate Train played from 9 to 9:30 PM. The occasion was ordinary for everyone except Seth, Hank, and Lance. For them, the show was an important step into the white power music scene. After the show, Hank said, "We needed to do something like that. We knew it wasn't going to be a big show or anything. It was more a way of officially announcing we're here and we're ready to start playing music for white people."[5]

What happened in the following months caught them all by surprise. Seth promoted the band locally and also with prominent Aryan music companies, such as Resistance Records. Word of their sound and style spread among southern California Aryans and into the broader white power music scene.

Two months after their first show, SkinFest organizers invited Hate Train to their white power festival in Texas. Seth now refers to this as their "first real show" because, as he saw it, the performance really "put them on the map" as a legitimate band in the movement's music scene.

SkinFest was only the beginning. White power promoters got wind of that successful performance, and Hate Train received invitations to more prominent gigs. The band played at large bar shows in Southern California and was then invited to play the first Hammerfest. The festival, organized by the Hammerskin Nation, drew about 600 Aryans to a private farm in rural Georgia where they heard a lineup of the most popular bands in the Aryan music scene.

Within a year of their first bar show, Hate Train gained a wide following in the white power music scene. Fans gravitated to the band's punk spirit, their theatrical performances, and the inventive transformations of well-known pop songs into Aryan-themed songs. They recorded two CDs and continued to play at a series of major Aryan festivals. Enthusiasm for their music spread to Europe, and the European National Socialist online fanzine, *Blood and Honour*, wrote glowing reports of their performances.

Hate Train's popularity among European skins led to bar concerts and festivals in England, France, Italy, Germany, and the Czech Republic. In the summer of 2004, a European extreme right-wing party invited Hate Train to headline one of their rallies, which drew more than 5,000 neo-Nazis. Seth, Hank, and Lance saw this as a tremendous honor and felt they had arrived.

HATE BANDS AND HATE MUSIC

White power music in the 1990s grew as a pervasive form of racist expression. New hate bands and the music companies that promoted them spread rapidly. The bands mainly play rock, heavy metal, country and western styles, or Aryan folk sounds.

White power rock represents the most popular Aryan music style. The sound morphed from the punk and Oi! styles of 1960s and 1970s English working-class culture. Punk and Oi! use hard guitar and drums, simple musical structures, and vocals that resemble fast-paced chants.

Contemporary white power versions of Oi! draw direct influence from the late-1970s British band Skrewdriver, the first premier Aryan rock band, whose members veered from punk anarchism toward racist politics.[6] Skrewdriver appealed to a growing number of American skinheads who moved toward extreme right-wing politics and Aryan ideology during the 1980s.[7]

Skrewdriver had a major influence on white power music. We interviewed dozens of Aryans who told us about the importance of the band in their racial awakening. Dave, a Volksfront member from St. Louis, vividly recalled the moment, saying, "The first time I heard Skrewdriver was it. Every skinhead can tell you about that. It was a bootleg of a bootleg of a bootleg and the sound wasn't worth shit, but it was still magical. It was instantaneous."[8] Andy, a skinhead from Vancouver, Washington, recalled:

> The first white power song I ever heard was "White Power" from Skrewdriver in high school on a shitty fifth- or sixth-generation cassette copy. It [the song] totally floored me. Once I heard that, it took over me. That was the attitude and feeling I had been looking for. I was already racially aware, but Skrewdriver motivated me.[9]

Veteran white power musicians like Tom also claim Skrewdriver was their inspiration: "A friend gave me this bootlegged tape and I started listening to it and couldn't believe how powerful it was. I knew I had to become a skinhead once I listened to that tape. The tape was Skrewdriver."[10]

There are now more than 100 American white power bands and more than 200 hate bands spread over twenty-two other countries, and the number of bands appears to be growing.[11] Although the sounds and styles of racist music—rock, heavy metal, country and western, folk, and other genres—are distinguishable from one another, the lyrical themes in the songs highlight Aryan nationalism, white power, race war, anti-Semitism, anti-immigration, anti-race-mixing, white victimization, and racial loyalty. Songs like Skrewdriver's "Race and Nation" paint a clear picture of the Aryan nationalist vision so central to the movement.[12]

The Bully Boys, Max Resist, Final War, and Youngland are among the most popular American white power bands. The Bully Boys, a Dallas, Texas, band, mirror Skrewdriver's punk and Oi! sound. They were one of the first bands to closely align themselves with the Hammerskin Nation. Detroit-based, Max Resist and the Hooligans also align themselves with the Hammerskins. The band's singer, Sean Suggs, is a notorious skinhead leader known by Aryans across the country.

The Bully Boys' song "Jigrun" is a prominent white power anthem that imagines a night terrorizing blacks.[13] One of Max Resist's most popular songs among Aryans, "Boot Party," refers to stomping racial enemies to death.[14] Final War and Youngland, bands formed in Orange County, California, sing about Aryan honor, brotherhood, *volk*, white pride, and white heritage. Their songs sustain the movement by promoting commitment and unity in hard times. Final War's "Pride and Tradition" describes problems Aryans face and a need to battle for the righteous truths of Aryan destiny. Aryans from across the movement's branches embrace Youngland's "Stand One, Stand All." This song is a short, powerful statement of Aryan idealism and unity.[15]

Prussian Blue is a unique and widely publicized white power music group. The duo consists of teenaged fraternal twins Lynx and Lamb Gaede, referred to by Aryans as the white power Olsen twins, in reference to the mainstream pop celebrity twins Mary-Kate and Ashley Olsen.

A Gaede performance in 2001 at an Aryan festival caught the attention of National Alliance leader and Resistance Records owner William Pierce, who immediately signed them to a recording contract.[16] The Gaedes combined Aryan folk themes and bubble-gum pop-rock to create a buzz among Aryans. The Gaedes recorded several CDs with songs written by the bands Rahowa and Brutal Attack.

The Gaedes' original songs include "Sacrifice," which honors Robert Mathews, founder of the white power terror cell the Silent Brotherhood, and Nazi leader Rudolph Hess. The Gaedes wrote the song, "The Lamb Near the Lane" after exchanging letters with imprisoned Aryan terrorist and convicted murderer David Lane.

Prussian Blue has garnered popular media attention, including feature segments on ABC's *Primetime* and *Good Morning America* and has been a subject of articles in *Newsweek*, *Gentlemen's Quarterly*, *Elle Girl*, and the *Los Angeles Times*. The Internet is replete with videos of the group, and the Prussian Blue website offers merchandise, photos, essays, and other paraphernalia.

Consciousness-Raising Music

Activists revere white power bands as icons and their songs fuel Aryan rage. Hate rock's seductiveness can be gauged by members' accounts of how they joined the white power movement. Aryan music fans talk about how the music helps them feel unique and superior to those people still blinded from the truth of the white power vision. Biggie, a Colorado skin, identifies the music-based defining moment of his racial awakening:

> I had some racist views before I started listening to [white power] music, but once I heard that first Skrewdriver song, I was sold. It really did change my life. I started going to white power shows whenever I could, and I'd drive anywhere. . . . It connected me to other people who were willing to say, "You know, I'm a racist. So what? I'm proud of who I am."[17]

Sociologist Kathleen Blee noticed a similar pattern of music's impact on Aryans' enlightenment. As a California skinhead girl told her, "How I really started believing, thinking, in that white separatist sense and then got all white supremacist, it was really through the music. . . . It gives you an identity . . . you're special, you know, because you're white."[18]

This sense of being "special" draws from a privileged knowledge Aryans have about the true nature of the world. Aryans think of themselves as among the few who see through and reject mainstream society's effort to destroy white culture and the white race. They consider music a tool to show other whites, and especially young members, the righteous way.

Kenny, a SoCal Skin, envisions music as a powerful way to reach white youth: "It's good for us to have music that raises consciousness of white kids as opposed to listening to all the other crap the mainstream gives out. Music is a good tool, you know. It helps with motivation to get more education about what is going on."[19] The message in music is easy to disseminate secretively as well.

> Music has the potential to get through to the kids like nothing else. The great thing about music is, if a kid likes it, he will dub copies for his friends and so on. This has the potential to become a grassroots, underground type movement, which we see happening already.[20]

Some bands consciously create music that will appeal to potential recruits. Samuel, a veteran white power band member in Seattle, explained his band's strategy to perform low-key racist music, which will not be too shocking for new recruits but eventually draws them into more extremist white power culture. Samuel said, "We try to keep our lyrics fairly approachable for people that may not pay a lot of attention to racial issues in order to try and persuade them to think about things. Once they're on our side they can listen to groups with real hardcore lyrics."[21]

Figure 5.1   A White Revolution member's young son clutches at his Blue Eyed Devils fan T-shirt. The Blue Eyed Devils are a popular band in the white power music scene. March 30, 2003, Van Buren, Arkansas.

Photo by David S. Holloway/© Getty Images

Bands and the music scene are thus key elements in the white power movement. The free spaces in which the bands play become sites of intense recruitment as members and newcomers create collective experiences to celebrate hate. When bars host white power music shows they become Aryan free spaces.

WHITE POWER BAR SHOWS

We begin our analysis of these music free spaces with an ethnographic narrative that takes us into a Southern California white power bar show.

"You're sure my name is on the list?" I said into the phone while driving alone to the suburban strip mall outside Garden Grove, California. "Yeah man, no worries. You're on there," Seth assured me.

I was still worried that Seth might have forgotten to add my name to the guest list. Security would be tight for Hate Train's show, as it usually was for gigs at larger venues like the Lotus Club, where they were playing tonight. These big bar shows could attract protesters and police. The entry list was one way that organizers tried to keep the space inside the bar free for Aryans to congregate and party. I could expect a hassle if my name was not on the list.

Security was tight, as I expected. I drove past the club's parking lot to scan the scene and prepare myself for the walk to the door. Outside the club entrance I saw four burly skinheads. Down the sidewalk a group of about ten to fifteen protesters held signs reading "Nazis go home" and "Diversity Is Our Strength." I parked a block away, took a deep breath to gather my wits, then strode toward the bar trying to exude an air of confidence.

"Hey! Don't go in there you fucking Nazi! You hater!"

I ignored the protesters, looked straight ahead, and quickly stepped past the doorman into the small lobby entrance to the bar. A small line had formed as two doormen wearing black "American Front Security" T-shirts checked names and collected the cover charge. I stepped up, said my name and held out a twenty-dollar bill. After a couple of seconds, the skinhead looked up, grabbed my money and said, "Enjoy the show, brother." I stepped forward to be patted-down by the other doorman, and then walked inside.

I moved quickly to the edge of the bar to get my bearings. The place was buzzing with conversations, and the bar's stereo primed the audience by playing National Socialist Black Metal, a hard-hitting Gothic style of hate rock. The club was one large room, with a bar full of high tables and chairs on the left and a music stage on the wall opposite the bar. Handbills from local punk and hip-hop bands adorned the walls.

It was a half hour before show time, and the crowd had already topped more than seventy people. They were mostly male neo-Nazis between twenty and thirty years old. Some older veterans were there as well, along with some teenage fresh cuts.

Most of the men had close-cropped or fully shaved heads and tattoos covering their bodies. Some wore traditional skinhead garb—tight blue jeans, Doc Marten steel-toed work boots, tight T-shirts, and colored suspenders. A group of eight high schoolers wore plain white T-shirts on which they had written in dark ink "Las Vegas Skins." Others wore plain shirts or ones emblazoned with band insignia or swastikas and other hate symbols.

Two other Aryan styles stood out in the bar. One group sported an urban style with knee-length trouser shorts sagging at the waist to show their boxer shorts, white tank tops, tube socks pulled knee-high, and athletic shoes with thick shoelaces. Another group presented a more polished GQ look, with styled hair, designer jeans, and polo shirts.

The men outnumbered the women four to one. About ten women chose a fairly conventional punk look, with heavy mascara, and short, stylishly unruly hair. The others did not clearly mark themselves as punk or Aryan.

The show organizers lined up several tables along the wall near the entrance and filled them with CDs, T-shirts, books, hats, posters, and other merchandise. Some of the T-shirts were from Aryan groups such as the National Alliance, Hammerskins, and World Church of the Creator, while others were specific to white power bands, such as Max Resist, Angry Aryans, and Skrewdriver. One table was strewn with pamphlets, cards, and Aryan books.

Paul, an Aryan musician I had met before, stood nearby. He was in his late twenties, medium height and build, and his dark hair was usually shaved down to little more than stubble. He wore a green Ireland T-shirt with navy Dickie shorts. White power tattoos decorated his arms and legs: a German iron cross tattoo on his left calf, and Nordic warriors sketched across both arms.

I joined Paul at the bar and asked what he thought of the crowd. "Great!" he said, pointing out the different groups and cliques that had come out. He turned to me with a smile, winked, and said, "Diversity is our strength, you know?"

I laughed as I thought of the irony in that statement. Neo-Nazis claim their world has been turned upside down by diversity policies and multicultural attitudes. Sometimes they use conventional phrases like "strength in diversity," to support their worldview.

I tagged along with Paul as he ambled over to a group of skinheads and Klansmen who were talking about the protesters outside the club. Tim, who I would shortly discover was a local Klan leader, looked nothing like a stereotypical Aryan. He was dressed in slacks, a dress shirt and a tie. His medium-length brown hair and a neatly trimmed mustache belied his extremism. He knew everyone in the group but me, quickly extended his hand and said, "I'm Tim. Good to meet you. Here, take my card."

I glanced down and saw what resembled a standard business card, except for the logo of a hooded Klansman riding a horse, and his official title, "Grand Dragon."

He said, "I was just out there with those faggot bastards! I kept trying to get them to step off the sidewalk to get 'em arrested for trespassing." Tim described the confrontation when Donny, a white power music promoter, approached and handed each of us flyers, "I gave these to the media outside."

It was a surprisingly well-written paragraph about free speech that painted the protesters as fascists trampling the rights of "American patriots to gather peacefully for music and fun."

"Peacefully" was the word that stuck out to me. White power music shows in Southern California had a reputation for violence. For several years, music organizers in the Southern California white power music scene had given up on bar shows because so many of them had been marred by brawls and stabbings among boisterous Aryans.

Violence is part of the music scene culture and the wider movement. Hate music weaves violent lyrics with driving beats that build excitement and tension. Skinheads prance, posture, and slam dance in the pit fronting the stage. Their antics can quickly turn from mock fights to real ones. Personal disputes or intergroup conflicts that Aryans bring to the shows exacerbate this tendency.

The tightly organized security team at tonight's show reflected past violence. Several band members playing the gig had commented that the organizers really "had it together." Through websites, leaflets, and word of mouth, promoters implored attendees to set aside any differences for the music and the spirit of Aryan brotherhood.

The emphasis on "peace" did not affect some of the more belligerent groups. Seth told me the day before that one of his Aryan friends known as Mackie had "screwed over" some members of Public Enemy Number One (PEN1) in a drug deal. PEN1 responded by giving members a "green light" on Mackie, meaning that they were to attack and punish him.

Seth said, "I'm good friends with Mackie but I'm also close with a lot of PEN1 guys, and I understand that this is business and Mackie shouldn't have fucked with 'em like that." He said he'd be "on guard" at the show in case Mackie showed up. He wanted nothing to do with him while he was green-lighted. Although Mackie did not attend the music show that night, he wasn't able to avoid the green light for long. Within a few weeks a member of PEN1 brutally stabbed Mackie.

When the first band, Aggressive Force, hit the stage at 8 PM, the lead singer, a burly middle-aged skinhead whose arms were sleeved with white power tattoos, grabbed the microphone and began yelling at several dozen skinheads standing ready in front of the stage. "You're a white power skinhead. Always fight! We'll never die!"

The music began and the group fronting the stage began to move suddenly, bodies jerking side to side. They then formed a circle and began stomping in unison, throwing their elbows wildly. Most of these skins were already shirtless, exposing tattoos on their chests, stomachs, and backs. The next song began. The circle broke down and the skinheads started a new dance with their bodies flailing in all directions. Aggressive Force finished its set by leading the crowd in *Sieg heil* salutes and chants of "Skinhead! Skinhead!"

The next band, Final War, was led by two veteran skinheads, joined by two newcomers not far removed from high school. Their brand of hate rock was surprisingly clear compared to most bands, whose heavy bass and screamed vocals render the lyrics almost totally unintelligible: "I'm hated by society. . . . Fight to the end for a world in which our race could never die. . . . Fight with fists. . . . Never surrender . . . the Zionists will soon be beat." A later tribute to Nazi idol Rudolph Hess was slow and melodic. "*Sieg heil* for Rudolph Hess. . . . Your courage never dies. . . . Heroes never die."

The show continued for more than three hours, mixing six bands with Aryan leaders, such as Tom Metzger and the Aryan Front music promoter who organized the show, rallying the crowd with speeches and Aryan-themed chants including "White power! White power! White fucking power!"

The infamous Max Resist closed out the show. They finished their set to loud applause and a chorus of "*Sieg heil*" that went on for several minutes. When the chants died down, some of the audience started making their way for the door. Many Aryans stayed around to talk with each other and visit with the bands. They took photos, exchanged phone numbers and e-mail addresses, and sought out the organizers to compliment them on the night's success.

An hour later, the bar owners ushered the stragglers out, although a dozen of us stayed behind for an after-hours party. I remained in the bar because of my connection with Seth. I then saw the strangest circumstance of the night.

Seth introduced me to one of the bar owners, Joel, a Lebanese man with long, dark, kinky hair, an olive complexion, and a thick accent. "How can this guy be standing here among these racists. He's the epitome of what these skinheads call a 'sand nigger,'" I thought. Sensing my surprise, Seth told me that Joel was "okay" and that his partner was an associate of the Hells Angels.

Later, I asked Joel about the Aryans playing a show in his bar. He said that while he didn't completely share their politics, he did share their anti-Semitism. "It's obvious the fuckin' Jews are causing so much of the problems in the world. Fuck them. If these guys want to annihilate them, I say do it." Joel felt that letting neo-Nazis play music shows at his bar was supporting freedom of speech: "I let everyone else play here. Why shouldn't I let them play too?"

Bar shows are core events of the white power music scene and one of the main occasions movement organizers use to bring white power activists together. Most bar shows are local affairs that draw different branches of Aryans from the surrounding city and local region. The smallest of these events draw between 20 and 30 people, while shows in larger clubs can bring together up to 300. The more elaborate multi-day festivals draw between 400 and 600 racists from local, national, and even international white power networks.

Figure 5.2   The white power band Intimidation One performs for a crowd of several hundred supporters at the National Guard Armory on August 24, 2002, in Towson, Maryland.

Photo by David S. Holloway/© Getty Images

A Place to Let Go

Organizers promote Aryan music shows to encourage a sense of purpose and fellowship among a broad range of Aryans. Music spaces provide activists a place to let go. For the night or weekend, these events promote cathartic releases of racist emotions and displays of hate. Rick, a veteran WAR skinhead and Aryan musician, explains:

> When you're at a show you get to do things you normally can't do, and it just feels great to let go and be what you are [as he points to audience members simultaneously performing *Sieg heil* salutes to the band on stage]. We're all here because we're white and we want to be somewhere where that's not a crime . . . and that's hard to find today.[22]

Finding places to have white power music shows is no easy task. Most club owners are hostile to white power. Even those who do not immediately reject the idea of an Aryan concert are typically cool to the prospect and want to avoid the negative publicity, fights, and other hassles. Their reluctance vastly limits the number of venues available for white power shows.

Despite the obstacles, Aryan promoters have cobbled together a small network of club owners like Joel who are either sympathetic to the cause or interested in the money the shows bring in. The Southern California scene is made up mostly of shows played in dive bars that typically host nonracist punk, gothic, and metal bands. A handful of more upscale clubs will periodically host white power shows.

The largest bar shows pull in racists from different states and, sometimes, different countries. Many of these racists come from their own vibrant local scene and bring information about their favorite bands, styles, and movement experiences. Kenny, an L.A. County skinhead, explains that his concert experiences provided a sense of a much larger Aryan community, which encouraged him to increase his level of participation.

> Before ninety-three I didn't really hang out with others [in the WPM] much. I pretty much did my own thing. But then I went [to a large bar show] and that's when it started to change. That show helped build so much unity. There were people from all over. It was all 'cause of this show.[23]

Aryans talk about feelings of unity and commonality as part of the typical experience at white power music shows. Lance, a SoCal Skin, feels camaraderie among Aryans as well as anger and hatred toward nonwhites and Jews, which reinforces his connection to other white power members. Lance said: "When I hear [white power music] it ignites something in me. The live shows are energizers for racial pride; they just fill you up with love and hope for the future."[24]

Aryans' descriptions of the music scene reveal an unmistakable sense of enjoyment and satisfaction derived from white power music shows. These concerts fill Aryans with a sense of defiance and self-respect.[25] The very existence of hate concerts and their participation in them symbolize Aryans' capacity to act for their beliefs in the face of mainstream oppression.[26]

Music Rituals and Member Recruitment

Aryans attribute pride, pleasure, and solidarity to both the music and the associated activities. These feelings are amplified through collective rituals performed by bands and audiences. The most common rituals are chants and forms of dance. The chants are usually straightforward calls and responses: "*Sieg heil!*" "White power!" and the variation "White fucking power!" complemented by Nazi salutes. The collective experience of shouting taboo expressions is exhilarating and appears to enhance their sense of fellowship.

Group dance rituals raise the communitarian spirit of the events. Skinheads perform a semi-choreographed, ritual boot-stomping dance that evokes power, violence, and militarism. The dance usually involves ten to twenty people stomping and rotating in a circular formation. Sometimes, one person moves to the center, crouching and stomping, circling in the opposite direction, and growling or shouting at the other skinheads. Often, the center skinhead will then run into the circled Aryans in a feigned but very physical attempt to break free. After several minutes a new skinhead moves to the center and the ritual repeats.

Slam dancing in front of the stage is less choreographed, but no less ritualistic. The slam dance involves aggressive pushing and crashing and acting out moves of a mock fight as part of a violent stylistic performance. Slam dancing sometimes escalates into actual brawls between two or more Aryans, which the other dancers usually break up after a minute or two. Less frequently, the brawls spread to the larger group of dancers and can escalate out of control. To an outsider, the fights can seem like a sign of discord among Aryans, but in most instances the fighting is just another part of the ritual experience that Aryans use to distinguish themselves as violent warriors.

Aryans combine their chants and dances with displays of hate symbols. Audience members wear tank tops, and some men go bare-chested, to flaunt their racist tattoos. Others wear jackets and T-shirts with white power patches that indicate their affiliation with local or national groups.

Concert organizers stay active during the shows. They distribute movement materials and talk with attendees about their beliefs. They stock the bar with white power CDs, stickers, patches, band T-shirts, fanzines, and white power literature. Some bar owners do not allow this sort of open marketing of the movement. In that case, veteran members will cruise the bar to covertly distribute to concertgoers flyers with contact information for white power groups. Bands work with movement recruiters by encouraging newcomers to sample the merchandise, carouse with band members, and befriend other activist "brothers and sisters." Recruiters stress themes of racial love, pleasure, and fellowship among Aryans as much as they stress themes of anger and racial hate.

FESTIVALS

Aryans revel in the private spaces of white power music festivals. Festivals are the largest and most elaborate and notorious music spaces. Festivals unite Aryans for days at a time to live the pure white relationships and experiences they fantasize about. The festivals are typically set on remote private property as protection from protesters and authorities.

Aryans called it a music festival. Although tiny in comparison to mainstream music festivals, they were right in that there was a crowd of people camped out to hear music and carouse. Festivalgoers had been instructed through a password-protected website to meet at a grocery store parking lot, where organizers would screen them, sell them thirty-dollar tickets, and then give them specific directions to the site. The festival was a two-day and two-night event with eight bands scheduled to play.

I stood in front of my tent and scanned the groups. Kids ran among the campsites where the early arrivals had circled lawn chairs around beer coolers. A constant stream of Aryans walked around the grounds. Occasionally one raised a drink and yelled, "White power!" or "Rahowa!" prompting others to yell back in approval.

Hours earlier I had met Seth and Paul by the car rental counter at the Atlanta airport. We were to meet several other Aryans there as well, grab lunch, and then follow them to the festival. I wasn't exactly sure where our Aryan guides were taking us. Organizers had kept the festival's specific location a secret in an effort to keep authorities and anti-Aryans from infiltrating the scene. Seth and Paul were band members and had received directions, but they felt more comfortable following local neo-Nazis to the property.

After lunch we loaded up for a ninety-minute drive into the Georgia countryside. We turned off the state highway onto a dirt road that led to a gate marked with a sign: "Whites Only!"

We rolled past the gate into a clearing surrounded by pine woods. More than a dozen tents had already been set up beside several RVs in a back corner of the clearing. I rolled down my window and heard a stereo blaring Skrewdriver across the grounds—"You are the diamonds in the dust. You stand out from the crowd."

Vendors busily set up long tables under canvas tent covers loaded with CDs, books, T-shirts, and Nazi memorabilia. I saw a skinhead stroll by with a T-shirt I'd seen many times before. The shirt's ominous image and message always gave me pause. It showed a portrait of Hitler and lettering that read, "Next time . . . No More Mr. Nice Guy!"

Skinheads, Klan members, and neo-Nazis from around the country spread themselves across the grounds. They reveled in the freedom to display their beliefs. They joked and caroused in ways that closely mimicked the Aryan Nations World Congresses in Idaho that were my first experiences at large Aryan gatherings.

We parked, pitched our tents, and then wandered over to the beer stand where a short line had formed. Seth broke into his usual mock Ebonics talk to anyone who would listen. "You be sayin' what? I gonna call Shanagaway. Shanagaway, you know what dis white boy just said? Said I smell funny." He then shifted tone and in mock response said, "Well, honey, ya know I always said dem whiteys are da devil. Dey brought us here in chains, dey always keepin' us down. You know what you need to do honey? You need to putta cap in his ass."

A skinhead at the front of the line punctuated the end of this performance by shouting, "Fuck the niggers!"

Others laughed and hollered, "Fuck them!" in reply.

We got our beers and went to a food line that sold hamburgers with chips for two dollars. We grabbed our food and wandered over to sit with a group of skinheads Seth recognized. I sat next to Vicki, a blonde woman in her mid-thirties. She told me that she was from Southern California and had known Seth since they were teenagers. In fact, she had married one of Seth's old friends.

I explained that I was here for research and she seemed eager to talk, especially about her husband. "He wasn't able to come 'cause he couldn't get the time off from work and he has to be careful about these events. He's been locked up a couple times and he doesn't need any problems with cops messing with him like they do sometimes at these shows." She said she was eager to bring her kids to a festival, to "show them who we are and how many believe in the cause."

After Vicki left, a young skin sat down and introduced himself as, "Casper from Indiana." I listened to his tales about the time he had spent in Southern California drifting from one skinhead crashpad to another. It was clear that he knew Seth and others from his time in California. After half an hour of conversation, he turned and asked, loud enough for everyone in the circle to hear, "So you're a researcher? So what do you think about us racists? I mean do you think we're all crazy or what?"

I tried to think of a quick answer that would shift attention from me when Seth suddenly interrupted, "Hell, he's more racist than I am. He knows we're right."

Casper laughed, "Well, of course, he's racist! You'd have to be blind not to be!"

I was thankful for Seth's comment. It gave me some cachet to have him vouch for me, and, more important, the group's attention shifted from my beliefs to the issue of how so many whites were blinded from the truth. Yet, I was also worried. I knew that Seth wanted me to be racist. He wanted all white people to be racist. Maybe I had crossed a line somewhere and he thought I believed in his cause?

As I mulled this over, the group broke up and people shuffled off to their tents. Tomorrow was the big day. More Aryans would arrive, and the music would start in the late morning and go deep into the night, punctuated by the swastika and cross burning planned as the finale. As Seth and I lay in the dark waiting for sleep to come he turned and reminded me, as he had other times before, to watch myself tomorrow. There would be a lot of Hammerskins at the show and things could get volatile. His mantra was "just watch and listen and look like one of us."

After breakfast the next morning, I walked over to the stage area to watch the first band set up. Nearby, about twelve burly skinheads were busy arranging an area for the "strongest man contest," where they would compete in the dead lift, bench press, tire lift, and other tests of strength. Hate Train didn't play until the afternoon, but Seth, Paul, and the others were already busy rehearsing, so I was on my own.

I planned to make my way around the field striking up conversations with people I'd met the night before. Things began uneventfully. I met a couple of Casper's friends who had come down with him from Indiana. Dave, a soft-spoken, middle-aged man, with graying hair, wore a blue work shirt with the sleeves cut off and showed no visible tattoos. Casper's other friend, Rich, was short, stocky, and clean-cut. He wore a Max Resist tour shirt and jean shorts. He looked to be in his late twenties. Dave immediately asked where I lived. When I said "Las Vegas," he asked about how many nonwhites lived there. I replied, "quite a few." He nodded in disgust and said,

> Yeah I used to be a taxi driver down in L.A. God what a cesspool! All the filth! Driving taxis and seeing what all these nonwhites were doing, I lived in this shit hole apartment near Watts and these black motherfuckers used to harass me all day long. People were banging on my door all night. My place got broke into four times in the year that I lived there. I finally couldn't take it anymore.

Just then, the first band of the day, Intimidation One, started to play. We stopped our conversation and walked over toward the stage to join the crowd.

The audience near the stage was mostly skinheads. Within minutes they started slam dancing—knocking into one another, pushing and stomping. A few Klansmen and other neo-Nazis formed a half-circle around them, nodding their heads to the music and giving *Sieg heil* salutes toward the band.

Casper, Dave, and I stood at the back of the crowd about twenty-five yards from the stage. A young skinhead approached us between band sets. His head was freshly shaved and he was full of swagger. He was short, about five-seven, and wiry. A huge plug of chewing tobacco protruded from his lower lip. Without hesitating, he said, "Hey!" and started telling us about a recent incident that happened in his hometown in Oregon.

I wasn't sure if he knew Casper or Dave. They didn't seem to greet him with any recognition. We listened as he told us how two of his friends had recently beaten a gay man in a warehouse.

"My buddies asked this fag if he wanted to get fucked up the ass and then they rammed a baseball bat right up his ass," he said excitedly with a cocky smirk. His eyes were brown and dull and he stared intently at us. Was he looking for approval? I wondered.

He went on. "They just beat this fag and left him for dead."

I considered that he might be testing us, looking for a reaction. Maybe he thinks one of us is an infiltrator. Maybe he thinks it's me.

He continued to tell us that the police had recently hauled him in. "It was funny. They tried to pin all these phony charges on me, but they never mentioned the one thing I did do. I axed this nigger up a while back with a hatchet and they never even mentioned it." He said it in a matter-of-fact way, as if he were telling us the score of last night's ballgame.

Was this guy for real? I wondered. If he did this, is he really stupid enough to tell a group of strangers about it. I remained silent, watching him, and trying to convince myself that he was talking tough just to impress us.[27]

At a lull in the skinhead's story, I broke away and moved to the other side of the stage. I watched the next band, Jewslaughter, set up their equipment. They were to be followed by a Klan leader speaking about lone-wolf activism. Hate Train would then take the stage. I decided to return for the speech and Hate Train's set. For now, I headed to my tent to decompress and write down my observations.

By midafternoon, festival organizers announced that more than 400 Aryans were in attendance. The camping area was full of tents. Vendors did brisk business. The audience at the front of the stage grew in size and energy, and during Hate Train's set, three injured skins were pulled out of the dancing area.

The last band in the lineup, Angry Aryans, finished their final song around 10 PM. The audience readied for the swastika and cross burning which was scheduled to close the evening's festivities. Klansmen in full regalia led the ceremony. The group was hushed as they began the ritual. I watched the hooded men feeling like I'd been transported directly back to the 1950s, when KKK grand wizards and their followers held sway in the Deep South. A small girl interrupted my thoughts when she turned to her mother in a voice loud enough to be heard across the crowd, "Mommy these guys are kooks!" Her mother looked horrified and scolded her, "Don't talk like that, just watch." I couldn't help but smile.

While the cross and swastika burned, the robed Klansmen led the crowd in hymns and chants. I was tired, but most of those in the crowd seemed energized by the ceremony. Some clasped shoulders and sang or chanted in unison. Others stood alone, mouthing the words and gazing into the fire. The sense of fellowship, shared feeling, and purpose among them was obvious. It struck me that, however short-lived these events were, they seemed crucial to help participants invigorate their hate and press on with their struggle. Before long, I headed to the tent for some sleep, eager for tomorrow's flight home.

Figure 5.3   A group of boys follow a man across a field at the White Heritage Days Festival, which was held on private land, September 18, 2004, near Scottsboro, Alabama. The crosses on the ground were later erected and burned in a cross-lighting ceremony.

Photo by David S. Holloway/© Getty Images

Since 1998, both the size and frequency of white power music festivals have dramatically increased.[28] The two most prominent festivals are *Hammerfest*, organized by the Hammerskin Nation, and Nordic Fest, produced by the Imperial Klans of America and factions of Blood & Honour. The events have been held annually since 2000 and draw between 300 and 600 activists from both the United States and Europe.[29] The events usually include up to a dozen bands, speeches from WPM leaders, workshops on Aryan heritage and activism, ritual swastika and cross lightings, sporting competitions, and sales of a wide array of white power merchandise.

AryanFest is a newcomer to the festival scene. Inaugurated in 2004 by the Oregon-based Volksfront and Panzerfaust Records, the event offered attendees nine bands, three featured speakers, two free beers, a barbeque dinner, and on-site camping all for a thirty-dollar ticket. Proceeds from the festival helped Volksfront purchase two plots of land for an all-Aryan community in the Northwest.

A Chance to Build Unity

Activists talk enthusiastically of the empowering communitarian spirit they feel at the festivals. The privacy of the festival setting is crucial to create a space where Aryans feel comfortable displaying white power pride and unity. Being together with so many Aryans gives Otto, a SoCal Skin, a sense of Aryan power and inspiration. "When people come together at the music shows, we're telling each other that our beliefs can withstand all of the bullshit out there and we don't have to cave in, we don't have to give up."[30]

Likewise, Garth, an Idaho Aryan, explains: "The shows really bring people together. They keep you strong, they keep you feeling like you're part of something, part of the movement, and if we can keep together, then there's hope that we can save the white race from destruction."[31]

The privacy at the festivals allows Aryans to openly express white power beliefs. Activists set up temporary tent towns where Aryans from many locales can connect. Participants joke and carouse with one another in ways that contradict the stereotypes of intense, menacing, vitriolic Nazis brimming with animosity and hatred. Aryans feel comfortable to let down their guard at festivals like this. Festivals also bring together different ages of white power activists, creating a powerful context for sustaining and transmitting the movement's culture across generations.[32] Sammy, a Colorado Aryan, describes a visceral, unifying spirit at the festivals, saying, "[The festivals] are great. We get dressed up [in Aryan regalia] with all these great white families, and that's what is really important . . . a chance to build unity and remember why we do all of this. It's for racial kinship."[33]

WHITE POWER MUSIC COMPANIES

We close this chapter with a discussion of how white power music companies organize and produce hate music. Aryan recording companies organize and support white power music festivals with money, space, and volunteers for the events. They also widely promote the shows through their extensive Internet presence.

More than forty North American companies are involved in the multimedia hate music culture.[34] They include small two- to three-person Internet outlets that stock and distribute Aryan music, as well as larger, independent labels that sell merchandise and organize live concerts and festivals. Aryan music company organizers see their role as raising the communitarian spirit among white power activists. Joey, an Aryan music distributor, says:

> The music we produce lets them express their anger for those working against their people. The music helps them develop strong racial rootedness and feel part of a large community of white people who care about the same things they do—a community who isn't afraid of being called names or not being "politically correct"; a community that is not afraid to stand up for their race.[35]

Figure 5.4   Stacks of Panzerfaust Records' "Project Schoolyard" CDs waiting to be shipped at the Panzerfaust Records office in Newport, Minnesota. Project Schoolyard was launched in 2004 as a recruitment plan to distribute 100,000 free CDs to kids aged thirteen to nineteen at schools. After a change in leadership in 2005, Panzerfaust Records was renamed Free Your Mind Productions.

Photo by David S. Holloway/© Getty Images

Resistance Records and Free Your Mind Productions are the two most prominent white power music distributors. Their goal is to create a racist alternative to mainstream music. Resistance Records is an arm of the National Alliance, and Free Your Mind Productions grew out of the Hammerskin Nation. The two record companies have elaborate national and international Internet distribution networks for their music and merchandise.

Resistance Records emphasizes youth recruitment. The late National Alliance leader and Resistance Records CEO, William Pierce, told his followers:

> Our aim is to make Resistance music have a much bigger impact on young people in the future than it has had in the past. . . . We want millions of young, white Americans and Europeans to make resistance music their music of choice, instead of the Negroid filth churned out by MTV.[36]

Resistance Records bills itself as "the soundtrack for the white revolution."[37] The company offers more than 700 music titles that span all the WPM music genres. Themes of violence and racist hatred aimed at African Americans, Jews, Asians, and immigrants are expressed in the songs, cover art, and band names, such as Fueled By Hate, Aryan Terrorism, Brutal Attack, Blue Eyed Devils, Angry Aryans, Racist Redneck Rebels, and RaHoWa.

The company appears to do modestly well compared to other small, nonracist independent music labels. The Anti-Defamation League reported that Resistance sold up to 50,000 white power CDs per year before legal troubles in 1997.[38] In 1999, Pierce bought the Swedish company Nordland Records, reportedly doubling Resistance's inventory to 80,000 compact discs.[39]

The acquisition also gave Resistance an immediate presence in Sweden, "one of the world's largest producers [and consumers] of racist rock."[40] Sales rebounded by 2000 when Resistance reportedly received about fifty orders per day, averaging seventy dollars in merchandise, equaling more than $1 million in annual sales.

Free Your Mind Productions has a short, tumultuous history. Anthony Pierpont and Eric Davidson founded the company as Panzerfaust Records in September 1998.[41] They cultivated close links to the Hammerskin Nation, Volksfront, and White Revolution. But Panzerfaust changed hands after these three organizations withdrew their support from the company because of internal disputes over money combined with Pierpont's legal troubles and claims about his impure racial heritage. Bryant Cecchini and others seized control of the Panzerfaust website and reorganized it in early 2005 as Free Your Mind Productions.

Free Your Mind Productions describes their mission as offering white people opportunities to find and embrace their true Aryan identity. Anthony Pierpont explained that before he was forced out, the music company's role was to provide places for disaffected whites to connect with an authentic, indigenous racist culture: "You'd be amazed at how many [white] people are looking for an outlet to be something different, where they don't have to feel guilty about being white or act like a nigger to be cool. . . . We give them that opportunity."[42]

Aryans order compact discs and MP3s through the Resistance Records and Free Your Mind Productions' websites. These websites offer access to twenty-four-hour streaming radio, music reviews, Aryan books, videos, jewelry, clothing, and links to additional websites where members can connect to other dimensions of white power culture.

The music websites created by the companies are retail clearinghouses for Aryan music and merchandise and spaces where committed fans and activists and even the mildly curious can talk to one another through online chatrooms. These technologies create opportunities for "bring[ing] distant isolated groups and individuals together [to] reach an audience far beyond any they could reach with their traditional propaganda."[43] James, a Southeast Aryan who runs a small Internet music site, explained: "We think a lot about how to reach a wider audience, with the [mainstream] media pushing all this antiwhite propaganda. We can't let that media define us. We've got to find ways to get the message out. The websites help connect people to something larger."[44]

★

Music theorist Tia DeNora says that music is a way of living ideas.[45] WPM activists use music as a form of aesthetic expression to establish themselves as true Aryans. The music itself evokes multiple emotional appeals that activists draw upon to support and sustain their commitment. The songs express racial hatred and violence along with potent emotions of pride, honor, love, and movement unity.

Aryans experience white power music's inspirational imagery. The sense that there are many other racists who listen to the same music with the same convictions helps anchor Aryan commitments. Greg, a veteran Northern Hammerskin, explains:

> What it does to people who listen to white power music, it gives them a certain level of confidence when they're trying to keep their jobs or to raise a child. You know you can get through your day with the whole world against you instead of giving up or selling out. We say, "You know what, we're racists and nobody likes us, but we don't care and we're not gonna go away, and tomorrow is another day."[46]

White power activists use music as a major ideological and organizational resource, uniting racists in festivals, bar concerts, and parties. Bar shows cater to local activists in specific locales, while larger concerts and festivals draw together members from widely scattered Aryan scenes.

The hate music scene is growing, but "not all racists agree on what forms of racist culture are appropriate [and] the question of music can provoke especially hot disputes."[47] Some factions see the music scene as a distraction from real movement politics and the limit of most members' activism rather than a stepping-stone to deeper commitment.

Our analysis shows that white power music is far more powerful than the superficial stylized packaging of Aryan ideas.[48] Potential recruits may start in the scene by just hanging around without the pressure of delving too far into the ritual culture of hate. But one visit to a festival or bar concert can lead to more, and eventually recruits may dive headlong into hate culture. And for those who are already committed to the movement, their music scene experiences help to further sustain their involvement.

Aryans' contact with the white power music scene extends beyond the shows. Musicians and promoters use cyberspace to enhance access to and involvement in the Aryan scene. In the next chapter we discuss the ways that Aryans use the Internet to extend their participation in white power hate culture.

6

Virtual Hate

The net has provided us with the opportunity to bring our point of view to hundreds of thousands of people. . . . [White power websites] which are interactive, provide those people who are attracted to our ideas with a forum to talk to each other and to form a virtual community . . . and that's the beauty.

—Don Black, founder of Stormfront.org[1]

The survival and growth of the white power movement depends on the Internet. Hundreds of Aryan websites offer easy and anonymous access to white power culture. Members build and extend personal relationships with one another online. They chat, post videos, download music, visit racist parenting and education websites, and play online hate games. They also use this virtual realm to organize and extend real-world activities, such as house parties, concerts, and festivals.

In this chapter, we explain the critical role of cyberspace as an Aryan free space. We describe how white power members use the Internet and what they experience on white power websites. Specifically, we describe how Aryans use cyberspace to access hate culture and immerse themselves in a "lived, communicative environment" with other Aryans.[2] The Web has given Aryans a new place to assemble in expansive cyber-communities[3] where they preserve racist and anti-Semitic narratives and build virtual social solidarity. Online forums are echo chambers for hate.[4]

ARYAN HATE CULTURE ONLINE

Aryan culture online is only microseconds away. Keyword searches such as *Aryan* or *white power* on any search engine bring up an array of virulent racist and anti-Semitic websites. The first webpage that the Google search engine lists using the key words *white power* is www.whitehonor.com, a website operated by neo-Nazi Axl Hess that gives readers Aryan propaganda. The site's home page shows an iconic image of Oklahoma City bomber Timothy McVeigh in an orange prison jumpsuit. The photo is inscribed by McVeigh himself: "My head is bloody, but unbowed. May 2001." Hess frames the picture with a call to arms.

> For those with hope,
> For those with courage,
> For those who have finally realized that nothing
> short of a Violent White Revolution will save our
> Race,
> Supreme White Power
> Doing whatever it takes for Total Aryan Victory.[5]

An audio file in the background broadcasts a rousing Adolf Hitler speech.

One click reveals Adolf Hitler's image with the proclamation, "Extreme Violent Racism. White Revolution is the FINAL Solution." A banner announces that the website is "Powered by Hate." Swastikas frame the words. Nazi and Confederate flags fly on the page.

The "Opening Statement and Purpose" tells the reader:

I created this website with the intent of providing White Racists with information on what we can do to effectively secure the existence of our people. . . . Peaceful methods . . . have tried and failed. . . . This is not a game we are talking about; this is our Fight and Struggle for our mere Existence on this Earth. . . . God gave the White Race the brains to make guns and weapons, but He won't pull the trigger for you. Axl Hess 88/14[6]

A link entitled "Important Articles" catalogs texts under ominous themes.

- Articles Dealing with Our Understanding of the Current Struggle and Explaining the Necessity to Fight
- Articles on Lone Wolf of the Century: Timothy James McVeigh, April 23, 1968–June 11, 2001. R.I.P. Brother for You Have Well Earned Your Place In Valhalla. We will Never Forget Your Sacrifice For Freedom.
- A Selection of Essays by Revolutionary Racist Grant Bruer.[7]

"Heil Hitler," written in blood-red font, follows the cursor across the site's pages.

One of the longest-running white power websites, Stormfront.org, offers streaming StormfrontRadio shows, "Town Hall Talks," among Aryan leaders and rank-and-file activists, and fifty-four forums where Aryans post information, ideas, and communiqués. The forums range from the chat room "For Stormfront Ladies Only" to Classified Ads, Homemaking, Money Talks, Culture and Customs, Strategy and Tactics, and White Singles Networking. Fifteen additional forums categorized by country are dedicated to connecting members around the world.

Stormfront.org is one of the largest Aryan websites, claiming 133,000 international members.[8] On the night of Barack Obama's election as the U.S. president, a massive onslaught of Web hits knocked Stormfront.org offline.

Aryanwear.com offers a catalog of white power clothing, accessories, collectibles, and books, along with "news from the frontlines." The site's home page graphics are dominated by an animated war scene of tanks, skulls, and blown-out buildings. A young blond female model poses seductively in a white power T-shirt and necklace. The words *Aryan Wear* shine above her. One click on her image sends you to Girls Gear and another female model posing in an "88" shirt surrounded by a catalog of AryanWear items for white power women.

Micetrap.com, a white power music website, has an extensive music catalog that begins with the band Stormtroop 16 and their recording *Steel Capped Justice*. The CD's cover art shows four skinheads wearing steel-toed boots kicking a black man on the ground.

The list of Aryan websites goes on for pages, with a few anti-Aryan links, such as the Anti-Defamation League and Southern Poverty Law Center, scattered among the pro-white power websites. Each Aryan website also hosts links to more racist pages. White power cyberspace is truly an interlinked web of hate.

Easy access to hate is meaningful to white power activists. Aryan websites show idealized Aryan families. Children are posed in Klan robes and SS uniforms with arms raised in Nazi salutes. Trey, a SoCal Skin, reflected on the meaning of access to white power Web images and paraphernalia:

> It's really cool how you can get all this shit off the Net now. Ten years ago there really wasn't that much, but now you've got all the music, the clothes. I bought my daughter a toy figure of Hitler from a website. I mean you're not going to find that at Wal-Mart.[9]

Aryans use the Internet to weave movement culture into their daily lives and access the movement anywhere there is an Internet connection. At home and work, in coffee shops and bars, Aryans participate in white power culture by chatting with other Aryans, listening to streaming hate rock, shopping white power retail websites for Aryan merchandise, reading inspirational texts, or playing racist video games. Members consume these symbols and experiences and thereby authenticate their commitment to the movement.

Selling the Aryan Aesthetic

White power music companies are among the savviest online distributors of hate culture. Resistance Records and Free Your Mind Productions use online catalogs to market hate music and white power style to activists. They fill their catalogs with images of Aryan style represented in clothing, activities, and mementos. The Free Your Mind Productions website has links to photo galleries of racists at concerts. Concert-going Aryans display attire, tattoos, jewelry, and other symbols of Aryan authenticity for viewers to admire. Resistance Records markets their clothing brand, Aryan Wear, through both Resistance.com and Aryanwear .com.

Online white power merchandisers mimic mainstream Web retailers. Resistance Records and Free Your Mind Productions websites are easily navigable for customers. Each item on the Resistance site has an adjacent Buy Now button for quick and easy checkout. Free Your Mind Productions has a currency conversion calculator to simplify foreign transactions. The companies also emphasize customer satisfaction, ensuring patrons the best selections, lowest prices, safe access to their products, and quick, discrete delivery.

Lifestyle materials of Aryan membership create revenue streams for white power movement coffers. Eric Davidson, co-organizer of Panzerfaust Productions, said, "When you support Panzerfaust, you're not pouring money into a hole, you're helping finance a very serious fight."[10] Aryan Web enterprises promote the idea of online purchases as an easy way to contribute money to the movement.[11]

Aryan Cyber-Games

Online racist video games offer especially potent Aryan socialization experiences.[12] Racist images and ideas are conveyed via games with titles such as, Aryan 3, Shoot the Black, White Power Doom, ZOG's Nightmare 2, and Ethnic Cleansing. Games draw both novice and longtime racists to interactive versions of Aryan racial extermination and white domination fantasies.[13]

In Ethnic Cleansing, the race war has begun. Players must defend their city, which has been overrun by blacks and Latinos controlled by a Jewish boss. Each player dresses their avatar in KKK robes or as a skinhead. Avatars roam city streets and subways to take back the city by killing racial enemies. Monkey and ape sounds accompany black killings, while poncho-wearing Latinos shout, "I'll take a siesta now!" and "Ay carumba!" when they are destroyed.

National Alliance signs and posters appear on the virtual city streets. White power music comprises the soundtrack. The game concludes when a player confronts the Jewish boss, a rocket-wielding former Israeli prime minister, Ariel Sharon, who taunts players: "We have destroyed your culture!" and "We silenced Henry Ford." When Sharon is killed he says, "Filthy white dog, you have destroyed thousands of years of planning."

National Socialist Movement gamers developed the first-person shooting game ZOG's Nightmare 2, in which players make their way through an urban landscape populated by blacks, Latinos, and other nonwhites. Players must "liquidate all the non-white invaders and purify the NSM party headquarters, while Jew-controlled police hunt the player."[14]

Aryans use racist computer games as a critical recruiting tool. Charlie, a Southeast Aryan, proclaimed, "Online video games are a great idea for the movement. It's planting a seed. [We] need these games for what they say and do. There's just something about the visual part and being able to really get into it."[15]

Children's Virtual Indoctrination

Video games are just one part of the virtual realm that Aryans devote to racial socialization. White power websites are aimed directly at children, streaming racist cartoons, racist coloring pages, white power–themed puzzles, and Aryan children's stories.

WAU14.com, a website for Aryan families organized by Women for Aryan Unity, offers a link to a WAU Kids webpage. Here parents access Little Warriors coloring books with Viking and Celtic warrior images, battleships, and Pagan symbols. The "For Kids" section of ILoveWhiteFolks.com has Aryan crossword puzzles for young adults. Crossword questions emphasize Aryan supremacy. The website also contains original fairy tales such as "The Land of the White" and "The Magic Parakeet," a tale about a child who follows his father's advice to eradicate racial diversity.

Parents also find online support for racist homeschooling. Web-based teaching materials, such as lesson plans, workbooks, and children's literature, are available on several sites to download, print, and distribute. I Love White Folks—For Kids offers history lessons, such as "The March of the Titans," a pseudo-historical survey of the white race, including anthropological and archaeological research about Aryan racial evolution and white supremacy. Women for Aryan Unity and Stormfront.org also host chat rooms where Aryan parents discuss strategies for indoctrinating their children into hate culture.

White Power Video and Social Networking Sites

Aryans do not limit their Web presence to nonmainstream sites. Many use the popular video hosting site YouTube to upload scores of racist and anti-Semitic Aryan videos ranging from rallies, marches, and live concerts to MTV-style white power music videos. Aryans have also produced their own white power documentaries and infomercials that market hate culture and white power groups. Aryans use video blogs, such as Aryan Guard TV and Aryan Patriot, where the bloggers that operate these sites are filmed wearing ski masks and holding high-powered weapons while discussing the current state of affairs from their white power perspective.

The mainstream popularity of social networking sites like MySpace and Facebook motivated the National Socialist Movement to create its own social networking site for Aryans, New Saxon. Participants construct virtual identities through personal profiles, blogs, and photos and link to other Aryans based on their preferred ideological branch, music tastes, and other interests.

New Saxon organizers describe their site as a virtual place where

> people of European descent may enjoy many great features which will enable fun interaction among members. New Saxon is an excellent place to meet like minded people with high moral character, a love for their heritage and culture, have strong family values and are politically active in various grassroots projects.[16]

Thus, the Internet also offers a variety of ways to access extremist ideology. With a few clicks, white power Web surfers can move through virtual spaces full of taboo symbolism, racial violence, and social networks of people who hate. In the next section, we analyze what online hate culture means to Aryans and how they use it to sustain their devotion to Aryan ideology.

"IT KEEPS ME FEELING CONNECTED"

Even the most isolated members can feel they are an interactive part of a widespread community of racists using the Internet.[17] Jay, an Aryan Front skinhead, uses the Internet to allay his feeling of isolation from the movement.[18] As he points out, "I don't have much free time anymore to attend festivals, but e-mailing and the chat rooms make me feel a lot less alone. The Internet just makes it easier to be a racialist when you know people all over the world are fighting for pretty much the same thing you are."[19] And Scotty, also an Aryan Front skinhead, explained, "[The Internet] keeps me feeling connected to the movement and that gets pretty hard sometimes because I work two jobs and have a family."[20]

Aryans access a global online community. Veteran Hammerskins say that the Internet helped them better imagine an international movement of racists. Forrest, a Hammerskin, explained:

> Since we've been able to access the internet and email Hammers in other countries it's changed everything. We really see ourselves as part of an international movement. We communicate with each other on a regular basis, we coordinate events. It's really different than before we had the internet. We knew about [skinheads in other parts of the world], but it was more word of mouth and now we're actually working together.[21]

White power members build and sustain their connections online largely by sharing accounts of their struggles. Their online chats, videos, and writings detail injustices that they perceive and define the social, physical, and moral boundaries that separate them from racial enemies and non-Aryans. White power members imagine a future "cleansed" of their enemies.

Aryans pay close attention to how they present themselves online. Since skin color and other visual cues are not available in cyberspace, other signs of racial loyalty are crucial. The names they use in their postings are almost invariably pseudonyms that bear the mark of movement membership, such as Aryan Warrior, White Resistance, or Mudslayer. They fill their cybertalk with expressions of kinship and fraternity by using terms like *brother* and *sister* to evoke solidarity. Aryans also rely upon shared codes to establish their allegiance. Online postings about topics that might otherwise seem far removed from racialist themes, such as advice on troubleshooting computers or cooking recipes, often begin or close with phrases like "88," "*Sieg heil*," or "14 Words" to mark their white power affiliation.

Embracing the Aryan aesthetic and conveying that commitment to others online sustains members' identification with the collective "we" of the movement.

Discovering Aryan "Truth"

Aryans' virtual conversations are often organized around how they became enlightened to the true racialized nature of world affairs and the forces out to destroy the white race. Like the conversations that dominate real-world house parties, Aryan enlightenment stories tend to highlight a personal trauma that triggered their racial awakening. Members trigger online conversations about these moments by posting questions like, "When did you realize you hated niggers?" and "What made you hate Jews?" The responses contain some of the most emotion-laden discussions among Aryans that we tracked online.

We note below a sample from a typical day of postings in a Panzerfaust.com chat room. This Aryan online conversation highlights racial awakening. The thread of interaction began when a veteran member posted the question: "When did you become a racist?" Then he told his own enlightenment story. Within twenty-four hours he received twenty-one responses about personal traumas caused by "nonwhites."

when i was in 1st grade i was dragged into the boys room by 4 niggers was beat to a pulp then pissed on by all 4 of them. . . . I learned to stand up for myself and realize now I have good reason [to hate]. TruckingSkinhead

I personally just have always seen around me how we are much different than non-Whites and liked that I was white. But, what made me a "pure racist" so to say is when I attended middle school which was 90% niggers. HateMachine

When I was a child I never had non-white friends, because here in my small town were no niggers or other alien shit. And later when I was 13 or 14 years old, I began to hate these fucking bastards . . . because they come to our nice quiet town and to school and began trouble. We built our first racist groups and tried to resist, against all these turkeys (here in germany there are millions of turkeys, more than niggers) and other scumbags. NorthernHammerskin

Hmmm, when did I start to hate spear-chuckers? . . . All the coons I came across in high school were annoying and cared more about their fucking shoes. Pathetic. By my senior year, I had enough to the point that I felt like dismembering everyone and everything in my sight. Now I am in college, and I see all these gatorbaits all over the place. Always remember that hatred is purity. AKHate[22]

These accounts define moments that mark each member's step into racial extremism. The narratives pivot on school-age conflicts with racial enemies and a deep-seated feeling of white superiority. Whether or not the stories are true matters little in this context. Their potency lies in reinforcing Aryan cultural norms through the telling of them.

Betrayal, Dispossession, and Violence

White power members demonize and scapegoat enemies.[23] Aryan cybertalk mainly blames blacks, Jews, and Hispanics for marginalizing whites. Aryans identify themselves as victims betrayed and dispossessed by multiculturalist ideology. They single out blacks and Hispanics as perpetrators of innumerable rapes, beatings, and murders of whites. They repeatedly lament the loss of clean, safe, white neighborhoods and cities to dirty minority incursions.

Now we are the minority. They are breeding us out. Killing us off and we let this shit fucking happen? BULLSHIT!!! Where can my daughter play? Today I can't believe how organized we [racist skinheads] all are and bringing everyone together! Special thanks to the net and the creators of the HSN [Hammerskin Nation]!!! Grab your brothers and sisters and MAKE them see. Make us all a safe neighborhood for all our children of tomorrow. And to all who are fighting the good fight and aren't falling for it but can stand up proud . . . THANK YOU! Thanks for letting me vent. I just can't take it anymore! 88Rocker[24]

[In] any big city you name, the nonwhites are flying into the airports like crazy. New families are arriving in the big cities with their suitcases in hordes each day. We're not winning the war, only perhaps slowing it down somewhat. Those foreigners and especially the blacks loveeeee the BIG CITIES to death. Chicago . . . BLACK. New Orleans . . . BLACK. Memphis . . . BLACK. Atlanta . . . BLACK. St. Louis . . . BLACK. NO COUNTRY in the world will be oblivious to the non whites unless it's the country we as WN's (White Nationalists) come together to form. WhiteInstinct[25]

Aryans level blame at nonwhites for all manner of social ills. In doing so, Aryans build extensive and elaborate threads of fantasies about racial cleansing and white domination. A common theme in these fantasies is killing racial enemies; however, the scale of violence in these dreams varies from random individual victims to fantastical final solutions to the "nonwhite problem" as illustrated by a post on Whiterevolution.com:

> Niggers don't have the ability to think. Lets put those fuckers on a rape table and beat them with chains and clubs, kick them shock them, hang them. Let's wall off an entire state, add the spics and jews in for good measure, and let them kill each other. I guess I have just about had it with all the bleeding hearts that refuse to see the truth. . . . I'm scared of not having another White person left in this shithole of a country who will stand up for what is right. We are the minority friends. Viking-Blood[26]

Aryans sometimes link violent fantasies to reality by posting models of real-world Aryan violence. Members post articles on Aryan actions, hate crimes, and ethnic conflicts around the world, framing them as inspirational stories to help them keep the faith. A member of a Free Your Mind Productions forum posted a news article with photo images and a video clip of a Gay Rights march in Belgrade, Serbia. Discussion focused on the melee that erupted during the march when racist skinheads and Serbian nationalists attacked and severely injured several marchers. A small sample of the discussion thread shows how members enthusiastically hailed the skinhead violence:

> 8fuckin8! thats the idea smashing queers and zog enforcers. Viking88

> Damn those pics are great. If anyone deserves a good beating its that lot. Takes me back to the good ole days of my youth. Three cheers for the brothers taking care of business. . . . Fag bashing by moonlight oh god don't it feel so right. Battlefront

> that scene where that one skin kicks that Anarchist/Red fag is funny as fuck. Hate-crime

> that was awesome. way to go for our boys over seas! WhiteLaw

> Fag bashing? I don't know. Id be afraid to get their blood on me. Really if you think about it, God only knows what these people got and all it takes is some blood getting splashed on your person. NordicThunder

> That's why you're supposed to bash fags with bricks. I feel the same way about nigger blood. I always carry a pair of leather gloves. Hate Crimes Pass the Time! Odinsdaughter

> Don't worry they can't win, still breathin, kick em again! Believe me they're better off dead. KikeKiller

Don't waste good leather gloves on a nigger, what if you can't get the stains out? Just use cheap fake leather mits and a long steel pipe or crow bar. That way you can whack them in the head and such from a distance and not even get any bodily fluid on you. Aryanfront[27]

These Aryans celebrate hate violence as a blow against ZOG, blacks, and others. They extol the virtues of exacting punishment upon their enemies. Rioters like those in Belgrade are icons whose acts represent the Aryan courage, violence, and heroism needed to win the race war.

Declarations of Faith

Racists use online discussion forums to openly declare their faith and find others who support their radical beliefs. Many postings appear to come from new recruits who have lurked a while in the Web forums without posting.

With anonymity assured, Web forums are the safest space for new recruits to come out to others about their beliefs. Newcomers declare their faith with detailed confessions of how they discovered "Aryan truth." In White Revolution's chat room Forum 14:

Hey my white brothers & sisters,
  After far too many years of sitting back and doing nothing, I've finally come around! I can't take the damn niggers, spics, ragheads, fags and kikes taking over our country. Who gives a damn about the white man? We do!!! And I'm glad to be a part of it. Over the course of many years, I felt so alone and powerless and wondered if there was anyone like myself who could see what was happening. Then I sought out others on the internet. . . . It's great to be a part of WR! Thank you everyone for the warm welcome. . . . Wishing you all 14 words. whiteusa[28]

Newcomers typically find enthusiastic support from others:

Mike, you are so welcome here. We have a lot of good people here, all happy to meet you, and converse with you. . . . There are people of all ages . . . and we are all of one mind . . . enjoy your participation on this forum. Lucy[29]

Welcome buddy! I can't help but notice that you're from "Dixie." I live here in the heart of it myself. Indeed, there is much work to be done . . . which is why I must ask which southern state you live in. We gotta make this southeastern network stronger! SouthernMan[30]

Hi Celtic and welcome to the forum. You should be very glad that you have learned the truth, and are going to be living the white way now. You have two precious little girls, who are your responsibility. You must start NOW training them correctly. You have a big job ahead of you. . . . Welcome, join in the posting, and get to know the people here. Wolf1488[31]

Aryan interactions in cyberspace deal with more than just racial enlightenment, dispossession, hatred, and violent fantasies. Members also use cyberspace as a source of virtual therapy for easing the burden of carrying such a stigmatized, deviant identity.

ARYAN CYBERTHERAPY

Communication among activists in cyberspace helps them sustain their commitment in the face of oppositional social pressure. Recurring posts emphasize the value of virtual connections that link isolated activists to the broader movement. Aryans often end their entries with an uplifting statement about drawing strength from others in cyberspace.

> Thanks everyone. I take heart in knowing that there are others like me all across the world and that even though I am alone in a sea of mud and liberal scum I am a rock. 14/88. IronCross[32]

> i thank you all very much. i really enjoy posting seems like i could do it all day. i like hearing the opinions of others this is just about the first place i have ever had such a warm welcome i hope we can grow close and stick together in this war we are fighting. i get so tired sometimes fighting for our race but it helps when you know others are in the fight and feel the same way you do. AryanAngel[33]

Aryans weave the fraternal quality of these exchanges throughout most of their online conversations. Users constantly encourage one another to ask questions about the movement and find ways to be more involved. These statements seem to be directed specifically at young recruits to push forward their political socialization.

> Feel free to ask any questions you might have. I may not have the answer but someone will. Just jump in with both feet. We are glad that you and the other younger folks are here. If you don't ask, you don't learn. American Anglo88[34]

Advice flows freely among the posters who seek and give guidance to one another on ways to spread the movement's messages, parenting strategies, finances, and relationship problems. Frequent postings advise on disputes with romantic partners and acquaintances who oppose a member's extremism.

> Hi my name is Chris and I am 18 and I been in the movement for almost a year but I've always been racially aware of what's going on. Anyways I wanted to get your opinion on a problem I have. See my girlfriend is mad as hell at me for being racist because i just told her and she said if i stay racist she will break up with me. so i just wanted to get some peoples opinion. Painless Brutality[35]

Chris's post drew sixteen responses in less than twenty-four hours. All were empathetic and many suggested various strategies ranging from gradually intro-ducing his girlfriend to Aryan ideology to violent strategies intended to demon-strate the virtues of Aryanism.

> Same deal with me mate, my girl is German and very anti nazi's. But talk to her, try to educate her. My girl is slowly coming around now. red neck nzr[36]

Another suggested:

> Take her for a walk in a nigger ghetto. Take the ass-beating and then see if she becomes racist. Vegas h8s Spearchuckers[37]

Chris expressed his gratitude to the respondents and vowed to "keep them posted."

Coming Out to Non-Aryans

Online conversations focus on how Aryans should come out about their extremist beliefs to nonracist family and friends. A primary theme in Aryan postings is racial kinship.

> Hey, sorry I have to rant. My sister hates everything we stand for. I know it should be expected because the jews have so much control today, but I just don't understand how your own flesh and blood can turn on you for realizing the truth. I have tried to explain everything to her, but she never listens she just yells over me. I just can't do it anymore. What would any of you do in this situation? Aryan88chick[38]

> I recently talked to my cousin online, that I used to love, and she used to love me. But once I expressed my love for the white race, she just flipped out on me. That's what happens when people grow up on the nigger loving mtv jew box their whole life. . . . She may not agree with me and say bad things about me and my people, but she is still my cousin. What to do? Zogslayer[39]

> I joined this forum because I'm hurt and confused. I'm seventeen and I've never exactly been fully white pride. I'm DAMN proud of my ancestry, but not actively racist. Now my blonde, nordic cousin WILLINGLY slept with a nigger. I'm hurt and getting angrier as I write. My whole family, they're all so proud of her. So proud of her betrayal. For the first time in my life, I'm ashamed of my family. None of my friends understand my horror. I don't know where to turn. I joined here hoping some of you could help me decide what to do. WhitePride[40]

Each of these postings quickly generated between fourteen and twenty replies from other members who relayed similar personal experiences. Respondents empathized that they could relate to the posters' situations and feel their pain.

They stressed the sanctity of their Aryan beliefs over all else. These replies reinforce the idea that an Aryan's true friends and family are found only inside the movement. Empathy is evident in members' responses to the last post above:

> Such appalling news brought tears to my blue eyes. . . . I'm thankful you have asked us for comfort, for we are willing to give it. Remember, you are not alone. Focus on your beliefs, ignore the nay-saying and great things will become of you. I'm positive that this is true, for I have been clinging on to my beliefs for five years through dirt, blood, sweat, and tears, and still my dreams shine brightly without any dwindle. Jenocide[41]

> I feel your pain but you must understand that family is good, but when it is spoiled by some nigger fucking inferior, that there is a giant WP family waiting for you, and will help you. . . . As far as your family making you ashamed, well then try and open your door to them a bit and show them your point of view. If they are angered and don't want to hear the truth then you have to accept that you are superior to all of them. RACE FIRST! Hitler's Aryan Ghost[42]

Activists idealize white power faith. Consequently, Aryans fill their online conversations with admonitions to keep the faith in the face of mainstream social pressure and affirm white power attitudes by glorifying white racial kinship.

Dependency and Loneliness

Cyberspace helps Aryans affirm their commitments to white power identity. Aryans open up to others about their virulent hatred and find support for their beliefs. Advice on coping with loneliness flows freely through the chat rooms. Members assure one another that they are not alone in their fight and express mutual moral support and concern to ease the strains of their stigmatized social status as Aryans.[43]

Aryans depend on Web forums to connect to the broader WPM community. Just how deeply dependent some members are becomes especially apparent when the websites go offline for technical upgrades or reorganization. After a temporary shutdown of the forum board on Free Your Mind Productions, members expressed their deep disappointment about the downtime and exhilaration about the forum board's return. Responding to others' frustrations about the brief hiatus, a forum participant wrote:

> Damn right!!! I kept clicking on it like someone with a broken remote. Lol Glad to see everyone back here. Kinda gives ya a warm feelin' knowing there's other people out there that think like you. Spring Demon[44]

Another responded:

> Me to [*sic*], bro! I really enjoy posting in this forum with others who share my faith and knowledge of the true nature of race and nation. Without it I get lonely. There

is so much trash hurled at us through the media that is meant to isolate us. . . . I for one am glad to find a place like this. AryanPrincess[45]

Aryans build a sense of community online. The online connections are not confined to the virtual world, but also extend to real-world activities. We end this chapter by explaining the ties between Aryan virtual free spaces and their real-world spaces of hate.

CYBERSPACE TIES TO REAL-WORLD ARYAN SPACES

Aryans "do not neatly divide their worlds into two discrete sets: people seen in person and people contacted online."[46] The relationships Aryans develop online add layers of interaction to social connections they already make in the real-world spaces where they meet. Aryan websites support activist networks and are tied to real-world activities. Major white power groups such as the Hammerskin Nation, White Revolution, Imperial Klans of America, and Volksfront use the Web to promote national and regional gatherings. Local groups of activists coordinate house parties and campouts via e-mail and chat rooms. Aryans also extend their interpersonal relationships using e-mail, networking sites, and Internet forums.

Aryans even participate vicariously in real-world gatherings through the Web. The largest and most prominent Aryan gatherings, such as white power music concerts, typically have an extensive Web presence. Members who cannot attend can still be involved through live blogs, streaming broadcasts, and audiovisual recordings of the performances.

Attendees also report directly to one another about concerts, festivals, and even campouts as a way to spread access to members in cyberspace. Aryans' enthusiastic descriptions of movement events affirm a vibrant movement community. Thrilled attendees of the 2006 Unity Fest in Northern California filled the forum group CaSkinhead with descriptive exchanges of the event.

> Let me tell you about the beginning of what had to be one of the most memorable weekends of my entire life. Up in the beautiful, mountainous areas not far from my own home, I took part in one of the most welcoming, exciting and enthusiastic events that any Aryan could experience: Unity Fest. This one had it all: great food cooked to perfection, raffles with bitchin' prizes, entertainment for the kids, and most importantly, numerous White brothers and sisters ready for fun, all located in the coniferous mountains of California. FightforFreedom[47]

Aryans also create many virtual extensions of their real-world interpersonal relationships.[48] Virtual contact among Aryans continues when a concert is over or a party winds down. Members extend their opportunities to interact by sharing e-mail addresses and Web-forum information where they can be reached.

Online connections in Web-forum groups become real-world meetings among

Aryans. Chat room participants ask one another how to connect offline. Web-forum group organizers are especially quick to respond with invitations. In a typical exchange, a nascent WPM member, whitewarrior, asked:

> Do any of you guys ever meet up in the real world? I live in Farmington. If any of you guys would like to get together, please feel free to contact me. whitewarrior[49]

A membership coordinator for the state branch of White Revolution responded within minutes.

> White Revolution members actually get together quite often. Sometimes for cook-outs, but mostly for our meetings. We will be having a meeting later on in the month. If you feel comfortable enough to send me your email, I can put you on our email list so you can stay up to date on what we are doing.[50]

Queries from members who move to a new area are also common in chat rooms.

> i am a skingirl planning on moving to south city in the middle of april and i dont know many people there. it would be good to meet some like minded folk. email me if you get some time. Hail Victory! skingirl14[51]

Responses to this posting were quick and inviting. Most responders congratulated her on the move and offered to bring other Aryans to meet her when she arrived.

★

We have seen that Aryans use cyberspace as a safe and efficient way to communicate their virulent racist and anti-Semitic challenges to mainstream culture and to display Aryan norms that members are encouraged to reflect in their own lives. Many websites are channels to real-world movement spaces, giving activists opportunities to connect with fellow Aryans.

The white power movement's Web presence symbolizes an Aryan community. Activists might have a hard time regularly connecting outside cyberspace. Val Burris and his colleagues point out that the Internet seems to hold a "special attraction for those [Aryans] in search of 'virtual' community to compensate for the lack of critical mass in their own [locale]" and to extend their otherwise sporadic participation in the movement's real-world free spaces.[52]

Some Aryans never connect to others through the Web, while others may limit their involvement in the movement by secretly surfing white power websites and lurking in chat rooms. In fact, some activists have coined the term "net-Nazis" to castigate members who spend the bulk of their time posting in Web forums and chatting online while avoiding more public activism. Yet, as white power activists craft more and more virtual spaces to support and encourage the unconstrained expression of radical racism, they help to amplify and sustain more members' involvement in the movement.

In the next chapter, we shift our focus to private Aryan communities. These settlements are the most restricted Aryan free spaces. In residential communities, white power members participate in a microcosm of the idealized Aryan separatist world they desire.

7

Private Aryan Communities

During the last few decades, white power groups have formed a small number of private communities where members live in racially exclusive Aryan free spaces. Some settlements contain as few as a dozen members, while others host up to 100. The most notorious private Aryan communities include the 346-acre National Alliance grounds near Hillsboro, West Virginia; Elohim City, a 1,000-acre white-separatist community in eastern Oklahoma; and the now-defunct 20-acre Aryan Nations compound in Hayden Lake, Idaho. These devoutly racist compounds house Aryan worship centers and white power libraries stocked with Aryan literature and movement paraphernalia. Compound members practice Aryan educational, religious, and paramilitary training.

The compounds are hubs for white power networking. Activists make pilgrimages to the communities, which host large gatherings where devotees experience a "pure" Aryan settlement. These communities serve as way stations for traveling WPM activists, some of whom are on the run from authorities.[1]

Private Aryan communities are repositories of hate culture. White power members talk of these communities as the truest form of mainstream defiance and commitment to white racial kinship. Aryan communities symbolize an independent, enduring, and righteous resistance against their racial enemies. Members organize the settlements to represent a small-scale, racially exclusive, anti-Semitic world. In private Aryan communities, white power extremists have planned some of the most notorious acts of Aryan violence.

We begin this chapter by describing the origins, history, and organization of several private Aryan communities. Two of the most publicized, albeit disbanded, private Aryan communities are The Covenant, the Sword, and the Arm of the

Lord (CSA) and Aryan Nations. Elohim City and the National Alliance persist. We discuss the disbanded communities because they are powerful symbols that continue to serve as inspiration to Aryan resistance and as models for present-day Aryan gatherings.

Private communities are the most secretive Aryan free spaces. Few outsiders have studied their day-to-day activities. Much of our discussion here necessarily relies on secondary sources because we have the least direct observational experience with private Aryan communities. However, we do draw upon our own fieldwork data from the Aryan Nations compound and the Aryan congresses held there.

PURE ARYAN SPACE

Prior to the major civil rights desegregation efforts in the 1960s, white supremacists had no immediate need to wall out the mainstream world. Racial exclusivity was the norm in many regions across the United States. According to James Loewen, "'sundown towns'—those towns that systematically excluded African Americans and other minorities, often with signs at the city limits that usually said 'Nigger, Don't Let the Sun Go Down on You in [Whitesville]' were everywhere in America."[2] Loewen wrote:

> Most independent sundown towns expelled their black residents, or agreed not to admit any, between 1890 and 1940. Sundown suburbs arose still later, between 1900 and 1968. By the middle of the twentieth century, it was no longer rare for towns [ranging from a few hundred to many thousands] to be all-white. It was common, and usually it was on purpose.[3]

While sundown towns still persist today, most have dissolved, as civil rights policies curtailed the most overt racist practices. In the aftermath of these changes and in the context of spiritual-religious revivalism, Aryans established private communities to wall themselves off from the cultural turmoil of the 1960s and 1970s.

The Covenant, the Sword, and Arm of the Lord

From its formation in 1971 until its destruction in 1985, The Covenant, the Sword, and the Arm of the Lord was one of the most active and notorious Aryan settlements. CSA became a model for later private Aryan communities. Texas minister James Ellison founded CSA on more than 200 acres near the Missouri-Arkansas border. Their geographical isolation separated CSA families from the taint of mainstream society, and the area's isolated and rugged terrain made monitoring by authorities especially difficult. The property's location on state borders also complicated jurisdictional responsibilities.[4]

Ellison started CSA as a Christian fundamentalist community. He drew together fifteen families committed to simple living and purity in their spiritual and physical lives.[5] Early CSA members committed to strict dietary standards that included occasional fasting and prohibitions on alcohol, drugs, and smoking.

During the late 1970s, after Ellison claimed to have a vision of a coming race war that would engulf America, he and his followers turned to Christian Identity principles and transformed the property into a white supremacist, paramilitary training camp. The group adopted the name The Covenant, the Sword, and the Arm of the Lord to reflect their increasing radicalization. Ellison began characterizing "the CSA mission as establishing an 'Ark for God's people' for the coming race war. God's people were white Christians [while] Jews, he told his followers, were not really God's chosen people, but rather a demonic and inferior race."[6]

The insular CSA community stressed collective experiences. The community met for praise meetings three or four times per week and had at least one extended Bible study meeting each week.[7] For a short time the group experimented with polygamy and, according to former CSA member Kerry Noble, used the Bible meetings to develop justifications for the practice.[8] Members followed traditional gender roles, with the males, known as "the Cedar Boys,"[9] working outside the home cutting timber on the property, farming, and doing carpentry. CSA women homeschooled their children and tended to household chores.[10] Some members also held jobs outside the compound in local businesses, such as a sawmill and a department store.

The CSA settlement built a church, a communications center, workshop, munitions storage bunker, and member houses.[11] Each family lived in their own twenty-four-square-foot residence without electricity and running water. Reflecting their apocalyptic worldview, members strategically positioned their homes in three separate directions from the main settlement as defensive vantage points in case of attack.[12] Families also prepared for attacks with underground storage and safety bunkers.

Members created paramilitary training areas that included a mock village called "Silhouette City . . . complete with pop-up targets of blacks, Jews, and police officers wearing Star of David badges"[13]

In 1982, the Federal Bureau of Investigation suspected that CSA had just over 100 active members living on or in close proximity to the compound.[14] Others estimated the number at closer to 200.[15]

CSA members often attended gun shows in their preparations for the race war. Here they met and formed alliances with members of Aryan Nations, Silent Brotherhood, Posse Comitatus, local Ku Klux Klan chapters, Elohim City, and the Christian Patriot Defense League.[16] CSA members used these connections to increase their weapons and food stockpiles.

These networks also allowed Ellison to enlist survivalist combat coaches for his paramilitary training program on the CSA compound. He called survivalist training the "Endtime Overcomer Survival Training School." The survival school gave courses in "urban warfare, riflery and pistolcraft, military tactics, Christian martial arts, and wilderness survival."[17]

To supplement their income, CSA members traded semiautomatic rifles, silencers, and other weapons on the gun-show circuit.[18] Ellison prodded his followers into thievery and pawning personal goods that were not crucial to warfare and survival. Followers even pawned their own wedding rings.[19] Such income increased the CSA stockpile of weaponry, chemicals, explosives, food, and first-aid supplies.[20]

Ellison and his CSA followers originally stockpiled weapons and did survivalist training as defensive preparation for racial conflict. But in the early 1980s, CSA planned several terrorist plots.[21] In 1983, federal marshals killed Christian Identity adherent Gordon Kahl in a shoot-out. After that event, CSA declared the compound "an arms depot and paramilitary training ground for Aryan warriors."[22] CSA planned the assassinations of a local FBI agent and a U.S. district judge, and plotted the poisoning of municipal water supplies, arsons, and bombings.[23]

The original plan to destroy the Alfred P. Murrah Federal Building in Oklahoma City was hatched by CSA members nearly twelve years before Timothy McVeigh and his accomplices bombed it to complete the mission.[24] Although CSA failed to execute most of their terrorist plans, CSA members and their associates bombed a Missouri community church known to support homosexuality and an Indiana Jewish community center. CSA radicals also detonated explosives near a natural gas pipeline in Arkansas, robbed and murdered a pawnshop owner they thought was Jewish, and murdered an African American Arkansas State Trooper.[25]

CSA's spree of violence ended in April 1985. Ellison and other CSA followers surrendered at CSA's compound following a four-day standoff with federal agents.[26] The FBI's search of the CSA compound uncovered nearly 200 firearms, including land mines, machine guns, assault rifles, thousands of rounds of ammunition, antitank rockets, and a large supply of cyanide.[27]

In September 1985, CSA leaders James Ellison and Kerry Noble and four other CSA activists were sentenced to federal prison on racketeering and weapons charges, which effectively destroyed the group and the settlement.[28] After his release from federal prison, Ellison took up residence at Elohim City.

Elohim City

Founded in 1973, Elohim City is the oldest major racialist community still operating in the United States. Robert Millar moved to the United States from Canada in the 1950s and organized eighteen Christian Identity members to build a settlement on 400 acres near Muldrow, Oklahoma, an isolated and mountainous area along the Oklahoma-Arkansas border. Millar and his followers planned an insular

Christian Identity community. They named it Elohim City, or "City of God" while waiting for the Rapture.[29]

Elohim City residents are notoriously secretive about their beliefs and activities and shield their racialism from outsiders. The city hosts a population that reportedly fluctuates between seventy and ninety residents. Members focus on "pure" living, shunning the outside world and its decadence, which they claim will bring the apocalypse to cleanse the world of all impurities.

Elohim City believes devoutly in racial separatism. Prior to his death in 2001, Millar preached separatism as a strategy to avoid conflict and strengthen bloodlines and kinship ties among "true, pure Aryans." Millar's son John now leads the community and continues his father's emphasis on racial separatism.[30]

The community includes a sawmill, trucking company, K–12 school, church, community medical service, armed patrol unit, and construction firm, which financially supports the community.[31] Elohim City members begin each day with a Pentecostal-type church service that may last several hours. Recreational activities are exclusively community events. The entire community, including children, participates in parties, picnics, canoe trips, and evening socializing.

After the 1995 Oklahoma City bombing reports linked the event to Elohim City and thrust the community into the national spotlight. Elohim members have cultivated ties with right-wing racial extremists, along with violent antitax and militia groups. Elohim's founders were also closely tied to The Covenant, the Sword, and the Arm of the Lord. In 1982, several Elohim members attended CSA's national convention at the group's compound, and Robert Millar preached several times during that gathering.

CSA founder James Ellison and his close associate Richard Wayne Snell repeatedly visited Elohim City in the early 1980s. When the FBI surrounded the CSA compound to arrest Ellison and his followers in 1985, they requested Millar's cooperation to mediate a peaceful surrender to the armed standoff. Robert Millar was Snell's spiritual adviser, and John Millar testified as a character witness when Snell was sentenced to death for the 1984 murder of an Arkansas State Trooper.[32] On April 19, 1995, the same day as the Oklahoma City bombing, Robert Millar visited Snell just before he was executed. Millar witnessed the execution and arranged for Snell's body to be buried at Elohim City.

Other extremist groups to whom Elohim City members have ties include Aryan Nations, the Aryan People's Republic, and White Aryan Resistance. Mark Thomas, former Pennsylvania minister for the Aryan Nations, who hosted meetings of neo-Nazis, skinheads, and other white racist groups on his Pennsylvania farm, helped organize the Aryan Republican Army and arranged for several of its members to live at Elohim City. Cheyne and Chevie Kehoe, who founded the small but violent Aryan People's Republic, reportedly sought refuge at Elohim City. Dennis Mahon, a former imperial dragon in the Oklahoma Ku Klux Klan and an organizer for White Aryan Resistance, kept a trailer at Elohim City. In June 2001, the *New York Post* reported that Elohim City members revere

McVeigh as a martyr, and pictures of him are displayed throughout the compound.[33]

Although Elohim City persists, its future appears tenuous. Robert Millar's son John remains as a patriarch and spiritual leader. But the community's population is reportedly declining as elders die and young residents leave the community for a less isolated and constrained life. Still, among white power devotees, Elohim City is a symbol of Aryan purity and persistence.

National Alliance

In the early 1970s, William Pierce founded the racist and anti-Semitic group National Alliance. Pierce attracted members with his cosmotheist philosophy, which promotes "the superiority of the white race and the unity of the white race with nature."[34]

In 1985, Pierce relocated the group's headquarters from Arlington, Virginia, to a 346-acre farm in rural West Virginia. He called the new compound the Cosmotheist Community Church and, for a time, received partial tax-exempt status for his religious activities. Pierce died in 2002. His protégé, Erich Gliebe, took over and, despite some infighting, the group continues to operate Resistance Records, National Vanguard Books, radio shows, and an extensive website.

The National Alliance headquarters is not an Aryan settlement in the same mold as Elohim City or the former CSA. The Southern Poverty Law Center reports that there are seventeen members of the Alliance's national staff, including experts in computer programming, Web design, video game technology, shortwave broadcasting, and film production. Few members live onsite. There are relatively few structures on the property apart from a church, Pierce's former house, a guesthouse, and a warehouse for Resistance Records and National Vanguard Books.[35] But, as Resistance Records sales grew, the company constructed a major new building with room to seat up to 400 people, offices for twelve staffers, and a video production suite.[36] National Alliance also enhanced its publishing efforts by acquiring new and "expensive office and printing machinery and its own diesel power plant, along with a flatbed dump truck and a log-splitting machine," presumably to use in building more structures on the compound.[37]

The National Alliance uses its West Virginia compound as headquarters to organize and register local National Alliance groups around the country. Pierce also held conferences there to which he invited between thirty and fifty Alliance members with "leadership potential" to teach them about the Jewish conspiracy and recruitment strategies.

At a National Alliance meeting in 1983, Robert Mathews delivered a fiery speech shortly after forming the violent Aryan terrorist cell, the Silent Brotherhood. Mathews had attended several National Alliance events and, through his contact with Pierce and the National Alliance, had come to believe that a violent racial revolution was needed to prevent white genocide. The National Alliance conferences and communiqués via the National Alliance website still offer ideas and resources to local Aryan leaders for organizing National Alliance members and sympathizers.[38]

Aryans also visit the National Alliance headquarters as pilgrims or fugitives seeking safe haven from law enforcement. The most notable of these fugitives is German neo-Nazi and Aryan musician Hendrik Möbus. Möbus was convicted of killing a fourteen-year-old boy in 1993 in the former East Germany. While in prison, Möbus promoted a genre of music known as National Socialist Black Metal (or NSBM), which combines neo-Nazi ideology with a gothic heavy-metal sound. German authorities released Möbus from prison after he served five years. Once out of prison, Möbus continued to produce and promote NSBM music, but in 1999 after a probation violation, which involved a public Nazi salute and demeaning public statements about his murder victim, he was to be rejailed. Möbus fled from Germany to escape incarceration and was active in neo-Nazi groups in the United States prior to befriending Pierce in 2000. He was arrested by U.S. marshals in 2000, outside the National Alliance compound, and sent back to Germany.[39]

Pierce died shortly after, and National Alliance's fate is unclear without his guidance. Almost a decade after his death, however, the group does not appear to be dissolving. National Alliance staff continues to coordinate the group's music and publishing efforts from the compound. National Alliance's sophisticated Web presence and radio broadcasts still draw a wide Aryan audience.

Aryan Nations

Prior to its demise in 2001, the Aryan Nations' headquarters was the most recognized white power community among Aryans and in the public eye. Aryan Nations members were relatively open to researchers and reporters. Consequently, the Aryan Nations compound became the most studied white power encampment.[40] In the following sections we draw extensively from our participant observation fieldwork at Aryan Nations, complemented by published reports from other observers.

Richard Butler established the twenty-acre Aryan Nations compound outside of Hayden Lake, Idaho, in 1974. The compound was "the prime nerve-center for the Aryan movement in the occupied United States,"[41] and quickly became "renowned as a gathering point for a wide range of white supremacist groups and individuals."[42]

Butler called it "the international headquarters for the white race." He held annual Aryan gatherings on the land between 1980 and 2000, and he imagined the community as "a national racial state," saying, "We shall have it at whatever price necessary. Just as our forefathers purchased their freedom in blood so must we. . . . We will have to kill the bastards."[43]

Butler's emphasis on violent solutions to the race problem remains front and center. The Aryan Nations website proclaims: "We are a worldwide Pan-Aryan crusade dedicated to the preservation and advancement of our Race—Our Race is Our Nation! Racial Purity is our Nations Security! Our Motto: Violence Solves Everything."[44]

In contrast to this rhetorical grandeur, the compound itself was quite unremarkable. From the state road, a dirt driveway led through native pines. Only after winding up to the guard gate was it clear that the area was an Aryan compound. A prominent sign at the guard gate welcomed visitors: "Whites Only." After passing through the gate, the compound came into view. There was Butler's modest farmhouse, an office, a visitors' bunk house, a work shed with a swastika painted on the roof, a watchtower, and the chapel of Butler's Church of Jesus Christ Christian. Adjacent to the church and work shed was a clearing where the Aryan faithful camped during mass gatherings. Butler's office had desks for him and his secretary, a printing press, and a workshop.

White power symbolism was emblazoned in the buildings. Butler's office displayed images of Adolf Hitler, along with many photographs of himself with white power movement leaders. Inside the chapel a stained glass window formed the Aryan Nations symbol. Butler had positioned wooden crosses, a bust of Hitler, and another swastika around the chapel. Aryan Hall, a space adjoining the chapel, was filled with Aryan and neo-Nazi imagery. Robert Balch wrote:

Figure 7.1   Front entrance to the Aryan Nations bunkhouse used by guests at the compound. April 22, 1997.

Photo by Pete Simi

Figure 7.2   Swastika painted on the work shed roof at Aryan Nations compound. April 22, 1997.

Photo by Pete Simi

Posters depicting Storm Troopers mingled with paintings representing AN's vision of the future: the Four Horsemen of the Apocalypse, Aryan Warriors battling ape-like mud people, and a youth, sword in hand, standing triumphantly over the corpse of a Jewish dragon while rays of light beamed down from Heaven.[45]

Butler and no more than a dozen people lived at the compound for extended periods. The director of security, a position that shifted hands regularly, was a common resident, along with his immediate family if he had one. Butler hosted Aryan pilgrims and provided them a haven in which to retreat, worship, and invigorate their racist commitments. Butler's prison outreach efforts housed racist ex-cons who needed a place to stay after their release. He invited white power leaders for periodic visits to the settlement. Butler also hosted Aryan Nations members who lived in communities in and around Hayden Lake and visited on Sundays for church service and communal fellowshipping.

Congresses and Youth Assemblies

Aryan Nations came to prominence in the white power movement during the late 1970s when Butler began an outreach strategy to draw new members and veteran

Figure 7.3   Interior view of Aryan Hall at the Aryan Nations compound, Hayden Lake, Idaho. April 22, 1997.

Photo by Pete Simi

white supremacists to Idaho. He churned out racist and anti-Semitic literature and ran ads in right-wing magazines. In them "[he touted] the attractions of the inland Northwest. Butler also organized meetings with other Identity leaders to promote a [white] separatist agenda [and took] the bold step of inviting [into his group] representatives of the Ku Klux Klan and neo-Nazi groups who ordinarily did not mix with Identity people."[46]

Butler's efforts culminated in the first Aryan Nations World Congress, held at the compound in 1980. He wanted to draw Aryans from all branches into a single setting where they "could set aside their sectarian differences and work together for racial preservation."[47] Held consistently from 1980 to 2000,[48] the congresses drew up to 500 activists per gathering from across the country.

The meetings attracted a veritable "who's who" of prominent extremists.[49] We observed leaders of Oregon's National Socialist Vanguard; Aryan Nations members and branches from Ohio, Pennsylvania, New York, Montana, California, Georgia, Alabama, Kansas, and Missouri; leaders and rank-and-file members from the National Alliance, Ku Klux Klan, and skinhead organizations; and representatives from white power media organizations such as Panzerfaust Records and 14 Words Press.

Butler also sought to organize young Aryan activists. During the 1980s, he ran an Aryan Nations Academy to teach the group's philosophy to children of local

Aryans. Although it is difficult to confirm the claim, an information packet that Butler mailed out in 1982 said, "the 'academy' had 15 full-time students."[50] One of these children, David Tate, eventually became a member of the terrorist cell, the Silent Brotherhood, and is now serving a life sentence for murdering a Missouri State Trooper.[51]

Between 1989 and 1996, Aryan Nations also hosted gatherings Butler called the Aryan Youth Assembly, which was part of the outreach effort to support new WPM members. The assemblies highlighted the importance of cultivating the next generation of Aryans by building a force that would carry the movement forward. Although the assemblies were explicitly youth oriented, many veterans of the congresses also attended and created a setting where veterans socialized young recruits.

One of the most notable differences between the congresses and youth assemblies was the prominence of white power music. While music was a part of the larger congresses, it was much more central to the assemblies, whose main attendees were young skinheads. To attract young Aryans, Butler hosted popular white power bands, such as Bound for Glory and Odin's Law.

A Place to Be "True White Men"

Butler imagined the congresses and youth assemblies as "consciousness-raising events intended to create and sustain a collective Aryan identity, transcending barriers, of class, religion . . . and factional allegiance."[52] The gatherings were one of the few places where movement activists could directly experience a large group of white power adherents from across the movement and hear WPM leaders' speeches about racism and anti-Semitism. Butler explained that the congresses were one of the few places WPM members could openly flaunt their beliefs: "They allow us to be true white men. We can say nigger and not have to worry about losing a job and having someone scream racist. It used to be this way in all of America not just places like here."[53]

As attendees arrived at each congress, guards checked their names against a registration list, handed each person a schedule of speakers and events, and then directed them to the parking area. Most Aryans milled around on the first Friday morning of congresses, talking, drinking coffee, and setting up their camping spots. Conversations began as people introduced themselves, identified where they were from, and then described their locale's racial makeup and Aryan politics. Aryans also gathered around tables covered with white power books, music, magazines, T-shirts, films, flags, paintings, sculptures, military uniforms, and bumper stickers.

A period in the early afternoon on the first day was set aside for an official press conference; only Caucasian reporters had access to the grounds for these couple of hours. Butler stood with several key staff members on a wooden deck adorned with Nazi, Confederate, and Aryan Nations flags and spoke in grandiose terms about the goals of the weekend and of the broader movement. When the press conference ended, Aryan Nations security promptly escorted the reporters off the grounds.

The congresses then began in earnest. Butler gave a keynote address, and other movement leaders spoke as well. Much of the weekends were given to speeches and workshops on movement ideology, recruitment strategies, athletic contests, and, for a time, survivalist training and guerilla warfare. Although we did not observe this, James Aho describes "nigger shooting" contests, during which armed Aryans shot at "among other targets, crude facsimiles of running black men and enlarged photos of despised Jewish faces."[54]

Butler scheduled times for "fellowshipping," periods of informal networking among the attendees. Dinner marked the official end of each day. Then attendees gathered around bonfires to carouse or left the compound to attend parties at local Aryan homes.

After sundown on the last full evening of each congress, Butler convened a grand ritual of cross and swastika lighting. Aryan-themed prayers were followed by ritualistic chants of "*Sieg heil*," "Rahowa," "14 Words," and "White power." The next morning offered chapel services, followed by a Soldier's Ransom ritual in which men pledged their allegiance to the movement and reaffirmed their commitment to the cause. By lunchtime on the final day attendees packed up and began their trip home.

Despite Butler's best intentions to carry off disciplined, well-ordered weekends, things did not often go as planned. Drawing together racists from different factions was a challenge. Butler and his staff did not manage it seamlessly. Some attendees, particularly neo-Nazi skinheads, flaunted Butler's prohibitions on guns, alcohol, and drugs. The security patrol was a rag-tag outfit. Events often failed to start on time.[55] Balch argues that "[Aryan Nations] events may have been good [public theatre, but] the script lost its punch because the cast, crew, and director could not deliver a convincing performance."[56]

Balch's perception is valid but also incomplete. The congress's theatre may have been weak, but its practical and symbolic significance was powerful. Those who attended the congresses and youth assemblies found an Aryan social scene where they could meet face-to-face and form alliances in a rare whites-only context.

We interviewed Aryans at Hayden Lake about their unique feeling of being insulated from the outside world. Charlie, an Aryan Nations veteran, said, "Right now we're here together as a people and, you know, that's what's going to allow us to defeat the Zionist Occupied Government. These [congresses] help us build our solidarity and bring people together. It gives us time away from everything else."[57]

Attendees told us how this time spent fellowshipping renewed their commitments and strengthened their resolve to persist as Aryans. Mike, a longtime visitor to the compound, explained: "These congresses are a good time for us to come together in one place where we can feel some comfort being around proud white people. These few days make it possible to get through the rest of the year."[58] Likewise, Gary, another Aryan Nations veteran, said, "If we don't do things like this, then how are we going to keep the movement together?"[59]

Russ, an Alabama Klan member with five Aryan Nations World Congresses under his belt, emphasized the special draw the events held for him and others, saying, "Aryan congresses are a time for us to come together, a special time. And we recognize how special this is how much this event signifies and how much it means to keeping our race alive."[60]

A strong indication of the importance the Aryan gatherings had for the movement was their two-decade lifespan. The congresses and youth assemblies were no short-lived experiment. Movement activists saw such gatherings as symbolic of enduring Aryan righteousness. And the rituals buttressed their faith in this idea.

Aryan Nations Rituals

The congresses and youth assemblies generated excitement, power, pride, and a collective affirmation of white power identity. The symbolism combined hatred and violence toward racial enemies as well as love and kinship among Aryans. Rituals portrayed romanticized visions of Aryan traditions anchored by Nordic warrior and religious themes.

Speeches by white power leaders were the congresses' most frequent ritual activity. Most speeches, like Neuman Britton's described below, were fire-and-brimstone sermons designed to agitate Aryan hate.

I listened as Pastor Neumann Britton seethed in racist anger before the packed church on the Aryan Nations compound. It was the second day of the Aryan Nations Annual World Congress, and the attendees were primed for his hate sermon. "The Jews are bloodsuckers! They must die! We need to fill the streets with their blood," he bellowed, face red from exertion. He paused and the crowd responded in unison: "White power! *Sieg heil*! Hail victory!"

For the first ten minutes of the sermon I stared straight ahead, trying not to look at the others around me. I had seen most of the congregation earlier in the day as I wandered around the compound. Then, I mainly felt a sociologist's curiosity about them. But now, sitting among this group of true believers chanting for blood, I was simply scared. As Neumann Britton fumed in explosive rage, I wondered if the parishioners all felt the same intense hatred as him. They all listened intently. The young neo-Nazis in the audience seemed particularly mesmerized.

I was struck with how much his tirade and the audiences' interest contrasted with the morning's opening speech. Then, an elderly man droned on about ZOG for what seemed like hours and literally put almost half of the audience to sleep. No one shouted "White power!" or "Hail victory!" The glassy-eyed audience just sat quietly, waiting for the end. But Britton had everyone's attention. The pastor's face looked warped as he spewed his racist vitriol: "The race traitors will be the first to hang—it's the white race mixers who are really ruining this country!" At times, I felt like he was speaking directly to me, targeting me, "the race traitors, some are in this very room!"

Britton ended his forty-five-minute sermon and the congregation broke up. I walked straight outside to get some fresh air. The Aryan Nations Compound was surrounded by tall, fragrant pine trees that swayed in the soft summer breeze. Aryans from around the country milled about, chatting, drinking coffee and sodas. I sat down on a bench at the edge of the encampment and considered the irony of such a tranquil place being used for building a movement of extreme hate.[61]

The most dramatic rituals at the congress were cross lightings ignited by robed and hooded Klansmen. Attendees circled a swastika and cross and listened as leaders explained the meaning of the cross and swastika lighting. The lighting was a deeply religious ritual that continued eons of Christian and Aryan heritage. Cindy, an Aryan Nations member said, "When we light the cross we think of how much we love our people. We love them enough to die for them, like Christ. The lit cross is an ancient Aryan symbol."[62]

Steven, a Kentucky Klansman, described how the ceremony created a feeling of peacefulness and release, saying, "I always feel so peaceful when the crosses are lit. I guess kind of just at ease or something like the natural order the way it's supposed to be."[63]

The Soldier's Ransom ceremony performed on the congress's final day marked the collective meaning of the gathering and left participants with renewed commitment to the movement. Men lined up for the ceremony in the chapel's center aisle and then passed a broad sword along the line, each kissing the hilt and pledging their allegiance to the Aryan cause. Each man stated his own pledge in turn.

I pledge my life to the racial struggle.
I will give my life in honor of our white heroes and warriors who have gone
    before me and given the ultimate sacrifice:
The Order,
Gordon Kahl,
Ian Stuart.
These are my forefathers and I will do everything in my power to meet their
    standards and to make our white homeland a reality.

Heil Hitler!
Heil Bob Mathews!
White power!
Rahowa!

Following this pledge, each man stepped aside to be blessed by an Aryan Nations pastor. The pastor dipped his thumb in oil then rubbed a cross symbol on the man's forehead.

Dylan, an Aryan from Oregon, talked about his reverence for the ceremony.

> I've done the Soldiers Ransom ceremony once before, but it's time to do it again and really get the feelings renewed. During the year it's easy to forget about our responsibilities to our race and just get caught up in the daily crap that all of us have to face. But looking into Pastor Butler's eyes and thinking about everything he's given us, that really puts a lump in my throat. It's these times that get me through.[64]

Throughout the congress weekend, attendees sang racialized hymns, wore symbolic Aryan regalia, and participated in crude military exercises. These are the activities that strengthen devotees' commitment by reaffirming collective grievances. Rituals generate and amplify activists' solidarity "high,"[65] which sustains commitment to a risky cause.[66]

Pilgrimage

The trip to the Aryan Nations compound for a congress or youth assembly, or at another time of the year, was a spiritual pilgrimage and badge of honor that signaled deep commitment to the white race. Attendance at Butler's gatherings grew during the 1980s. Their notoriety and reverence grew among white power members from all the movement's branches.[67] Rachel, a Washington State Skinhead, said:

> Aryan Nations is a gathering place for the movement; there's no doubt about it. It's kind of one of those places that every racialist has to come to. Just to be here and feel part of this that's so much bigger than you. It tells that you're not alone and there are others who see things the same as you.[68]

Attendees talked of their visits as a way to pay homage to Butler and the movement. Upon arriving, first-timers often sought out Butler to express the honor they felt being in his presence and at the compound. Those who eventually made it to a congress, like Charley, a skinhead from Sacramento, frequently lamented the fact that they should have come sooner to experience the movement in a pure white space: "Yeah, this is my first time up here. I just had to make it. I should have come up here a long time ago, but I'm going to start coming up here more now."[69]

Regular attendees were often quick to express that their commitment to attending the congress overshadowed much in their lives. Bill, a Southwest Aryan Separatist, said, "I used to have to drive sixteen hours just to go to congress and I'd never miss 'em. If I couldn't get the time off from work, I'd go anyway, just leave. I lost a few jobs doing that, but it was worth it; it was always worth it."[70]

Once they were on the compound, members devised ways to express their commitment and reverence for the gathering and Butler. A young skinhead told a group at Aryan Nations of his plans to pay respect to Butler by wearing his grandfather's Nazi SS uniform to the congress in order to "honor Pastor Butler and what he's done here."[71]

Aryan Nation's Legacy

In the mid-1980s, Aryan Nations came under intense scrutiny from law enforcement and media. Congresses grew in popularity, and testimony in the trials of several members of the Aryan terrorist cell the Silent Brotherhood revealed close ties to Aryan Nations. The compound also faced strident opposition from human rights groups as well as local authorities, business leaders, and the public. Local and state police harassed and arrested congress attendees. Federal agents and human rights organizations, such as the Anti-Defamation League and the Southern Poverty Law Center, stepped up their infiltration efforts and organized protests at the gate.

By the mid-1990s, most of the group's original members dropped out to avoid attention from authorities.[72] Butler still held the congresses, but the main attendees were neo-Nazi skinheads who were volatile, unpredictable, and challenged the family atmosphere Butler intended for congress weekends.[73] Butler ended the youth assemblies in 1995.

The knockout blows to Aryan Nations were landed in 1999 and 2000. In 1999, former Aryan Nations security guard Buford Furrow "went on a shooting rampage in California wounding five people at a Jewish community center, and later killing a nonwhite postal worker."[74] As news of the incident and Furrow's history with Aryan Nations spread, Butler became embroiled in a civil suit prosecuted by the Southern Poverty Law Center on behalf of Victoria Keenan and her son Jason. Aryan Nations security guards had chased the Keenans' car, ran them off the road into a ditch, and threatened them at gunpoint. The guards reportedly claimed that the Keenans fired at the compound as they drove by. In 2000, the jury levied a $6.3 million judgment against Butler.

Butler soon filed for bankruptcy, and the compound was sold at auction in 2001. The buyer burned all the buildings and removed all traces of Aryan Nations from the property.[75]

Stripping Butler of his property forced a hiatus on the annual events that had been a white power institution for twenty years. Butler continued to lead Aryan Nations from a small house in Hayden, Idaho, and posted messages on the group's website.[76] The Aryan Nations World Congress was reconstituted in 2003 at a campground in Farragut State Park near the former compound. Seventy-five attendees gathered with an ever-defiant Butler. He told a reporter, "What you're seeing here today is the awakening of the white race."[77]

Butler officially anointed activist Ray Redfeairn as his successor at the 2003 day-long event, which was reported on a number of white power Internet sites.[78] Representatives attended from groups such as the Aryan Nations Knights of the Ku Klux Klan, White Revolution, and the National Socialist Movement.[79] However, attendance plummeted to forty people at the 2004 congress. Butler died two months later.

Aryan Nations has since been embroiled in a struggle over leadership, and no large-scale congresses have since been held.

Inspirational Symbol

Aryan Nations lives on as an inspirational symbol to many in the movement. Other white power groups have used the congresses and youth assemblies as models for their own gatherings. Some of these meetings are openly touted as white power gatherings in the same vein as the Aryan Nations. The growing neo-Nazi group Volksfront holds an annual AryanFest, a white power music festival that Butler himself attended in 2001. Volksfront's Oregon contingent also claims to own two plots of land in the Northwest and intends to build a "folk homeland" to draw Aryans together in gatherings and permanent communities there.[80] Volksfront claims Butler's ideal as their vision: to turn the Pacific Northwest into an all-white separatist Aryan homeland.

Another group, the Imperial Klans of America, owns a heavily wooded fifteen-acre site in Dawson Springs, Kentucky. The gated property has living quarters and a stage for speeches and music shows. The Imperial Klans of America annually hosts the infamous Nordic Fest music festival, which has drawn an international audience of more than 400 Aryans.

Other gatherings also draw on the Aryan Nations legacy. Those are disguised as family-oriented festivals celebrating European heritage, Nordic culture, or Anglo-Celtic history. These festivals draw veteran white power activists, but their toned-down racist rhetoric and covert inferences of "culture" and "heritage" are aimed at recruiting new members who might initially be turned off by more aggressive displays of Aryan ideas. The Southern Poverty Law Center estimates that now some 200 of these festivals are held each year.

★

Private Aryan communities are organized as the purest of Aryan free spaces, set apart from mainstream culture and insulated from the outside world. Permanent residents of communities like Elohim City imagine themselves to be taking the most extreme step into committed racialism by devoting themselves to living full-time in a racially pure society.

The communities differ in their insularity, economic autonomy, and openness to outsiders. The Covenant, the Sword, and the Arm of the Lord was the most tightly controlled settlement, while Aryan Nations was quite open to outside observers. National Alliance has created less of a community atmosphere than the others but uses its property as an outpost to disseminate white power hate culture.

The violent radicalism associated with CSA, Elohim City, National Alliance, and Aryan Nations brought them close scrutiny by law enforcement authorities and anti-Aryan groups. Nevertheless, Elohim City and National Alliance continue to sustain their activities, although the deaths of their founders curtailed aspects of the communities' activities.

Private Aryan communities envelope their members in a culture that stokes conspiracy, paranoia, and racial violence. The most ominous legacy these communities leave behind is the violence they encourage. Terrorism was the death knell for CSA and Aryan Nations.

Members of these communities led some of the most notorious Aryan-organized crimes in U.S. history:

- Plans for bombings, thefts, and murders carried out by CSA members were hatched inside the CSA settlement.
- William Pierce and the National Alliance housed violent Aryans and were implicated in a number of incidents, including inspiration for Timothy McVeigh's bombing of the Murrah Federal Building in Oklahoma City, a plan that originated at CSA years earlier.
- Nearly a decade later, McVeigh was linked to members of Elohim City, some of whom might have also helped McVeigh bring his twisted plans to fruition.[81]
- Elohim City was the seedbed for other violent radicalism and provided refuge to Aryans implicated in a range of racial hate crimes.
- Aryan Nations has been a spark for racial violence; they harbored violent racists and provided a context that encouraged racial and anti-Semitic violence.
- The Silent Brotherhood drew members from the Aryan Nations, National Alliance, Ku Klux Klan, and CSA.

The communities also created a second powerful symbolic legacy that continues to influence Aryans from all branches. Defunct Aryan communities such as CSA and Aryan Nations are martyrs for the cause. White power activists interpret attacks on white power communities as evidence of the ZOG conspiracy to eliminate the white race. Thus, these Aryan free spaces live on as cultural symbols that Aryans use to bolster their defiance against an anti-Aryan world.

The networks that these communities helped build, especially through Butler's annual congresses, also persist, although their contact now is made in other Aryan spaces, such as white power websites, concerts, and festivals. Based on their research of Aryan extremism, Jeffrey Kaplan and Leonard Weinberg write: "[Aryan Nations and the annual congresses] provided a relatively stable communal experiment. . . . Pastor Butler established important connections . . . that will continue to flourish long after the Hayden Lake compound is but a memory."[82]

With only a few exceptions, efforts to form and sustain permanent private Aryan communities like Elohim City or Aryan Nations appear to be fading. Now, more temporary large-scale gatherings of music festivals are replacing the role private Aryan communities once played in the white power movement.

Broad-based social networking on the Internet is the norm among Aryans. Music gatherings, house parties, and white power online networks are now the main hidden spaces of hate where Aryans sustain their vision of racial violence and a white power world. These new forms of community have implications for the persistence of Aryan hate culture and the potential for racial and anti-Semitic violence from white power extremists.

8

Enduring White Power Activism

Estimating the Aryan Threat and What to Do about It

Politicians, pundits, and newscasters tell us that terrorism is an external threat. Their proclamations are accompanied by images of bearded, weapons-bearing Muslims in the Middle East. Of course, the reality of the September 11, 2001, attacks on the World Trade Center and the Pentagon, followed by the "war on terror" in Afghanistan and Iraq, has fueled this imagery.

The idea that terrorism equals Middle Eastern violence seems indelibly etched into our collective imaginations. But we should not forget another important moment in our nation's recent past—April 19, 1995—the day Timothy McVeigh detonated the homemade bomb that destroyed the Alfred P. Murrah Federal Building in Oklahoma City and killed 168 people, including 19 children, and injured more than 500. Until 9/11, the Oklahoma City bombing stood as the deadliest act of terrorism on U.S. soil. The bombing horrified the nation, and in the immediate aftermath, many observers speculated that it was an act of foreign attackers.[1] The aftershock came when the bombing turned out to be an act of homegrown terror and the point-man was a young, clean-cut, white male and decorated Gulf War veteran with no prior criminal record. The natural question became—"What turned this All-American boy into a mass murderer?"

While observers focused on individual motivations and psychological explanations, most of their accounts failed to ask about the organization of extremist terror. What was McVeigh doing prior to the bombing? Years later, we know that McVeigh was deeply integrated into a potent culture of paranoia, conspiracy, and violence. He participated in the hidden spaces of radical racist and anti-Semitic culture. His journey from learning extremist views to taking radical action was guided by a persistent network of white power activists, including neo-Nazis, Christian Identity adherents, and Elohim City members who imagined they were waging a righteous war against a government and world gone bad.[2] In short, this "All-American boy" became America's most notorious homegrown terrorist after being integrated into Aryan free spaces that normalize ideas of extremist hate and violent insurgency. The potential for homegrown terror persists in Aryan hate culture found in white power families, Aryan house parties, the white power music scene, Aryan cyberspace, and private white power communities.

AN INFRASTRUCTURE OF HATE

Understanding violent extremism requires us to focus on much more than the violent incidents themselves. We must also pay careful attention to the settings and situations that precede violent acts. Ideas about racist and anti-Semitic violence are expressed, ritualized, and reinforced in Aryan free spaces. These are the backstage settings where extremists encourage violent action for the cause of white power.

The hidden spaces of Aryan hate provide members with the social supports they need to sustain their radical commitments. White power members use crashpads, concerts, backyard barbeques, and the Internet to meet, exchange ideas, and build solidarity with other Aryans. In these contexts, they express their collective hatred in their talk and concretize it in their rituals. Together they keep alive the vision of a future world where blacks, Jews, and other racial enemies are vanquished or destroyed. That vision nourishes violence, destruction, and death. Aryan free spaces are at the core of the contemporary white power movement.

Our up-close look at these contexts reveals that Aryans have built a bi-level infrastructure of free spaces that support distinct kinds of social ties and activities. White power families, racist parties, Aryan spiritual meetings, campouts, and skinhead crashpad gatherings nurture close-knit interpersonal ties among small networks of Aryans who typically live in the same town and connect regularly in face-to-face settings. They embed their racist and anti-Semitic ideals in collective activities that normalize racist and anti-Semitic hate in their lives. But these local pockets of Aryanism are also insular and can be fraught with the same sort of tensions as any small community. It is hard to imagine a geographically broad hate movement persisting with only isolated, local networks to sustain an activist culture.

White power ideology persists because activists connect with broader movement networks through the white power music scene and in cyberspace. Hate concerts and racist websites help link otherwise disconnected local activists into much broader webs of hate culture where they perceive a larger social movement of racists like themselves. Music shows give Aryans opportunities to meet others from across the country and even around the world who share their hate. Cyberspace provides Aryans the same opportunities in the virtual realm, as they connect through streaming audio and visual webcasts, fanzine reports, blogs, and chat rooms.

The act of connecting with other Aryans and the substance of those connections are both crucial to sustaining racist activism. Aryan free spaces provide experiences that are otherwise fleeting in most white power devotees' everyday lives. Most Aryans must live dual lives because their extreme racial and anti-Semitic attitudes are maligned at work and school and other mainstream settings in which they act out their lives. Aryan free spaces are among the very few social spaces where they can express their radicalism and find social and ideological support.

The relationships that Aryans build in these spaces brim with emotions that help bind them together. Anger and hatred galvanize Aryans against their racial enemies and they talk of "killing Jews to keep Hitler's dream alive" or "lynching the niggers and spics" as easily as most people discuss plans for dinner and a movie. But Aryans' lives are not consumed solely by hate. They also experience positive feelings of pride, power, efficacy, pleasure, love, and kinship in these contexts, which legitimate and intensify their connections to other white power believers. The combination of these emotions is the glue of Aryan solidarity that allows the movement to persist.[3]

ESTIMATING THE ARYAN THREAT

So what are we to make of Aryan persistence? Does the fact that white power culture endures in Aryan free spaces threaten civil society? And, if so, what kind of threat do Aryans pose?

Extremist elements clearly challenge American values of freedom, equality, and peace. Aryans are steeped in an ideology that glorifies brutality against racial enemies and envisions a race war as the final step toward white supremacy. Most Aryans will not act out their extremist fantasies, but some will. And as Aryans draw new members into their ranks through their hidden spaces, the odds of racist and anti-Semitic violence grows.

Consider the long histories of extremism by some of the Aryans in our research. We interviewed people who have participated in race riots, murders, bombings, robberies, drug dealing, money laundering, identity theft, and counterfeiting schemes to support Aryan causes. One member threatened to assassinate a U.S. Senator and made the claim on a nationally broadcast television program, no less. Some of the Aryan groups we discussed have stockpiled major weapons and other military equipment for the race war.

Also, consider the number of indictments involving Aryan extremists over the last two decades. Between 1984 and 2002, more U.S. federal indictments (187) were handed down to homegrown Aryan extremists than to international terrorists (185).[4] Between 2000 and 2002, Aryan indictments declined compared to international terrorist indictments as authorities turned their attention after 9/11 to threats from Islamic extremists. But Aryan radicals have not stopped planning violence. The Southern Poverty Law Center reports that, in the decade following the Oklahoma City bombing, Aryans and other right-wing extremists planned or carried out more than sixty terrorist plots, twenty-three of which occurred between 2000 and 2005.[5] The list includes:

> plans to bomb or burn government buildings, banks, refineries, utilities, clinics, synagogues, mosques, memorials and bridges; to assassinate police officers, judges, politicians, civil rights figures and others; to rob banks, armored cars and other criminals; and to amass illegal machine guns, missiles, explosives, and biological and chemical weapons.[6]

Authorities detected and quashed most of these plots before they were carried out, but at least twenty-two people died during this time as a result of organized Aryan violence.[7]

Even these worrisome facts do not fully capture the violence sown by Aryans. Racist skinheads frequently engage in low-profile street violence that does not draw much attention. Aryan gang violence and street fights often go underreported as white power crimes. At the same time, white power leaders have amplified their calls for lone-wolf action against Aryan enemies. The solitary nature of lone wolves like James von Brunn, a longtime white supremacist and anti-Semite whose June 10, 2009, armed attack at the U.S. Holocaust Memorial Museum killed a museum guard, makes it difficult to know how many Aryans will look to wage their singular race wars.[8] Finally, Aryans stockpile weapons and ammunition and play war games to prepare for racial combat. These preparatory efforts set the stage for future Aryan violence.

What catalysts might turn preparation into action? Extremist actions flow from perceived threats. As we write in 2009, severe economic problems, fears of Latino immigration, and anxieties about Muslim expansion feed Aryan angst. Combine these perceived perils with the new shift toward a liberal Democratic administration headed by an African American president and we appear to have a perfect storm of threats to galvanize Aryans. Religion and crime expert Phillip Jenkins observes that new waves of right-wing terror in the United States historically follow transitions to liberal administrations. By that measure alone, U.S. extremists are due for resurgence. As we write, Aryans are profoundly disturbed over President Obama and his administration.

The Southern Poverty Law Center sees anger and paranoia over President Obama's election as the spark for a wave of Aryan violence in 2009 that includes murders of three Pittsburgh police officers, two Florida sheriff's deputies, and a U.S. Holocaust Memorial Museum guard.[9]

Online Aryan chat rooms have also been buzzing since the election with discussion topics titled, "I Hate Obama" and "Obamination." The U.S. Department of Homeland Security's 2009 report on right-wing extremism warns of increasing signs of homegrown terrorism emanating from white power networks,[10] as well as of credible threats against President Obama's life.[11]

At the same time as Aryans lash out, they also imagine that Obama's presidency will generate a white backlash that will help Aryans recruit more members. To draw new members to the cause, Aryans hope to stoke white fears and exploit racist sentiments that still remain among many Americans. U.S. officials are concerned that white military veterans returning from Middle East conflicts with combat skills and experience will be susceptible targets of recruitment and radicalization efforts by white power extremists.[12]

White power groups are also strategically reframing their public message to change their public perception.[13] Their "new racist" rhetoric claims whites as minority victims who face the type of discrimination that contradicts the values of cultural pluralism. Aryans use this rhetoric to neutralize white power stereotypes with claims that they are merely interested in preserving their Southern or Nordic cultural heritage. In reality these efforts are a ploy to disguise their racial extremism and attract potential recruits.[14] Behind the scenes, in Aryan free space, their hate remains as vicious as ever.

Our main point is that when radical ideas endure, so does the potential for radical action. The potential for white power violence is nested in the movement's hidden cultural spaces, where Aryans wield potent ideas of hate. We do not presume a simple cause-effect relationship between exposure to hate culture in Aryan spaces and extremist violence. Most Aryans exposed to the radicalism in Aryan free spaces do not become violent race warriors. The relationship between free spaces and violence is more complex.

White power hate culture endures in fluid, transitory relationships among Aryan activists and groups that periodically coalesce in Aryan free spaces.[15] In a movement so focused on ideals of hatred, members' immersion in Aryan free spaces will inevitably encourage some to enact those ideals violently. Aryan violence may break out in spontaneous interpersonal street fighting as extremists battle enemies one-on-one or in small groups. It may also come in large-scale acts of terror by lone-wolves operating without clear and direct links to hate groups or by larger white power networks coordinating attacks. Whatever form Aryan violence takes or whoever perpetuates the acts, the inspiration will emanate from the culture of hate that endures in Aryan free spaces.[16]

WHAT TO DO

The white power movement endures, but it is in a precarious state, buffeted from the inside by ideological schisms and conflicts over strategy and tactics and from the outside by a long list of opponents. If Aryans maintain their infrastructure of free spaces where members support one another in their beliefs, white power culture will persist. At present, whatever vitality the white power movement possesses is reflected in the strength and persistence of Aryan free spaces where racist hate thrives.

Could eliminating the infrastructure of Aryan free spaces dismantle the white power movement? This logic imagines that if there are no Aryan free spaces, there is no movement and, consequently, no source for the promotion of extremist Aryan violence. This is the same logic that informs the strategy of most authorities and watchdog groups. Federal authorities and the Southern Poverty Law Center's successful efforts to strip Aryan Nations of their compound in 2000 brought the twenty-year run of the Aryan Nations World Congress to an end. This was a huge blow to Aryan radicalism, and it may provide some momentum for authorities to target other white power spaces. The Southern Poverty Law Center expects that its most recent legal victory against the largest U.S. Klan network, the Imperial Klans of America, will cripple the group and destroy its rural Kentucky headquarters.[17]

Yet, if we seek to dismantle all Aryan free spaces, we should prepare for the unintended consequence of more rather than less violent extremism, at least in the short term. The social ties that members cultivate in Aryan free spaces may help constrain their most radical actions. Aryan free spaces may act as pressure release valves that allow Aryans to let loose their frustrations among themselves rather than in overt violent acts against their enemies. In fact, we observed many Aryans stressing to one another the importance of staying true to the white power vision while also discouraging overt acts of violence and destruction that draw unwanted repression.

Repression increases the risks of losing the few supportive social environments where Aryans find positive status and experience feelings of joy, trust, reciprocity, racial kinship, love, and belonging with like-minded others. Thus, while Aryans sustain extremist ideology in their spaces of hate, they may also be tethered to them in ways that discourage higher rates of violent activism for fear of jeopardizing themselves and the movement. Should Aryans lose these spaces, some committed members might retreat further underground while newly isolated lone wolves and small terror cells could spin adrift and act on their violent fantasies.

Finally, questions about how to deal with racist and anti-Semitic extremism raise the vexing issue of how much a democratic society should tolerate from Aryans and other extremist groups. Any attempt to eradicate political free spaces inevitably pushes against the constitutional protections for freedom of speech, freedom of assembly, freedom from surveillance, and the right to privacy. The roll-back of civil liberties under the Bush administration's "war on terror" expanded state power in dangerous ways.[18] As authorities renew their focus on homegrown Aryan threats, we must carefully consider the implications of using expanded state powers. Do we continue to contest Aryans through the battle of ideas and strict enforcement of criminal sanctions, rather than seeking to deny them their constitutionally protected free spaces? Or do we push at any cost to eliminate the infrastructure of Aryan free spaces where hate culture persists?

We do not have definitive answers to these questions. But we know that any attempt to combat Aryan extremism requires a clear understanding of how white power hate culture persists. We hope that *American Swastika* will help us all better comprehend the organization and endurance of the contemporary white power movement and will feed discussions about how to counter the threat of radical racist and anti-Semitic ideas.

Appendix

Making Contact and Developing Rapport

One of the most asked questions about the research in *American Swastika* is how we made contact with Aryans and collected our data. Pete Simi performed the participant observations and interviews that we draw upon in the book. Pete first made contact in 1997 with the Southwest Aryan Separatists (SWAS) using a simple letter of introduction that identified him as a sociologist researching subcultures. Pete gained entrée to Aryan Nations via a series of phone calls requesting to visit and observe their gatherings. Aryan Nations granted access on one condition—that Pete was white. Contacts with other Aryans snowballed from there, producing the broad sample from which we draw in the book. Below, Pete describes making contact and developing rapport with Aryans.

I first made contact with the Southwest Aryan Separatists (SWAS) after a colleague found the group's post office box number and suggested I write them a letter asking to talk with SWAS leaders. Not expecting much to come of it, I addressed the letter to Erik, a SWAS leader, and sent it off. Erik responded almost a month later offering to meet for lunch in the small town near his home. He wrote, "We can talk and if you're ok I might show you the movement." A week later, I met with Erik and fellow SWAS member Darren at a small bar. I passed whatever litmus test they used to judge me. I think they mainly wanted to make sure I was Caucasian and not a cop. At the end of the lunch, Erik and Darren invited me for another visit and offered to put me up in their homes. My fieldwork began in earnest three weeks later when I took them up on their offer and stayed at Erik's house for two days.

Erik and Darren's status as SWAS leaders eased my entrée into the group. I was not hassled by any SWAS members, and they allowed me to ask questions and observe their lives. This openness might seem a bit surprising. Aryans live in a world that is hostile to their beliefs, and they are often antagonistic toward outsiders. They prefer secrecy to avoid conflicts with ZOG infiltrators, whom they perceive are out to destroy them. Yet they cannot totally close themselves off from the outside world. Aryans try to recruit new adherents, which requires them to be somewhat open to people they do not know well. I expect that Erik, Darren, and other Aryans who were open to participating in the research imagined that they might be able to recruit me into the movement or at least that this book might publicize and celebrate the movement.

I was invited to the 1997 Aryan Nations World Congress after I made several phone calls to their Idaho compound to request entrée as a researcher. The Aryan Nations office manager granted my request on the single condition that I was white. Following the congress, I visited the compound and Aryan Nations members around Hayden Lake, Idaho, to observe their informal gatherings and church services. Eventually I attended two other congresses and visited the Aryan Nations on another occasion when there was no large gathering planned. The initial contacts with SWAS and Aryan Nations began a snowball sample that spread into each of the main branches of the white power movement.

Gaining entrée and building rapport was much more difficult in other groups. White power movement networks are diverse and loosely structured. Levels of activism vary widely among participants, and some networks are more open to outsiders than others. Southern California's exotic assortment of racial extremists also offered some of the most difficult and riskiest attempts at entrée.

One of the people I met at the Aryan Nations introduced me to Seth, my most important contact in Southern California. Seth was active in the Southern California hate music scene and friends with members of several white power networks. Seth invited me into his home and introduced me to key members of White Aryan Resistance, Hammerskins, Nazi Lowriders, and Public Enemy Number One (PEN1). These introductions were invaluable, but Seth's assurances alone did not guarantee my safety. Racist gangs such as PEN1 and Nazi Lowriders contain career criminals who are both aggressive and paranoid toward anyone who does not appear to be part of the scene. Members who used drugs such as methamphetamine were especially unpredictable. Several times I was confronted by drugged-out or drunken Aryans who accused me of being a police infiltrator.

Most Aryans were willing to tolerate my presence so long as I did not disrupt their gatherings. If I arrived accompanying a white power member and then hung around unobtrusively at parties, concerts, and other gatherings, chances were low that I would be challenged. However, at some gatherings there were one or two members who I could tell were uncomfortable with my presence, as indicated by their continued glances my way and whispered conversations with other Aryans as they tried to identify me. I became very adept at spotting these Aryans and watched them closely for potential trouble.

One of my best assets for building rapport with racist skinheads was my ability to drink large quantities of beer while controlling my faculties. My willingness to imbibe was like a badge of acceptance that gained me a bit of insider status. Most important, however, was my physical appearance. As a relatively nondescript "white guy," I am of average height and weight and have no detectable spoken accent. In short, I did not stand out in the crowd and easily blended into Aryan gatherings, despite having no racist tattoos or white power clothing.

Participant observation in risky settings sometimes requires compromise of one's beliefs and values to avoid conflicts. At times, I outwardly portrayed myself as sympathetic to the Aryan cause, despite my deep personal opposition to racist and anti-Semitic beliefs. I found deception was necessary to build rapport with Aryans. I snickered at racist jokes that I found appalling or nodded vociferously in agreement when Aryans talked to me about white racial genocide. Despite this strategy, I was still occasionally threatened with bodily harm or death, although I was never attacked.

I frequently had to parry Aryans' efforts to recruit me into the cause. During the first few recruitment attempts, I directly answered that I was there only as a researcher with no intent to become an Aryan. Being rebuffed did not sit well with the recruiters, and they were quick to threaten me. They said that if I reported anything they considered unfair or inaccurate or revealed their identities, then I would be "hunted down and killed." After these threats, I usually tried to skirt the issue by changing the subject, or in the few instances that I felt particularly threatened, I would avoid conflict with a response of "We'll see," to create the impression than I might be recruited in the future. While I found this strategy thoroughly distasteful, it felt like a necessary survival response at the time.

Participant observations and interviews with Aryans were emotionally exhausting. Watching television with Aryans meant listening to constant banter about the inferiority of nonwhites and talk about how to control or kill their racial enemies. Trips to the grocery store meant the prospect of verbal harangues directed toward minority drivers or pedestrians.

I had to be careful when asking direct questions in these settings. Too many questions or queries that seemed too probing made Aryans wary of me and more likely that they would close themselves off. Some Aryans were overtly supportive of my research. On more than one occasion, Aryans who were aware of my research intentions commented on what they called "my laid-back approach" as a good way to research them. Evan, a North Carolina Klan member, once commented, "you seem to be doing this the right way; I like how you just hang out and sit back and ask questions just kind of casually." A small skinhead network in Southern California also took an active interest in my method. After five separate two- to three-day visits over a three-month period, several members asked me to tape record their conversations without letting them know ahead of time. They thought it would help them maintain a natural flow of conversation and give me better information.

Many, although not all, Aryan contacts were open to formal interviews. Aryans seemed to relish talking about their ideology, but they were much more guarded discussing their personal backgrounds. Pinning down respondents to provide in-depth accounts of their life histories was the most difficult task.

Scholars and other observers have questioned the ethics of building too much rapport with Aryans; getting close is akin to sympathy. To avoid this dilemma some researchers suggest using an open and honest approach, emphasizing to Aryans that they do not share the views of racial extremism and are not open to recruitment. However, this strategy compromises the degree of intersubjectivity the ethnography can reach. I tried as much as possible to understand Aryans from their point of view. I did not openly disagree with their claims and practices, and even befriend several contacts during the fieldwork. I felt a tremendous amount of internal guilt and discomfort. The perversity and illogic of their world astounded me. Yet, in many ways the form of Aryans' lives was far more ordinary than I expected. They work, play, raise children, attend school, surf the Web, and listen to music, among other routine, everyday activities. What differs is the ideological content of their experiences and the effort they give to sustain those radical ideas. Understanding strange and unfamiliar worlds is one of the main goals of ethnography. This understanding requires that researchers, to some extent, attempt to take on the perspective of their research subjects, if only for a time.

Glossary

14 Words	Aryan commitment pledge: "I must secure the existence of my people and a future for white children"
18	code for Adolf Hitler
88	code for Heil Hitler
AN	Aryan Nations
ANP	American Nazi Party
B&H	Blood & Honour
HSN	Hammerskin Nation
KKK	Ku Klux Klan
NA	National Alliance
NLR	Nazi Lowriders
NSM	National Socialist Movement
PEN1	Public Enemy Number 1
SWAS	Southwest Aryan Separatists
SWP	Supreme White Power
WAR	White Aryan Resistance
WPM	White Power Movement
ZOG	Zionist Occupied Government

Notes

PREFACE

1. Potok, Mark, "Rage on the Right: The Year in Hate and Extremism," *Southern Poverty Law Center Intelligence Report*, Spring, no. 137, available at: www.splcenter.org/get-informed/intelligence-report/browse-all-issues/2010/spring/rage-on-the-right (accessed 30 April 2010).

2. Thomas, Judy L., "Tea Party Rejects Racist Label, but Concerns Remain," *Kansas City Star*, 15 July 2010, available at: www.kansascity.com/2010/07/15/2087023/tea-party-rejects-racist-label.html (accessed 15 July 2010).

3. Damon, Anjeanette, and David McGrath Schwartz, "Armed Revolt Part of Sharron Angle's Rhetoric," *Las Vegas Sun*, 17 June 2010, available at: www.lasvegassun.com/news/2010/jun/17/senate-race-armed-revolt-angles-rhetoric-candidate (accessed 17 June 2010).

4. McNutt, Scott, "Militia Group Patrols Pinal Desert for Smugglers," TriValley Central.com, available at: www.trivalleycentral.com/articles/2010/07/06/front/doc4c2a0f90e6430737113138.txt (accessed 11 July 2010).

5. Bunkley, Nick, and Charlie Savage, "Militia Charged with Plotting to Murder Officers." *New York Times*, 29 March 2010, available at: www.nytimes.com/2010/03/30/us/30militia.html?_r = 1&scp = 2&sq = hutaree&st = cse (accessed 30 April 2010).

6. Potok, "Rage on the Right."

7. Zash, Chelsi, "Kody Britenham Sentenced for Threatening Obama," Digitriad.com, 17 June 2010, available at: www.digtriad.com/news/local/article.aspx?storyid = 143880&catid = 57 (accessed June 24, 2010).

8. Associated Press, "ATF: Obama Assassination Attempt Foiled," 27 October 2008, available at: www.politico.com/news/stories/1008/14988.html (accessed 7 July 2009).

9. Potok, "Rage on the Right."

CHAPTER 1

1. We use *Aryan* as a descriptor for all individuals who are involved in the white power movement. The term *Aryan* has a long history and signifies specific geo-cultural

groups. See also Romila Thapar, "The Theory of Aryan Race and India: History and Politics," *Social Scientist* 24 (1996): 3–29. Aryan was a name widely used in Nazi Germany as part of the Third Reich's "master race" theory. Contemporary white power advocates continue to use the term to describe themselves. There is some disagreement among neo-Nazis about what is and what is not Aryan. Over the last couple of decades there has been a shift toward "Pan-Aryanism," or the idea that despite variations among whites, all belong to a single racial family that stretches across the globe.

Research on the human genome shows no genetic differences between so-called races. DNA evidence demonstrates that humans are a single race, evolved in the last 100,000 years from the same small number of tribal groups that migrated out of Africa and colonized the globe.

2. It is difficult to distinguish hard-and-fast boundaries of white power hate culture. Like most movements, there are few absolute lines to be drawn. The different branches of the white power movement overlap with other subcultures that are not necessarily directly connected to white power ideals. For example, a large number of neo-Pagans reject white supremacist doctrine, while other neo-Pagan groups clearly endorse neo-Nazi and white supremacist ideals. For a fuller discussion of this point in regard to neo-Paganism, see Mattias Gardell, *Gods of the Blood: The Pagan Revival and White Separatism* (Durham, NC: Duke University Press, 2003).

3. We acknowledge that hate crime is a sweeping category of offenses that includes a wide range of offenses. For an in-depth discussion of the concept of hate crime, see James Jacobs and Kimberly Potter, *Hate Crimes: Criminal Law and Identity Politics* (Oxford: Oxford University Press, 1990). Specifically, we are thinking of activities explicitly carried out in the name of white power such as the violence of the group known as The Order and the Oklahoma City bombing. For a chronological listing of white power violence, see Michael Newton and Judy Ann Newton, *Racial and Religious Violence in America: A Chronology* (New York: Garland Publishers, 1991).

4. Sara Evans, *Personal Politics: The Roots of Women's Liberation in the Civil Rights Movement and the New Left* (London: Vintage, 1979); Sara Evans and Harry Boyte, *Free Spaces* (Chicago: University of Chicago Press, 1992); Francesca Polletta, "'Free Spaces' in Collective Action," *Theory and Society* 28 (1999): 1–38.

5. Erving Goffman, *Stigma: Notes on the Management of Spoiled Identity* (Englewood Cliffs, NJ: Prentice Hall, 1963).

6. James Aho, *The Politics of Righteousness: Idaho Christian Patriotism* (Seattle: University of Washington Press, 1990); Michael Barkun, *Religion and the Racist Right: The Origins of the Christian Identity Movement* (Chapel Hill: University of North Carolina Press, 1994); David Bennett, *The Party of Fear: From Nativist Movements to the New Right in American History* (Chapel Hill: University of North Carolina Press, 1995); Mitch Berbrier, "The Victim Ideology of White Supremacists and White Separatists in the United States," *Sociological Focus* 33 (2000):175–91; Chip Berlet and Matthew N. Lyons, *Right Wing Populism in America: Too close for Comfort* (New York: The Guilford Press, 2000); Kathleen Blee, *Inside Organized Racism: Women in the Hate Movement* (Berkeley: University of California Press, 2002); Sara Diamond, *Roads to Dominion: Right-Wing Movements and Political Power in the United States* (New York: Guilford Press, 1995); Betty Dobratz and Stephanie Shanks-Meile, *White Power! White Pride! The White Separatist Movement in the United States* (New York: Cengage Gale, 1997); Jeffrey

Kaplan, "Right-Wing Violence in North America," in *Terror from the Extreme Right*, ed. Tore Bjorgo (London: Frank Cass, 1995); Richard Mitchell, *Dancing at Armageddon: Survivalism and Chaos in Modern Times* (Chicago: University of Chicago Press, 2001); David Wellman, *Portraits of White Racism* (New York: Cambridge University Press, 1993); Joe Feagin and Hernan Vera, *White Racism: The Basics* (New York: Routledge, 1995); Abby Ferber, *White Man Falling: Race, Gender, and White Supremacy* (Lanham, MD: Rowman & Littlefield, 1998); Leonard Zeskind, *Blood and Politics: The History of the White Nationalist Movement from the Margins to the Mainstream* (New York: Farrar, Strauss, and Giroux, 2009).

7. See Michael Lewis and Jacqueline Serbu, "Kommerating the Ku Klux Klan," *Sociological Quarterly* 40 (1999): 139–57.

8. Blee, *Inside Organized Racism*; Kaplan, "Right-Wing Violence." See Cornell West, *Race Matters* (New York: Vintage Books, 1994). Mainstream racism in the United States shares some important assumptions with white power ideology, but there are also important differences. As Blee explains, "The ideas that racist activists share about whiteness are more conscious, elaborated, and tightly connected to political action than those of mainstream whites. . . . The difference between everyday racism and extraordinary racism [of the WPM] is the difference between being prejudiced against Jews and believing that there is a Jewish conspiracy that determines the fate of individual Aryans, or between thinking that African Americans are inferior to whites and seeing African Americans as an imminent threat to the white race" (p. 76). Moreover, notions of an impending "race war," a "Zionist Occupied Government," and the current "genocide of the white race" are core beliefs that are widely shared by WPM adherents, but have little salience with the general public. Perhaps the most telling indication of the WPM's marginalization from the mainstream is the tendency among "everyday" racists to disavow and disassociate themselves from the Klan, skinheads, neo-Nazis and other openly racist groups. See also Feagin and Vera, *White Racism*.

9. For similar arguments, see Aho, *Politics*; Blee, *Inside Organized Racism*.

10. Kenneth O'Reilly, *Racial Matters: The FBI's Secret File on Black America, 1960–1972* (New York: The Free Press, 1989).

11. Southern Poverty Law Center, "SPLC Wins $2.5 Million Verdict against Imperial Klans of America," 2008, available at: http://www.splcenter.org/news/item.jsp?aid = 345 (accessed 28 January 2008).

12. This circumstance reflects Doug McAdam's distinction between the substantial physical, social, economic, and legal costs incurred by "high-risk activism" and those incurred by "low-risk" forms against which intense and enduring repercussions are much less likely. Doug McAdam, *Freedom Summer* (New York: Oxford University Press, 2000), 208.

13. Tore Bjorgo, "Entry, Bridge-Burning, and Exit Options: What Happens to Young People Who Join Racist Groups—and Want to Leave," in *Nation and Race: The Developing Euro-American Racist Subculture*, ed. Jeffrey Kaplan and Tore Bjorgo (Boston: Northeastern University Press, 1998), 231–58; Blee, *Inside Organized Racism*.

14. See also Blee, *Inside Organized Racism*; Dobratz and Shanks-Meile, *White Power! White Pride!* 23.

15. Aho, *Politics*, and Blee, *Inside Organized Racism*, also make this point.

16. The relative infrequency of Aryan violence is hard to fully interpret. And while the

topic is exceedingly interesting, we want to bracket analysis of when and why Aryans choose to engage in conflict and fully express their hatred toward non-Aryans. A systematic analysis of violence is beyond our focus in this book, but several factors appear to influence whether individuals fully assert their Aryanism, including: age and experience, alcohol consumption, group reputation for violence, and the number of Aryans present during the situation. Based on our observations and interviews, however, the volume of these instances is minimal in comparison to the amount of concealment these activists perform on a daily basis.

17. James Scott, *Weapons of the Weak: Everyday Forms of Peasant Resistance* (New Haven, CT: Yale University Press, 1985); James Scott, *Domination and the Arts of Resistance* (New Haven CT: Yale University Press, 1990).

18. Pete Simi and Robert Futrell, "Negotiating White Power Activist Stigma," *Social Problems* 56 (2009): 89–110.

19. Blee, *Inside Organized Racism*, 167.

20. Simi and Futrell, "Negotiating Stigma."

21. Robert Futrell and Pete Simi, "Free Spaces, Collective Identity, and the Persistence of U.S. White Power Activism," *Social Problems* 51 (2004):16–42.

22. Anytime people feel constraint and coercion we can expect a "prosaic but constant struggle" to withstand or counteract the force. False compliance and backstage defiance are "weapons of the weak" used to mitigate or deny claims of the powerful. See also Scott, *Weapons*; Scott, *Domination*.

23. Steven Buechler, *Social Movements in Advanced Capitalism* (New York: Oxford University Press, 2000), 208; see also Hank Johnston, "New Social Movements and Old Regional Nationalisms," in *New Social Movements: From Ideology to Identity*, ed. Enrique Larana, Hank Johnston, and Joseph R. Gusfield (Philadelphia: Temple University Press, 1994); Verta Taylor, "Social Movement Continuity," *American Sociological Review* 54 (1989): 761–75.

24. Norman Denzin, *The Research Act: A Theoretical Introduction to Sociological Methods* (New York: McGraw-Hill Book Company, 1978).

25. There were more follow-up interviews than original interviews because we spoke with several informants three or more times.

26. Bruce Berg, *Qualitative Research Methods for the Social Sciences* (Boston: Pearson, 2004); John Lofland and Lyn Lofland, *Analyzing Social Settings: A Guide to Qualitative Observation and Analysis* (Belmont, CA: Wadsworth, 1995).

27. See also Aho, *Politics*; Blee, *Inside Organized Racism*.

28. The appendix provides more information on sample data.

29. See Blee, *Inside Organized Racism*, for an eloquent elaboration of this point.

30. Berg, *Qualitative Research*; Barney Glaser and Anslem Strauss, *The Discovery of Grounded Theory* (Chicago: Aldine, 1967); Mathew Miles and Michael Huberman, *Qualitative Data Analysis* (Thousand Oaks, CA: Sage, 1994).

CHAPTER 2

1. Mattias Gardell, *Gods of the Blood: The Pagan Revival and White Separatism* (Durham, NC: Duke University Press, 2003); Robert Balch, "The Rise and Fall of Aryan

Nations: A Resource Mobilization Perspective," *Journal of Political and Military Sociology* 34 (2006): 81–113.

2. Gardell, *Gods*, 71. See also Leonard Zeskind, *Blood and Politics: The History of the White Nationalist Movement from the Margins to the Mainstream* (New York: Farrar, Straus and Giroux, 2009).

3. Gardell, *Gods*, 73.

4. Kathleen Blee, *Inside Organized Racism: Women in the Hate Movement* (Berkeley: University of California Press, 2002); Betty Dobratz and Stephanie Shanks-Meile, *White Power! White Pride! The White Separatist Movement in the United States* (New York: Cengage Gale, 1997); Carol Swain, *The New White Nationalism in America: Its Challenge to Integration* (Cambridge: Cambridge University Press, 2002).

5. Alberto Melucci, *Challenging Codes: Collective Action in the Information Age* (Cambridge: Cambridge University Press, 1996).

6. The Southern Poverty Law Center projected an increase in the number of Aryan groups of 40 percent between 2000 and 2007. According to Mark Potok of the Southern Poverty Law Center, "the number of hate groups operating in the United States rose from 762 in 2004 to 803 [in 2005] capping an increase of fully 33% over the five years since 2000." Mark Potok, "The Year in Hate, 2005," available at: www.splcenter.org/intel/intel report/article.jsp?aid = 627 (accessed 4 July 2006). More recently, the *Christian Science Monitor* reports that "immigration levels helped boost the number of hate groups from 602 in 2000 to 888 in 2007." Patrik Jonsson, "After Obama's Win White Backlash Festers in U.S.," *Christian Science Monitor*, 17 November 2008, available at: www.csmonitor .com/2008/1117/p03s01-uspo.html (accessed 18 December 2008).

7. Allen Trelease, *White Terror: The Ku Klux Klan Conspiracy and Southern Reconstructionism* (New York: HarperCollins, 1971).

8. See Blee, *Inside Organized Racism*; David Chalmers, *Hooded Americanism: The History of the Ku Klux Klan* (Durham, NC: Duke University Press, 1987); Nancy McClean, *Behind the Mask of Chivalry: The Making of the Second Ku Klux Klan* (New York: Oxford University Press, 1994); Rory McVeigh, *The Rise of the Ku Klux Klan: Right-Wing Movements and National Politics* (Minneapolis: University of Minnesota Press, 2009); Leonard Moore, *Citizen Klansmen* (Chapel Hill: University of North Carolina Press, 1991).

9. David Cunningham, *There's Something Happening Here: The New Left, the Klan, and FBI Counterintelligence* (Berkeley: University of California Press, 2004).

10. Some observers prematurely predicted the Klan's demise. Certainly, since the 1960s the Klan has not been reinvigorated enough to draw the large following they enjoyed in the 1920s. The Klan has, however, remained an active branch within the larger WPM. Beginning in the mid-1970s, the KKK experienced a small revival purportedly heralding what some called the "new Klan." This "new Klan" was marked by two divergent trends: KKK leaders like David Duke and Donald Black tried to establish a more respectable, businesslike Klan ("hate with a pretty face"). Duke's efforts in politics led to his 1989 election to the Louisiana State Legislature as a Republican; however, he was narrowly defeated in a U.S. Senate election the following year and in his bid for the governorship in 1991. Duke's efforts garnered an immense amount of publicity, and in the gubernatorial race he received more than 700,000 votes, which included a majority of whites in Louisiana. Some Klan leaders shunned this attempt at "mainstreaming" the

Klan, instead opting for a more militant approach ("from robes to combat boots"). For example, during the 1970s and 1980s Glen Miller's North Carolina–based Carolina Knights of the Ku Klux Klan, which eventually became the White Patriot Party, terrorized minorities across the Carolinas and Virginia and stockpiled weapons and explosives in preparation for the coming race war. In 1979 Miller and an assortment of other Aryans from various groups opened fire on industrial workers and communists participating in a "death to the Klan" rally, killing five and wounding eleven others. Around the same time, Louis Beam's Texas Knights of the KKK was terrorizing immigrant Vietnamese fishermen in Galveston, Texas, burning boats and threatening violence if they did not leave the waters. Another force influential in promoting the revitalization and radicalization of the Klan was the former grand dragon of the Michigan Ku Klux Klan, Robert E. Miles, who received a nine-year sentence for his participation in planning the bombing of empty school buses that were to be used in a busing program in Pontiac, Michigan. From his federal prison cell, Miles began promoting a more paramilitary version of the Klan. For further discussion, see Patsy Sims, *The Klan* (Lexington: University of Kentucky Press, 1996).

11. Southern Poverty Law Center, "Hate Map," available at: www.splcenter.org/intel/map/hate.jsp (accessed 1 July 2009).

12. Mitch Berbrier, "The Victim Ideology of White Supremacists and White Separatists in the United States," *Sociological Focus* 33 (2000): 175–91.

13. Anti-Defamation League, "Ku Klux Klan Rebounds," 2007, available at: www.adl.org/learn/ext_us/kkk/klan_report.pdf.

14. The Southern Poverty Law Center dealt a blow to Klan resurgence in 2008 by winning a $2.5 million lawsuit for a Hispanic teen beaten by Imperial Klan members. The verdict has bankrupted the IKA and dismantled its compound. Imperial Klan leader, Ron Edwards, has vowed to continue the group and the Nordic Fest music festival.

15. Brent Smith, *Terrorism in America: Pipe Bombs and Pipe Dreams* (Albany: State University of New York Press, 1994).

16. For an in-depth discussion of Christian Identity, see Michael Barkun, *Religion and the Racist Right: The Origins of the Christian Identity Movement* (Chapel Hill: University of North Carolina Press, 1994).

17. SPLC, "Pagans and Prison," *Intelligence Report*, Spring 2000, available at: www.splcenter.org/intel/intelreport/article.jsp?aid = 270.

18. Dobratz and Shanks-Meile, *White Power!*

19. Gardell, *Gods.*

20. Gardell, *Gods,* 17.

21. Gardell, *Gods,* 1.

22. Prior to and during World War II a number of different Nazi parties and leaders surfaced in the United States. During the 1930s, more than 120 American fascist organizations started around the country, with the most notorious being the German American Bund, the Silver Shirt Legion, and the Black Legion. These groups' most lasting effect was their cross-fertilization of European fascism with traditional American nativism. These were the earliest predecessors to American neo-Nazis, who have been active since the 1950s. The National Renaissance Party (NRP) was the first U.S. neo-Nazi organization to form after World War II. Founded in 1949 by James Madole in Beacon, New York, the NRP gained notoriety in the early 1950s by organizing marches and rallies in which mem-

bers wore Nazi uniforms and regalia. The NRP's influence lay in its ability to garner media attention through spectacle displays (something later neo-Nazi organizations would emulate) and its role as a starting point for several neo-Nazi leaders. For histories of U.S. Nazism and proto-fascist groups prior to World War II, see Susan Canedy, *America's Nazis: A Democratic Dilemma* (Menlo Park, CA: Markgraf Publishers, 1990); and David Bennett, *The Party of Fear: From Nativist Movements to the New Right in American History* (Chapel Hill: University of North Carolina Press, 1995).

23. Frederick Simonelli, *American Fuehrer: George Lincoln Rockwell and the American Nazi Party* (Urbana: University of Illinois Press, 1999).

24. The Creativity Movement has also been a persistent presence in the neo-Nazi wing of the WPM. Although the group claims to be "a professional, non-violent, progressive pro-white religion" (www.creativitymovement.net/), its leaders promote a particularly extreme brand of hate based on race war ideology first touted by founder Ben Klassen in 1973. The Creativity Movement website welcomes all racists and provides them with contact information for Creativity chapters in the United States, Europe, and Australia. The group's Web forum, Skinheads of the Racial War, hosts articles on the race war, member discussions, and announcements for movement events. They have been active in recruiting young skinheads along with prison inmates to their cause. In 1999, Creativity member Ben Smith launched a three-day, one-man ethnic-cleansing campaign that killed two people and wounded seven. The groups' infamous leader, Matt Hale, was sentenced to forty years in prison for ordering the assassination of a federal judge. Many Aryans now see Hale as one of the movement's prisoners of war.

25. Pierce also wrote the novel *Hunter*, which depicts a government contractor moonlighting as a sniper who kills "racial enemies" in his spare time. Pierce dedicated *Hunter* to the racist serial killer and assassin Joseph Paul Franklin.

26. See Southern Poverty Law Center, *Intelligence Report*, "Descent into Thuggery: Neo-Nazi National Alliance Falls on Hard Times," available at: www.splcenter.org/intel/intelreport/article.jsp?aid = 1077 (accessed 2009).

27. *Volk* is a Germanic word that translates literally as "the people" of the German nation. Adolf Hitler used it as the concept of the national soul, which connotes spiritual connections among the Germanic people and German land. For the Third Reich, the Volk only included pure Aryans, which led to the extermination strategy toward Jews and other non-Aryans.

28. During the 1980s Metzger began producing the public access cable television talk show *Race and Reason*, featuring interviews with Aryan activists. He also published instructional handbooks on guerilla warfare and was a frequent guest on national talk shows. His son's appearances on *Geraldo* resulted in an infamous brawl that left the show's host, Geraldo Rivera, with a broken nose.

In 1990, Metzger's White Aryan Resistance was sued by the Southern Poverty Law Center (SPLC) on behalf of the family of Mulegata Seraw, who was murdered in 1988 by several members of Eastside White Pride, a local skinhead gang in Portland, Oregon. The jury agreed with the SPLC that members of Eastside White Pride were incited to racial violence by affiliates of White Aryan Resistance and awarded $12.5 million in damages to Seraw's family, which effectively bankrupted WAR and reinforced Metzger's advocacy of underground tactics. For further discussion, see Elinor Langer, *A Hundred Little Hitlers: The Death of a Black Man, the Trial of a White Racist, and the Rise of the Neo-Nazi Movement in America* (New York: Metropolitan Books, 2003).

29. Anti-Defamation League, "Extremism in America—National Socialist Movement," available at: www.adl.org/Learn/Ext_US/nsm (accessed 29 June 2009).

30. Skinhead culture began in Great Britain and developed in two waves through the 1960s and 1970s. The first skinheads emerged in Great Britain in the late 1960s as a response to deteriorating traditional working-class communities, a stagnating economy, and job competition with immigrants. While they did not explicitly associate with Nazism, they were ardently nationalist in political orientation and fervently opposed to foreign immigration, which was reflected by their affinity for violently attacking Pakistani immigrants, which they called "Paki-bashing." The first skinheads "were aware that they attended the worst schools, lived in the poorest districts, and had the worst jobs with the smallest wages. They perceived hippies and students as idle layabouts living off the state." Michael Brake, "The Skinheads: An English Working Class Sub-Culture," *Youth and Society* 6: 179–200 (quote at 184).

Early skinheads defined themselves along themes of nationalism, ultramasculinity, and working-class concerns about the lack of economic opportunity. They expressed their political sentiments primarily through stylistic imagery while distancing themselves from traditional, organized political ties and activities (for example, unions, political parties, marches, etc.). They became politicized as a second wave of English skinheads emerged in the late 1970s and explored associations with the National Front (NF) and the British National Party (BNP), extreme right-wing political parties who saw the utility of drawing disaffected white youth into their ranks. The second wave of skinheads spread beyond Britain and emerged in several other European countries as well as North America.

31. SPLC, "Nazis Rising," *Intelligence Report*, Spring 2006, available at: www .splcenter.org/intel/intelreport/article.jsp?pid = 1037 (accessed 19 March 2007); Langer, *Hundred Little Hitlers*.

32. Skinhead styles also vary from region to region. Some skinhead groups emphasize the idea of retaining the "authentic" and traditional appearance of the skinhead style, while in other areas (most notably Southern California) some skinheads blend a traditional style with a more contemporary "gangsta" style (for example, baggy pants, socks pulled up, etc.). Still other highly politicized skinheads encourage their brothers to play down the most noticeable aspects of their style by growing out their hair and covering tattoos to reduce their stigma and find legitimate jobs while covertly pursuing white power aims.

33. International braches of Hammerskin Nation are in Australia, Canada, Italy, New Zealand, Portugal, France, Germany, Sweden, Spain, Great Britain, Switzerland, and Hungary. Information available at: www.hammerskins.net/chapter.html (accessed 2 July 2009).

34. Volksfront claims chapters in Oregon, Washington, Idaho, California, Virginia, Florida, Pennsylvania, Ohio, Michigan, Massachusetts, Illinois, Missouri, Texas, Wisconsin, Arkansas, and Arizona. International chapters are located in Australia, Canada, Ireland, Great Britain, Germany, Spain, Croatia, and Switzerland. Information available at: www.volksfrontinternational.com/support.html and http://volksfronteurope.com/ (accessed 2 July 2009).

35. Information available at: www.adl.org/learn/ext_us/volksfront/default.asp?LEARN _Cat = Extremism&LEARN_SubCat = Extremism_in_America&xpicked = 3&item = volksfront (accessed 2 July 2009).

36. One schism within the movement centers on the issue of criminal activity and

whether white power gangs like the Nazi Lowriders and PEN1 are true Aryans. Aryans throughout the movement revere terror cells like the Silent Brotherhood, in part because they used money from their armed robberies to give direct financial support to movement organizations such as the National Alliance. However, some Aryans question whether the Nazi Lowriders and PEN1's criminal activity helps or hurts the movement because the groups do not seem committed to distributing the money they make from drug running, robberies, and other crimes back into the movement. Aryans who oppose the Nazi Lowriders and PEN1 say that the groups are not truly committed to the political cause of white power. Aryans who support the Nazi Lowriders and PEN1 consider the groups as frontline warriors fighting racial enemies and protecting whites in prison and on the streets.

37. Val Burris, Emory Smith, and Ann Strahm, "White Supremacist Networks on the Internet," *Sociological Focus* 33 (2000): 215–34.

38. Mitch Berbrier, "The Victim Ideology of White Supremacists and White Separatists in the United States," *Sociological Focus* 33 (2000): 175–91; Blee, *Inside Organized Racism*.

39. James Jasper, "The Emotions of Protest: Affective and Reactive Emotions in and around Social Movements," *Sociological Forum* 13 (1998): 397–424.

40. Verta Taylor, "Emotions and Identity in Women's Self-Help Movements," in *Self, Identity, and Social Movements*, ed. Sheldon Stryker, Timothy J. Owens, and Robert W. White (Minneapolis: University of Minnesota Press, 2000), 271–99.

41. Jasper, "Emotions of Protest."

42. Randall Collins as quoted in Jasper, "Emotions in Protest," 399.

CHAPTER 3

1. Darren, SWAS member, interviewed 22 January 1997.

2. See Hank Johnston, "New Social Movements and Old Regional Nationalisms," in *New Social Movements: From Ideology to Identity*, ed. Enrique Larana, Hank Johnston, and Joseph R. Gusfield (Philadelphia: Temple University Press, 1994), 267–86; Hank Johnston, *Tales of Nationalism: Catalonia 1939–1979* (New Brunswick, NJ: Rutgers University Press, 1991). Johnston notes that the intergenerational transmission of collective identity is essential for movement endurance in repressive contexts, and the control and anonymity available in the home ensures that identity work can proceed relatively unchallenged. Likewise, Richard Couto, "Narrative, Free Space, and Political Leadership in Social Movements," *Journal of Politics* 55 (1993): 57–79, explains that when the chance of repression is high for overt forms of political resistance, identity work occurs "in carefully guarded free spaces, such as the family."

3. H is the eighth letter of the alphabet, thus 88 represents HH, for "Heil Hitler."

4. Aryans use their homes for much more than child socialization. We leave other uses of the home to our discussion in the next chapter.

5. We studied Aryan families from all branches of the movement by staying in their homes, observing their daily patterns and their relationships with other families, and interviewing them about how they sustained their beliefs and socialized their children to carry on Aryan ideas. We visited Aryans living in small, rural towns and also spoke to Ku Klux Klan, racist skinheads, and neo-Nazi families attending large white power events such as

the Aryan Nations gatherings. We also interviewed Aryan Nations families who lived full-time near the organization's compound, devoting their lives to the Aryan Nations church and Pastor Richard Butler's vision of a white separatist nation in the Pacific Northwest. Finally, we observed and interviewed neo-Nazi families living in Southern California.

6. Seth, interviewed 19 September 2003.

7. Jessie is estranged from her fourth child, who lives in the Midwest with the parents of one of Jessie's ex-husbands.

8. Seth, interviewed 19 July 2004.

9. Kathy, SWAS activist, interviewed 26 June 1997.

10. We never directly observed physical punishment that crossed the line into child abuse; however, we recently discovered that Ronnie was placed in foster care due to child abuse charges stemming from Jessie hitting Ronnie with a blunt object across his back that resulted in injuries requiring medical attention.

11. Todd, interviewed 1 June 2002.

12. Anti Defamation League, "Public Enemy Number 1: California's Growing Racist Gang," 2007, available at: www.adl.org/learn/ext_us/peni.asp?LEARN_Cat = Extremism &LEARN_SubCat = Extremism_in_America&xpicked = 3&item = peni (accessed 19 February 2007); Pete Simi, Lowell Smith, and Ann Stacey, "From Punk Kids to Public Enemy Number One," *Deviant Behavior: An Interdisciplinary Journal* 29 (2008): 753–74.

13. Kate, interviewed 2 June 2002.

14. Randall Collins as quoted in James Jasper, "The Emotions of Protest: Affective and Reactive Emotions in and around Social Movements," *Sociological Forum* 13 (1998): 399. Hate and other "reactive emotions" are crucial to the relationships that galvanize WPM members against their enemies. But to fully understand WPM persistence we must also account for a range of "vitalizing" and "reciprocal" feelings such as friendship and camaraderie. For further discussion of these issues see Verta Taylor, "Emotions and Identity in Women's Self-Help Movements," in *Self, Identity, and Social Movements*, ed. Sheldon Stryker, Timothy J. Owens, and Robert W. White (Minneapolis: University of Minnesota Press, 2000), 271–99.

15. Ryan, Colorado activist, interviewed 29 June 2004.

16. Brandy, AN activist, interviewed 23 May 1997.

17. Beth, Christian Identity member, interviewed 12 June 2000.

18. Michelle, Colorado activist, interviewed 29 June 2004.

19. Kathleen Blee, *Inside Organized Racism: Women in the Hate Movement* (Berkeley: University of California Press, 2002).

20. Darren, SWAS member, interviewed 20 May 1998.

21. A small group of skinheads from Nevada and Arizona founded Southwestern Aryan Separatists (SWAS) in the late 1980s. The most prominent member, Darren, identified as a skate punk during his early teens, started a punk rock band when he was seventeen and became a skinhead after listening to some borrowed tapes with Christian Identity sermons that professed Aryan supremacy. Darren and his friends began to call themselves SWAS, got inked with swastika tattoos, met regularly at one member's crashpad, and began brawling with black and Hispanic gangs in Phoenix. They intimidated Jewish community organizations by crashing their meetings and holding small marches during which they chanted about Aryans being the true children of Israel. During the Ruby Ridge standoff in 1992, some of them traveled to Idaho to protest against the federal government, or what they called "Satan's forces." Some core members began calling for armed insur-

gency, although most in the group were not convinced the time was right for such extreme measures. The controversy splintered the group, with the majority moving to the rural Nevada area where we contacted them and were invited to visit.

22. Darren, SWAS, interviewed 13 August 1997.

23. Darren, SWAS, interviewed 13 August 1997.

24. Bill, SWAS activist, interviewed 22 January 1997.

25. Darren, SWAS activist, interviewed 30 March 1999.

26. Mindy, SWAS member, interviewed 23 January 1997.

27. Kathy, SWAS member, interviewed 26 June 1997.

28. The Operation White Care project is similar to the efforts of the group Women for Aryan Unity (WAU), which sponsors a number of movement activities including "Welcome to the World Little One," an initiative to secure the future of Aryan folk "one child at a time." The Aryan Unity project coordinates women throughout the movement to send gift packages to help new mothers with a newborn's first needs, such as receiving blankets, baby wipes, and diapers. The project is a way to "say thank you to all the moms and dads bringing new Aryan children into the world." WAU, at: www.w-a-u.net/baby.html (14 July 2005).

29. Blee, *Inside Organized Racism.* Blee's research demonstrated nuances in gender relations among movement members. Blee describes females who are often ideologically relegated to subordinate positions, but in practice they occupy important positions of power. Aryan women hold groups together by helping recruit new members and organizing events that retain existing members.

30. Andrew Macdonald [William Pierce], *Hunter* (Hillsboro, WV: National Vanguard Books, 1989).

31. A New Jersey couple reportedly did in fact name their son Adolf Hitler. The news came to light when a local grocery store refused to sign a birthday cake with the name. The couple also named their daughter Honszlynn Hinler Jeannie Campbell, after Nazi SS commander Heinrich Himmler. Douglas B. Brill, "Holland Township Man Names Son after Adolf Hitler," *Warren County News Express-Times*, 14 December 2008, at: www .lehighvalleylive.com/warren-county/index.ssf?/base/news-0/122 923112231930.xml& coll = 3 (accessed 5 January 2009).

32. Randy, SoCal Skin, interviewed 25 February 2001.

33. Cal, SoCal Skin, interviewed 20 August 2002.

34. Baxter, Aryan Nations activist, interviewed 23 May 1997.

35. Carrie, SWAS member, interviewed 27 January 1997.

36. Brenda, SWAS activist, interviewed 19 January 1999.

37. Stormfront.org, listserv (accessed 7 January 2001).

38. Melanie, Southern California neo-Nazi, interviewed 21 August 2002.

39. Cal, SoCal Skin, interviewed 15 July 2004.

40. Janine, Aryan mother, interviewed 20 June 2004.

CHAPTER 4

1. Darren, SWAS member, interviewed 13 June 1998.

2. We would remind the reader that extremists of any stripe need such gatherings for reinforcement against the mainstream.

3. Cal, SoCal Skin, interviewed 7 September 2002.

4. Right-wing extremists have a long history obsessing over the issue of purity and pollution and associating nature with racial characteristics. Hitler and Nazi Germany were especially reverent of nature, and neo-fascists sometimes overlap with "green" movements. For further discussion, see Boria Sax, *Animals in the Third Reich: Pets, Scapegoats, and the Holocaust* (New York: Continuum, 2000); Robert Paxton, *The Anatomy of Fascism* (New York: Vintage, 2005); Mabel Berezin, *Making the Fascist Self: The Political Culture of Interwar Italy* (Ithaca, NY: Cornell University Press, 1997).

5. Bill, SWAS activist, interviewed, 28 June 1997.

6. James, SWAS activist, interviewed 13 March 1999.

7. Erik, SWAS activist, interviewed 21 January 1997.

8. Darren, SWAS member, interviewed 21 January 1997.

9. Gus, Aryan Nations activist, interviewed 9 July 1997.

10. Darren, SWAS member, interviewed 21 January 1997.

11. Sarah, Aryan Nations activist, interviewed 17 April 1997.

12. Although we do not include them as a separate analytical section above, racist and anti-Semitic jokes permeate conversations among activists at just about every setting where Aryans gather. The jokes dehumanize their racial enemies, usually by imagining extreme violence against them. Aryan hate humor is extremely racist, but without the gravity that usually accompanies racist speech. The jokes convey and reinforce Aryan ideals among members in a more casual and, for them, entertaining way than the heavy, incendiary polemics of a racist speech or white power publication. For more on racist humor, see Michael Billig, "Humour and Hatred: The Racist Jokes of the Ku Klux Klan," *Discourse and Society* (2001): 267–88.

13. Dylan, Southern California activist, interviewed 21 November 2002.

14. Paul, SoCal Skin, interviewed 30 March 2002.

15. Betty Dobratz and Stephanie Shanks-Meile, *White Power! White Pride! The White Separatist Movement in the United States* (New York: Cengage Gale, 1997).

16. Mattias Gardell, *Gods of the Blood: The Pagan Revival and White Separatism* (Durham, NC: Duke University Press, 2003), 68; Kathleen Blee, *Inside Organized Racism: Women in the Hate Movement* (Berkeley: University of California Press, 2002); Dobratz and Shanks-Meile, *White Power!*

17. Gardell, *Gods*, 68.

18. Trent, Orange County Skin, interviewed 3 August 1998.

19. Blee, *Inside Organized Racism*, 35.

20. Aryan stories about conversion often segue into talk of how to enlighten and draw others into the movement. After Scotty, an Orange County Skin, told of his entrée into racist extremism, he explained how he had identified neighbors who had moved in across the street as potentially sympathetic to the cause. He saw a Confederate flag hanging in their garage. "I thought these guys might be interested, but we let them come to us. Eventually they came over for a few beers and we started playing the right kind of music to see what was up. If that works, then we start talking politics. It doesn't even matter if they're white power or not, but if we can get them moving in the right direction then we're doing our job." Stories of recruitment strategies range from the fantastical to the more practical. Sometimes these stories reveal big dreams of a societal or worldwide Aryan conversion through momentous actions, such as commandeering global media outlets and presenting the "facts" of the white power worldview. While these scenarios are all but impossible,

white power advocates seem to revel in a collective imagination of what it might be like to accomplish such monumental acts. Most stories focus on more realistic strategies such as leafleting public areas, schools, and concerts with white power pamphlets; placing white power stickers in obtrusive places; and creating signs, slogans, and persuasive arguments to gain potential recruits.

21. Matt, Aryan Nations activist, interviewed 3 July 1999.

22. Jack, Hammerskin, interviewed 17 March 2002.

23. Kim Voss, "The Collapse of a Social Movement: The Interplay of Mobilizing Structures, Framing, and Political Opportunities in the Knights of Labor," in *Comparative Perspectives on Social Movements*, ed. Doug McAdam, John D. McCarthy, and Mayer N. Zald (Cambridge: Cambridge University Press, 1996), 227–60.

24. Ross, Southern California activist, interviewed 30 May 2001.

25. Roger, WAR activist, interviewed 30 March 2002.

26. Some of their fortifying myths suggest that there is a group of secret Aryans—the hidden faithful—located throughout major social institutions such as the police, military, government agencies, and even corporate America. Bill, a SWAS member, claimed: "Of course I know a lot of people in law enforcement, military, high up positions in their company. There are a lot of people out there that were never involved in the racialist movement, never involved, that still agree with us, but when the time comes, they know they would be on the right track." These faithful remain hidden, even from other Aryans, because they are infiltrating institutions that ZOG controls. Recent U.S. military investigations suggest these sorts of claims are not entirely fanciful. In a 2006 Southern Poverty Law Center report, a Department of Defense gang investigator tells of an internal investigation that uncovered 320 Aryan extremists at Fort Lewis, Washington, alone. Investigators also uncovered an online network of 57 Aryans on active duty at five different Army and Marine installations. Aryans believe they have "friends in high places," a sort of reserve army that they envision rising up when the race war begins.

27. Also see, Mark Hamm, *In Bad Company: America's Terrorist Underground* (Boston: Northeastern University Press, 2002).

28. Seth, interviewed 18 February 2003.

29. For an in-depth discussion of the relationship between staging areas and gang violence, see Elijah Anderson, *Code of the Street: Decency, Violence, and the Moral Life of the Inner City* (New York: W. W. Norton & Co., 1999).

30. A few of these crashpads, then, operate as much more than ideological havens for Aryan skins to gather. Some are used as safe houses for fugitive Aryans hiding out from law enforcement or storage sites for stolen money, guns, explosives, ammunition, and other equipment. Aryan terrorist cells, such as the Silent Brotherhood and the Aryan Republican Army, utilized safe houses as part of their criminal operations, which included assassinations, bank and armored car robberies, as well as bombings of Jewish synagogues, gay nightclubs, and government buildings. The Silent Brotherhood was particularly adept at this in the mid-1980s, developing an extensive network of crashpad safe houses across the Western United States. One of these served as a telephone message center that allowed members indirect and covert contact with other members. Members used the message center to locate other members and to pass information on to them about criminal operations and law enforcement surveillance.

31. Ace, PEN1 skinhead, interviewed 23 June 2002.

32. See Emile Durkheim, *The Elementary Forms of Religious Life* (New York: The Free Press, 1965 [1912]). Randall Collins, *Interaction Ritual Chains* (Princeton, NJ: Princeton University Press, 2004).

33. Collins, *Interaction*, 36.

34. Randy, Southern California activist, interviewed 19 March 2000.

35. Hank, SoCal Skin, interviewed 17 November 2002.

36. Cory, Hammerskin, interviewed 17 August 2002.

37. Anthony, L.A. County Skinhead and tattoo artist, interviewed 18 March 2002.

38. Evelyn Larrubia, "Prosecution Rests in Alleged Racial Killing," *Los Angeles Times*, 22 October 1999, available at: http://articles.latimes.com/1999/oct/22/local/me-25077 (accessed 22 May 2009).

39. Nick, L.A. County Skinhead and tattoo artist, interviewed 19 August 2002.

40. Lewis Coser, *Greedy Institutions: Patterns of Undivided Commitment* (New York: Free Press, 1974).

41. Pete Simi, "Recruitment among Right-Wing Terrorist Groups," Final Report-2006-IJ-CX-0027 (Washington, DC: National Institute of Justice, 2008).

CHAPTER 5

1. Mike, Midwest Aryan, interviewed 1 September 2001.

2. Ron Eyerman and Andrew Jamison, *Music and Social Movements: Mobilizing Traditions in the Twentieth Century* (Cambridge: Cambridge University Press, 1998).

3. Hank, interviewed 14 June 2001.

4. Hank, interviewed 14 June 2001.

5. Hank, interviewed 14 June 2001.

6. Nicholas Goodrick-Clarke, *Black Sun: Aryan Cults, Esoteric Nazism and the Politics of Identity* (New York: New York University Press, 2002). Vron Ware and Les Back, *Out of Whiteness: Color, Politics, and Culture* (Chicago: University of Chicago Press, 2002).

7. Skrewdriver's lead singer, Ian Stuart Donaldson, died in car accident in 1993, and white power music bands and concert organizers have since immortalized him with memorial music shows that honor his life, Web-based biographies and discographies, and CD compilations of Skrewdriver's music.

8. Dave, Volksfront skinhead, interviewed 14 July 2000.

9. Andy, Washington skinhead, interviewed 25 April 1997.

10. Tom, Aryan musician, interviewed 9 July 2001.

11. Southern Poverty Law Center, "White Power Bands," www.tolerance.org/news/article_hate.jsp?id=403 (accessed 30 May 2002).

12. *Modified* lyrics for Skrewdriver's song "Race and Nation" can be retrieved from: www.metrolyrics.com/race-and-nation-lyrics-skrewdriver.html (accessed 15 November 2007).

13. *Modified* lyrics for Bully Boys' song "Jigrun" can be retrieved from: www.splcenter.org/center/splcreport/article.jsp?aid=115.

14. *Modified* lyrics for Max Resist's song "Boot Party" can be retrieved from: www.lyricstime.com/max-resist-boot-party-lyrics.html.

15. *Modified* lyrics for Youngland's song "Stand One, Stand All" can be retrieved from: www.lyricsondemand.com/y/younglandlyrics/standonestandalllyrics.html.

16. Their mother, April Gaede, a veteran Aryan activist and their manager, actively pushed the girls into the Aryan scene. She homeschooled them through sixth grade then enrolled them in a Bakersfield, California, junior high where their Aryan ties were unknown for some time. They apparently fit in well at school until word spread of their involvement in white power activism. Their mother moved the family to a small Montana town to avoid tensions they faced in Bakersfield.

17. Biggie, Colorado skinhead, interviewed 23 August 2002.

18. Quoted in Kathleen Blee, *Inside Organized Racism: Women in the Hate Movement* (Berkeley: University of California Press, 2002), 162.

19. Kenny, Aryan activist, interviewed 21 February 2002.

20. Neo-Nazi activist quoted in Blee, *Inside Organized Racism*, 161.

21. Samuel, Seattle activist, interviewed 29 June 2004.

22. Rick, WAR skinhead and Aryan musician, interviewed 15 July 2002.

23. Kenny, L.A. County skinhead, interviewed 28 March 2002.

24. Lance, SoCal skin interviewed 23 June 2003.

25. For similar points see Derrick Bell, *Faces at the Bottom of the Well: The Permanence of Racism* (New York: Basic Books, 1992); and Elisabeth Jean Wood, "The Emotional Benefits of Insurgency in El Salvador," in *Passionate Politics: Emotions and Social Movements*, ed. Jeff Goodwin, James Jasper, and Francesca Polletta (Chicago: University of Chicago Press, 2001).

26. Wood, "Emotional Benefits."

27. A few days later I talked to a journalist who tracks hate crimes in the United States. After checking with his contacts in law enforcement, he found nothing to confirm the skinhead's story and expected that it was just brash talk from an attention seeker.

28. Southern Poverty Law Center, "Present at the Creation," *Intelligence Report*, Fall 2001, www.splcenter.org/intel/intelreport/article.jsp?aid = 179 (accessed 30 March 2002).

29. Anti-Defamation League, "The Consequences of Right-Wing Extremism on the Internet," 2002, available at: www.adl.org/internet/extremism%5Frw/cord_rock.asp (accessed 5 February 2002).

30. Otto, SoCal Skin, interviewed 13 August 2000.

31. Garth, Idaho Aryan, interviewed 12 July 1999.

32. For similar findings, see Mark Hamm, *In Bad Company: America's Terrorist Underground* (Boston: Northeastern University Press, 2002), 85–93.

33. Sammy, Colorado Aryan, interviewed 19 February 2001.

34. Center for New Community, "Soundtracks to the White Revolution: White Supremacists' Assaults on Youth Music Subcultures," www.turnitdown.com (accessed 13 February 2003).

35. Joey, Aryan music distributor, interviewed 11 June 2004.

36. William Pierce, "*Resistance* magazine," http://resistance.com/magazine/ (accessed 2 August 2003).

37. George Burdi created Resistance Records in 1993. An early hate music pioneer and leader of the Canadian World Church of the Creator, he first sold music out of his home in suburban Windsor, Ontario. He then moved his operation to suburban Detroit a year later to avoid strict Canadian laws against hate propaganda. A 1997 joint U.S. and Cana-

dian raid on Burdi's home and office stopped record sales until William Pierce and the National Alliance acquired Resistance Records in 1999. Pierce died in 2002 leaving his protégé, Erich Gliebe, to run both the National Alliance and Resistance Records.

38. Anti-Defamation League, "Deafening Hate: The Revival of Resistance Records," 2000, www.adl.org/resistance_records/Reviving.asp (accessed 5 February 2002).

39. Anti Defamation League, "Deafening Hate."

40. Tore Bjorgo, "Entry, Bridge-Burning, and Exit Options: What Happens to Young People Who Join Racist Groups—and Want to Leave" in *Nation and Race: The Developing Euro-American Racist Subculture*, ed. Jeffrey Kaplan and Tore Bjorgo (Boston: Northeastern University Press, 1998), 231–58; According to a 1997 survey of eight thousand young Swedes between the ages of twelve and nineteen by the Centre for Migration Studies and the National Council of Crime Prevention in Sweden, 12.2 percent reported listening to white power rock "sometimes or often." See Helène Lööw, "White Noise—an International Affair," www.freemuse.org/sw6649.asp (accessed 30 May 2002).

41. The term "Panzerfaust" refers to a Nazi-era antitank weapon and can be literally translated as "armored fist"—a concept Pierpont and Davidson used to communicate the idea of white power music as "the audio ordnance that's needed by our comrades on the front lines of today's racial struggle. "About Panzerfaust Records," www.panzerfaust.com/about.shtml (accessed 29 June 2003).

42. Anthony Pierpont, interviewed 14 July 2002.

43. David Hoffman, *The Web of Hate: Extremists Exploit the Internet* (New York: Anti-Defamation League, 1996).

44. James, Southeastern Klansman, interviewed 15 December 2002.

45. Tia DeNora, *Music in Everyday Life* (Cambridge: Cambridge University Press, 2000).

46. Greg, Northern Hammerskin, interviewed 1 September 2001.

47. Blee, *Inside Organized Racism*, 165.

48. For more on this point, see John Street, "Fight the Power: The Politics of Music and the Music of Politics," *Government and Opposition* 38 (2001): 113–30.

CHAPTER 6

1. Don Black, founder of the first major white power movement website Stormfront.org, appearing on ABC's *Nightline*, 13 January 1998.

2. Mark Nunes, *Cyberspaces of Everyday Life* (Minneapolis: University of Minnesota Press, 2006).

3. Howard Rheingold, *The Virtual Community: Homesteading on the Electronic Frontier* (Reading, MA: Addison-Wesley Publishing Company, 1993); Sherry Turkle, *Life on the Screen: Identity in the Age of the Internet* (New York: Simon & Schuster, 1995).

4. Suzanne Brunsting and Tom Postmes, "Social Movement Participation in the Digital Age: Predicting Offline and Online Collective Action," *Small Group Research* 33 (2002): 525–54; Mario Diani, "Social Movement Networks Virtual and Real," *Information, Communication & Society* 3 (2000): 386–401; Sherry Turkle, "Cyberspace and Identity," *Contemporary Sociology* 28 (1999): 643–48; Stephen Doheny-Farina, *The Wired Neighborhood* (New Haven, CT: Yale University Press, 1996); Donna Haraway, *Simians, Cyborgs, and Women: The Re-invention of Nature* (London: Free Association, 1991).

5. Axl Hess, "White Honor," www.whitehonor.com/FRAMEPAGE.htm (accessed 21 June 2008).

6. Hess, "White Honor."

7. Hess, "White Honor."

8. Heide Beirich, "White Supremacist Represents School for Poor Minority Children," 2008, available at: www.splcenter.org/blog/2008/07/09/white-supremacist -represents-schoolfor-poor-minority-kids/ (accessed 11 July 2008).

9. Trey, SoCal Skin, interviewed 14 June 2004.

10. Anti Defamation League, "Hate Rock Online: New Tool for Racists and Anti-Semites," 2001, available at: www.adl.org/extremism/intro.asp (accessed 20 May 2004).

11. Strategically promoting the indigenous character of the enterprises enhances members' sense of connection to economically viable movement institutions that support what they see as their much misunderstood and maligned Aryan aesthetic. In turn, WPM members directly contribute to the movement by providing a revenue stream through their purchase of the merchandise. Keeping members' money circulating in the movement nourishes and sustains the white power music scene. This relationship between WPM music enterprises and activists who participate produces a "co-op effect" similar to the way that progressive movements in the 1960s and 1970s established alternative service organizations such as food co-ops and community credit unions to serve those seeking cultural materials, lifestyles, and commercial options outside, and competitive with, the mainstream providers. Those organizations were sustained by members' participation and resources with the most successful becoming enduring indigenous institutions and lending a strong sense of efficacy to members' efforts. While certainly more clandestine than these organizations, WPM music and merchandising enterprises also appear to be establishing themselves as viable anchors for transmitting and supporting movement identity. Their success in this regard creates opportunities for activists to feel involved in an authentic, viable, self-sustaining alternative white power music scene that is their own and is seen as a legitimate rival to the mainstream music and culture.

12. Although we are not claiming there is a direct relationship between racist video games and violence, there is substantial research that demonstrates violent media images heighten aggressive behavior among individuals, especially children. For further discussion, see Greg Anderson and Karen Dill, "Video Games and Aggressive Thoughts, Feelings, and Behavior in the Laboratory and in Life," *Journal of Personality and Social Psychology* 78, no. 4 (2000): 772–90.

13. The WPM is not the only revolutionary movement to embrace the strategic use of video games. The militant Islamic organization Hezbollah markets a game to Arab children that awards points for killing Israeli soldiers, while a Syrian company sells a game that lets kids kill Jewish settlers. For further discussion, see Anti-Defamation League, "Hezbollah Releases Anti-Israel War Game," 17 August 2007, available at: www.adl.org/ main_Terrorism/special_force_2.htm (accessed 6 September 2008).

14. Anti-Defamation League, "Extremism in America: National Socialist Movement," available at: www.adl.org/Learn/Ext_US/nsm (accessed 29 June 2009).

15. Charlie, Southeastern Aryan activist, interviewed 28 June 2003.

16. New Saxon, www.newsaxon.org (accessed 29 July 2008).

17. Jeffrey Kaplan and Leonard Weinberg, *The Emergence of a Euro-American Radical Right* (New Brunswick, NJ: Rutgers University Press, 1998), 159; David Hoffman,

The Web of Hate: Extremists Exploit the Internet (New York: Anti-Defamation League, 1996), 72.

18. Some of these conversations extend into announcements for movement-focused services and tactical planning to disseminate the "word."

> Coming Soon the first pro-white credit union if your interested in learning more email me at floridabuilder@aol.com. . . . Stop feeding the beast and become a founding member of the first pro-white credit union. . . . Creating financial freedom and wealth for our people is a huge step in the right direction. PrideofaWhiteMan. (Retrieved from Stormfront.org, 13 March 2003)

> After recently completing some upper level web design training, I would like to offer my services to any white nationalist activists, organizations, and businesses. I do not provide web hosting, but would love to meet some people who do, and work together with them. To see a version of my handiwork go to pages.prodigy.net/lexo. ForVictory. (Retrieved from Stormfront.org, 13 March 2003)

On a Resistance Records bulletin board, discussion centered for a time around ways to extend Project Schoolyard, a Panzerfaust Records/Free Your Mind Productions program that distributed free racist (CDs at targeted U.S. high schools. This chat suggested members target college radio stations in their area as an outlet for Aryan music.

> I have an idea that I'm working on and hope that you join me as well in this endeavor. As we all know, "Project Schoolyard" has been a success and I have a similar idea. How about making white power music CDS and trying to get college radio stations to play the music? College radio stations aren't commercial and are pretty much free to play whatever they like as long as it falls within FCC guidelines. NoRemorse. (Retrieved from Resistance.com, 18 November 2004)

Seven forum users immediately affirmed the idea and several offered additional ideas.

> Actually, we do that, and there are more than a few college radio stations that play our stuff . . . some know exactly what we are about, some I suspect do not. A couple of our customers in college have gotten into the college radio stations as DJs or whatever, for the express purpose of playing our music. Ghostrider. (Retrieved from Resistance.com, 18 November 2004)

Announcing and discussing these aspects of activism gives members a sense that action is occurring in the broader movement and conveys a sense of strength, efficacy, and the wherewithal of Aryan activism.

19. Jay, Aryan Front activist, interviewed 27 June 2004.

20. Scotty, Aryan Front activist, interviewed 12 June 2004.

21. Forrest, Northern Hammerskin, interviewed 13 July 2002.

22. Postings on panzerfaust.com (accessed 27 November 2004).

23. Chip Berlet and Matthew N. Lyons, *Right-Wing Populism in America: Too Close for Comfort* (New York: The Guilford Press, 2000). Lane Crothers, *Rage on the Right: The American Militia Movement from Ruby Ridge to Homeland Security* (Lanham, MD: Rowman & Littlefield, 2003).

24. 88Rocker, post on White Revolution, www.whiterevolution.com (accessed 28 July 2007).

25. WhiteInstinct, post on Stormfront, www.Stormfront.org (accessed 20 July 2007).

26. VikingBlood, post on White Revolution, www.whiterevolution.com (accessed 20 August 2007).

27. Postings on Free Your Mind Productions, www.freeyourmindproductions.com (accessed 13 February 2004).

28. whiteusa, posted on White Revolution, www.whiterevolution.com (accessed 20 February 2006).

29. Lucy, posted on White Revolution, www.whiterevolution.com (accessed 29 July 2004).

30. SouthernMan, posted on Stormfront, www.stormfront.org (accessed 12 March 2006).

31. Wolf1488, posted on White Revolution, www.whiterevolution.com. (accessed 13 April 2005).

32. IronCross, posted on White Revolution, www.whiterevolution.com (accessed 31 January 2005).

33. AryanAngel, posted on Stormfront, www.stormfront.org (accessed 3 November 2005).

34. American Anglo88, posted on "White Revolution," www.whiterevolution.com (accessed 20 January 2005).

35. Painless Brutality, posted on Panzerfaust, www.panzerfaust.com (accessed 14 January 2005).

36. red neck nzr, posted on Panzerfaust, www.panzerfaust.com (16 January 2005).

37. Vegas h8s Spearchuckers, posted on Panzerfaust, www.panzerfaust.com (accessed 16 January 2005).

38. Aryan88chick, posted on Stormfront, www.stormfront.org (5 July 2006).

39. Zogslayer, posted on Stormfront www.stormfront.org (4 November 2005).

40. WhitePride, posted on Free Your Mind Productions, www.freeyourmindproductions.com (12 November 2005).

41. Jenocide, posted Free Your Mind Productions, www.freeyourmindproductions.com (12 November 2005).

42. All posted on Free Your Mind Productions, www.freeyourmindproductions.com (12 November 2005).

43. The support members find online is very similar what occurs in other Web-based support groups such as menopause groups, recovering alcoholics, and drug addicts. Barry Wellman and Milena Gulia, "Virtual Communities as Communities," in Communities in Cyberspace, ed. M. A. Smith and P. Kollock (New York: Routledge, 1998), 167–94.

44. Spring Demon, posted on Free Your Mind Productions, www.freeyourmindproductions.com (accessed 21 January 2005).

45. AryanPrincess, posted on Free Your Mind Productions, www.freeyourmindproductions.com (21 January 2005).

46. Wellman and Gulia, "Virtual Communities," 182.

47. FightforFreedom, posted on CaSkinhead, www.caskinheads.com (accessed 20 July 2007).

48. Mary Virnoche and Gary Marx, "Only Connect—E. M. Forster in an Age of Elec-

tronic Communication: Computer-Mediated Association and Community Networks," *Sociological Inquiry* 67 (1997): 85–100.

49. whitewarrior, posted on White Revolution, www.whiterevolution.com (accessed 24 January 2005).

50. AryanTerror88, posted on White Revolution, www.whiterevolution.com (accessed 24 January 2005).

51. skingirl14, posted on Panzerfaust, www.panzerfaust.com (accessed 22 May 2004).

52. Val Burris, Emory Smith, and Ann Strahm, "White Supremacist Networks on the Internet," *Sociological Focus* 33 (2000): 215–34 (quote at 232).

CHAPTER 7

1. Stuart Wright, *Patriots, Politics, and the Oklahoma City Bombing* (Cambridge: Cambridge University Press, 2007); Mark Hamm, *In Bad Company: America's Terrorist Underground* (Boston: Northeastern University Press, 2002); Kerry Noble, *Tabernacle of Hate: Why They Bombed Oklahoma City* (Prescott, ON: Voyageur Publications, 1998).

2. James Loewen, *Sundown Towns: A Hidden Dimension of American Racism* (New York: New Press, 2005).

3. Loewen, *Sundown Towns*, 9.

4. "The Encyclopedia of Arkansas History and Culture," available at: www.encyclo pediaofarkansas.net/encyclopedia/entry-detail.aspx?ent ryID = 4031 (accessed 2 October 2007).

5. Michael Barkun, *Religion and the Racist Right: The Origins of the Christian Identity Movement* (Chapel Hill: University of North Carolina Press, 1994); Noble, *Tabernacle*.

6. Encyclopedia of Arkansas History and Culture; MIPT (Memorial Institute for the Prevention of Terrorism) Terrorism Knowledge Base, available at: www.tkb.org/Group .jsp?groupID = 3226 (accessed 2 October 2007).

7. Noble, *Tabernacle*.

8. Noble, *Tabernacle*.

9. Noble, *Tabernacle*, 35.

10. Noble, *Tabernacle*.

11. Noble, *Tabernacle*.

12. Noble, *Tabernacle*.

13. James Corcoran as quoted in Wright, *Patriots*, 84.

14. Noble, *Tabernacle*.

15. Wright, *Patriots*.

16. Wright, *Patriots*.

17. The Nizkor Project, "Paranoia as Patriotism: Far-Right Influences on the Militia Movement," available at: www.nizkor.org/hweb/orgs/american/adl/paranoia-as-patriotism/ covenant.html (accessed 2 October 2007); Noble, *Tabernacle*.

18. Brent Smith, *Terrorism in America: Pipe Bombs and Pipe Dreams* (Albany: State University of New York Press, 1994).

19. Noble, *Tabernacle*; Smith, *Terrorism in America*.

20. Noble, *Tabernacle*; Kevin Flynn and Gary Gerhardt, *Silent Brotherhood: The Chill-*

ing Inside Story of America's Violent, Anti-Government Militia Movement (New York: Signet, 1990); Smith, *Terrorism in America.*

21. Noble, *Tabernacle.*

22. Smith, *Terrorism in America,* 64.

23. Smith, *Terrorism in America.*

24. Wright, *Patriots*; Noble, *Tabernacle.*

25. Wright, *Patriots*; Noble, *Tabernacle*; Smith, *Terrorism in America.*

26. Noble, *Tabernacle.*

27. Noble, *Tabernacle*; MIPT Terrorism Knowledge Base.

28. Kerry Noble, James Ellison's right-hand man, testified against Ellison, rejected Aryan ideology, and now writes and speaks publicly about the threat of domestic terrorism from extremist white power groups.

29. Anti-Defamation League, "Elohim City," available at: www.adl.org/learn/Ext_US/Elohim.asp?xpicked = 3&item = 13 (accessed 3 October 2007).

30. Robert and John Millar never publicly called for violence against racial others. In fact, they have both claimed that ethnic and racial cleansing is "ungodly" and "un-Aryan."

31. Summer Shook, Wesley Delano, and Robert Balch, "Elohim City: A Participant-Observer Study of a Christian Identity Community," *Nova Religio* 2 (1999): 245–65; Hamm, *In Bad Company.*

32. Snell was also subsequently convicted and sentenced to die for the 1983 murder of a pawnshop owner in Texarkana whom he mistakenly thought to be Jewish. Snell reportedly told a CSA colleague that the pawnshop owner was "a Jew who deserved to die."

33. Anti-Defamation League, "Elohim City."

34. Anti-Defamation League, "National Alliance," available at: www.adl.org/Learn/ext_us/N_Alliance.asp (accessed 3 October 2007).

35. Southern Poverty Law Center, "Facing the Future," *Intelligence Report,* Fall 2002, available at: www.splcenter.org/intel/intelreport/article.jsp?pid = 94 (accessed 19 August 2006).

36. SPLC, "Facing the Future."

37. SPLC, "Facing the Future."

38. The efforts have produced events such as the "Spring Buffet Dinner" and the "European American Cultural Fest" organized by members of the Cleveland, Ohio, National Alliance chapter. The events drew more than 100 people of all ages for food, drink, and Irish and Slovakian music and dance. They also featured talks by WPM leaders such as Pierce and White Aryan Resistance leader Tom Metzger. Likewise, the Sacramento, California, chapter sponsored the "Winter Solstice Celebration" and "Winter Thule," billing them as family events. WAR's Tom Metzger also attended and spoke at these events

39. Anti-Defamation League, "National Alliance."

40. James Aho, *The Politics of Righteousness: Idaho Christian Patriotism* (Seattle: University of Washington Press, 1990); James Coates, *Armed and Dangerous: The Rise of the Survivalist Right* (New York: Farrar Straus & Giroux, 1987); Flynn and Gerhardt, *Silent Brotherhood*; Raphael Ezekiel, *The Racist Mind: Portraits of American Neo-Nazis and Klansmen* (New York: Viking, 1995); Betty Dobratz and Stephanie Shanks-Meile, *White Power! White Pride! The White Separatist Movement in the United States* (New

York: Cengage Gale, 1997); Richard Mitchell, *Dancing at Armageddon: Survivalism and Chaos in Modern Times* (Chicago: University of Chicago Press, 2001); Robert Balch, "The Rise and Fall of Aryan Nations: A Resource Mobilization Perspective," *Journal of Political and Military Sociology* 34 (2006): 81–113.

41. Aryan Nations website, available at: www.aryan-nations.org (accessed 4 October 2007).

42. Kathleen Blee, *Inside Organized Racism: Women in the Hate Movement* (Berkeley: University of California Press, 2002), 196.

43. Anti-Defamation League, "Aryan Nations," available at: www.adl.org/learn/ext _us/Aryan_Nations.asp?xpicked = 3&item = 11 (accessed 3 October 2007).

44. Aryan Nations website.

45. Balch, "Rise and Fall," 86.

46. Balch, "Rise and Fall," 86.

47. Balch, "Rise and Fall," 86.

48. Butler canceled the congress in 1985 to lower Aryan Nations' profile after The Silent Brotherhood carried out a rash of robberies. Some of the Silent Brotherhood's members visited the Aryan Nations compound and Butler feared the media attention.

49. Anti-Defamation League, "Aryan Nations."

50. Anti-Defamation League, "Aryan Nations."

51. Flynn and Gerhardt, *Silent Brotherhood.*

52. Balch, "Rise and Fall," 89.

53. Aryan Nations leader Richard Butler, sermon, 29 June 1997

54. James Aho, "White Man as a Social Construct," *The European Legacy* 4 (1999): 62–72.

55. Mitchell, *Dancing at Armageddon.*

56. Balch, "Rise and Fall," 94; see also Mitchell, *Dancing at Armageddon.*

57. Charlie, AN activist, interviewed 2 July 1999.

58. Michael, AN activist, interviewed 22 July 1998.

59. Gary, AN activist, interviewed 3 July 1999.

60. Russ, Alabama Aryan, interviewed 3 July 1999.

61. This event took place on 8 July 1999.

62. Cindy, Aryan Nations member, interviewed 8 July 1999.

63. Steven, Kentucky Klansman, interviewed 8 July 1999.

64. Dylan, Aryan Front member, interviewed 9 July 1999.

65. Douglas McAdam, *Freedom Summer* (New York: Oxford University Press, 1988).

66. For similar description of Aryan National Congress rituals, also see Aho, "White Man," and James Aho, "The Recent Ethnogenesis of White Man," *Left Bank* 5 (1993): 55–63.

67. Pilgrimages to Aryan Nations were also for more instrumental purposes, such as running from the law. Butler was generous to Aryans in trouble with authorities, and offered his land as a refuge or hideout. As Carl, a skinhead who was living at the compound during one visit, told us, "I'm from New Hampshire, I was having some trouble with the law back there, so I came out here [AN property] to live for a while and stay out of trouble. Works out fine since I've been wanting to come out here for a long time now and I've been really grateful about spending time with Pastor Butler." Like William Peirce, Butler reportedly also gave refuge for a time to infamous German neo-Nazi musi-

cian Hendrik Möbus when he came to the United States in the late 1990s to escape jail time in Germany.

68. Rachel, Washington State Aryan, interview 25 April 1997.

69. Charley, Northwest skinhead, interviewed 22 April 1997.

70. Bill, SWAS member, interviewed 27 January 1997.

71. Tom, Washington State skinhead, interviewed 19 April 1997.

72. Balch, "Rise and Fall"; Mitchell, *Dancing at Armageddon.*

73. Balch, "Rise and Fall," 100.

74. Balch, "Rise and Fall," 106.

75. Balch, "Rise and Fall."

76. Balch, "Rise and Fall."

77. Kari Huus, "Aryan Nations Plots a Comeback at Idaho Campout," MSNBC, 16 December 2003, available at: www.msnbc.msn.com/id/3340524 (accessed 4 March 2004).

78. Huus, "Aryan Nations."

79. Huus, "Aryan Nations."

80. Heide Beirich and Mark Potok, "Two Faces of Volksfront," *Intelligence Report,* Summer 2004, available at: www.splcenter.org/intel/intelreport/article.jsp?pid = 786 (accessed 11 October 2007).

81. Hamm, *In Bad Company*; Wright, *Patriots.*

82. Jeffrey Kaplan and Leonard Weinberg, *The Emergence of a Euro-American Radical Right* (Piscataway, NJ: Rutgers University Press, 1998), 150.

CHAPTER 8

1. Stuart Wright, *Patriots, Politics, and the Oklahoma City Bombing* (Cambridge: Cambridge University Press, 2007), 6.

2. Wright, *Patriots.*

3. Randall Collins, "Stratification, Emotional Energy, and the Transient Emotions," in *Research Agendas in the Sociology of Emotions*, ed. Theodore D. Kemper (Albany: State University of New York Press, 1990), 27–57.

4. The largest number of Aryan indictments occurred in the mid-1980s, inspired by several groups' declaration of insurgency against the federal government called the "WAR in 84." Indictments rose again in the mid-1990s with the most notorious being the 1995 Oklahoma City bombing.

5. Andrew Blejwas, Anthony Griggs, and Mark Potok, "Terror from the Right: Almost 60 Terrorist Plots Uncovered in the U.S," *Intelligence Report*, Summer 2005, available at: www.splcenter.org/intel/intelreport/article.jsp?aid = 628 (accessed 15 October 2006).

6. Blejwas et al., "Terror from the Right," 1.

7. Blejwas et al., "Terror from the Right," 1.

8. Michael E. Ruane, Paul Duggan, and Clarence Williams, "At a Monument of Sorrow, a Burst of Deadly Violence," *Washington Post*, 11 June 2009, available at: www.washingtonpost.com/wp-dyn/content/article/2009/06/10/AR2009061001768.html (accessed 18 June 2009).

9. Joseph Williams, "Obama Election Spurs Wave of Hate Group Violence," *Boston*

Globe, 12 May 2009, available at: www.boston.com/news/nation/washington/articles/ 2009/05/11/obamaeelection_s purs_wave_of_hate_group_violence/#; Ruane et al. "At a Monument of Sorrow."

10. U.S. Department of Homeland Security, "Rightwing Extremism: Current Economic and Political Climate Fueling Resurgence in Radicalization and Recruitment," 7 April 2009, available at: www.fas.org/irp/eprint/rightwing.pdf. This report marks a major shift in perspective for the agency. As recently as 2005, the Department of Homeland Security concluded that white power extremists do not pose a substantial threat to domestic security. In response, the Southern Poverty Law Center warned:

> A draft internal document from the U.S. Department of Homeland Security that was obtained [in Spring 2005] by The *Congressional Quarterly* lists the only serious domestic terrorist threats as radical animal rights and environmental groups like the Animal Liberation Front and the Earth Liberation Front. But for all the property damage they have wreaked, eco-radicals have killed no one—something that most definitely cannot be said of the white supremacists and others who people the American radical right.

SPLC, "Terror from the Right," *Intelligence Report*, Summer 2005, available at: www .splcenter.org/intel/intelreport/article.jsp?aid = 628.

11. Lindell Kay, "Investigation Continues into Man Accused of Making Threats against Obama," ENCToday.com, 9 February 2009, available at: www.enctoday.com/arti cles/brittingham-62276-jdn-marine-service.html (accessed 20 February 2009).

12. U.S. Department of Homeland Security, "Rightwing Extremism."

13. Mitch Berbrier, "Impression Management for the Thinking Racist: A Case Study of Intellectualization as Stigma Transformation in Contemporary White Supremacist Discourse," *The Sociological Quarterly* 40 (1999): 411–33; Mitch Berbrier, "'Half the Battle': Cultural Resonance, Framing Processes, and Ethnic Affectations in Contemporary White Separatist Rhetoric," *Social Problems* 45 (1998): 431–50; Mitch Berbrier, "Making Minorities: Cultural Space, Stigma Transformation Frames, and the Categorical Status Claims of Deaf, Gay, and White Supremacist Activists in Late Twentieth-Century America," *Sociological Forum* 17 (2002): 553–91; Mitch Berbrier, "The Victim Ideology of White Supremacists and White Separatists in the United States," *Sociological Focus* 33 (2000): 175–91.

14. White power music culture and cyberspace appear to be especially potent points of contact for attracting new members. Hate rock intermingles highly racist and anti-Semitic ideas with familiar, pop-culture commodity forms such as music and clothing styles, jewelry, stickers, and other paraphernalia. We see evidence of a slow and stealthy seep of white power imagery and messages into the mainstream cultural landscape. Already the German iron cross, a staple image of neo-Nazi groups and white power bands, has become a very popular symbol in alternative clothing and advertising. For instance, the popular custom motorcycle shop West Coast Choppers uses the cross prominently in their promotions as a sign of rebellion and strength, but not to promote white power. The more that such cherished neo-Nazi symbols become familiar images, the greater chance Aryans have to attract unsuspecting visitors to websites and gatherings. Aryan cyberspace offers the easiest access to movement culture, where the merely curious can make contact, experiment with the ideas, and take steps into other Aryan free spaces where white power culture persists.

15. Alberto Melucci, *Challenging Codes: Collective Action in the Information Age* (Cambridge: Cambridge University Press, 1996).

16. The Olympic Park bomber, Eric Rudolph, is a case in point. Rudolph's attacks included detonating bombs at the 1996 Olympic Games in Atlanta, at abortion clinics in Atlanta and Birmingham, Alabama, and in an Atlanta lesbian nightclub. He killed two and injured 119 people. His exact motivations and links to other extremists remain somewhat mysterious. What is clear is that Rudolph is vehemently antiabortion, antigay, antifeminism, and anti-Semitic, and he feels that American culture is rapidly deteriorating (see Rudolph's writing on www.ArmyofGod.com). He has a long history of associations with Christian Identity adherents and other right-wing extremists. When Rudolph was eighteen he lived for six months at Pastor Dan Gayman's Christian Identity community, the Church of Israel, in Schell City, Missouri, where Gayman served as his mentor and considered Rudoph a potential husband for one of his daughters.

17. Courier-Journal.com, available at: http://m.courier-journal.com/news.jsp?key= 455989.

18. For a penetrating analysis of the unfulfilled potential of democracy and the agents who see to it that democracy remains but a dream deferred see Cornell West, *Democracy Matters: Winning the Fight against Imperialism* (New York: Penguin, 2004).

Bibliography

Aho, James. *The Politics of Righteousness: Idaho Christian Patriotism.* Seattle: University of Washington Press, 1990.

Anderson, Elijah. *Code of the Street: Decency, Violence, and the Moral Life of the Inner City.* New York: Norton, 1999.

Anderson, Greg, and Karen Dill. "Video Games and Aggressive Thoughts, Feelings, and Behavior in the Laboratory and in Life." *Journal of Personality and Social Psychology* 78, no. 4 (2000): 772–90.

Balch, Robert. "The Rise and Fall of Aryan Nations: A Resource Mobilization Perspective." *Journal of Political and Military Sociology* 34 (2006): 81–113.

Barkun, Michael. *Religion and the Racist Right: The Origins of the Christian Identity Movement.* Chapel Hill: University of North Carolina Press, 1994.

Bell, Derrick. *Faces at the Bottom of the Well: The Permanence of Racism.* New York: Basic Books, 1992.

Bennett, David. *The Party of Fear: From Nativist Movements to the New Right in American History.* Chapel Hill: University of North Carolina Press, 1995.

Berbrier, Mitch. "Making Minorities: Cultural Space, Stigma Transformation Frames, and the Categorical Status Claims of Deaf, Gay, and White Supremacist Activists in Late Twentieth-Century America." *Sociological Forum* 17 (2002): 553–91.

———. "The Victim Ideology of White Supremacists and White Separatists in the United States." *Sociological Focus* 33 (2000): 175–91.

———. "Impression Management for the Thinking Racist: A Case Study of Intellectualization as Stigma Transformation in Contemporary White Supremacist Discourse." *The Sociological Quarterly* 40 (1999): 411–33.

———. "'Half the Battle': Cultural Resonance, Framing Processes, and Ethnic Affectations in Contemporary White Separatist Rhetoric." *Social Problems* 45 (1998): 431–50.

Berezin, Mabel. *Making the Fascist Self: The Political Culture of Interwar Italy.* Ithaca, NY: Cornell University Press, 1997.

Berg, Bruce. *Qualitative Research Methods for the Social Sciences.* Boston: Pearson, 2004.

Berlet, Chip, and Matthew N. Lyons. *Right-Wing Populism in America: Too Close for Comfort.* New York: The Guilford Press, 2000.

Billig, Michael. "Humour and Hatred: The Racist Jokes of the Ku Klux Klan." *Discourse and Society* (2001): 267–88.

Bjorgo, Tore. "Entry, Bridge-Burning, and Exit Options: What Happens to Young People Who Join Racist Groups—and Want to Leave." In *Nation and Race: The Developing Euro-American Racist Subculture*, ed. Jeffrey Kaplan and Tore Bjorgo, 231–58. Boston: Northeastern University Press, 1998.

Blee, Kathleen. *Inside Organized Racism: Women in the Hate Movement*. Berkeley: University of California Press, 2002.

Brunsting, Suzanne, and Tom Postmes. "Social Movement Participation in the Digital Age: Predicting Offline and Online Collective Action." *Small Group Research* 33 (2002): 525–54.

Buechler, Steven. *Social Movements in Advanced Capitalism*. New York: Oxford University Press, 2000.

Burris, Val, Emory Smith, and Ann Strahm. "White Supremacist Networks on the Internet." *Sociological Focus* 33 (2000): 215–34.

Canedy, Susan. *America's Nazis: A Democratic Dilemma*. Menlo Park, CA: Markgraf Publishers, 1990.

Chalmers, David. *Hooded Americanism: The History of the Ku Klux Klan*. Durham, NC: Duke University Press, 1987.

Coates, James. *Armed and Dangerous: The Rise of the Survivalist Right*. New York: Farrar Straus & Giroux, 1987.

Collins, Randall. *Interaction Ritual Chains*. Princeton, NJ: Princeton University Press, 2004.

———. "Stratification, Emotional Energy, and the Transient Emotions." In *Research Agendas in the Sociology of Emotions*, ed. Theodore D. Kemper, 27–57. Albany: State University of New York Press, 1990.

Coser, Lewis. *Greedy Institutions: Patterns of Undivided Commitment*. New York: Free Press, 1974.

Couto, Richard. "Narrative, Free Space, and Political Leadership in Social Movements." *Journal of Politics* 55 (1993): 57–79.

Crothers, Lane. *Rage on the Right: The American Militia Movement from Ruby Ridge to Homeland Security*. Lanham, MD: Rowman & Littlefield, 2003.

Cunningham, David. *There's Something Happening Here: The New Left, the Klan, and FBI Counterintelligence*. Berkeley: University of California Press, 2004.

Daniels, Jesse. *Cyber Racism: White Supremacy Online and the New Attack on Civil Rights*. Lanham, MD: Rowman & Littlefield, 2009.

———. *White Lies: Race, Class, and Gender in White Supremacist Discourse*. New York: Routledge, 1997.

DeNora, Tia. *Music in Everyday Life*. Cambridge: Cambridge University Press, 2000.

Denzin, Norman. *The Research Act: A Theoretical Introduction to Sociological Methods*. New York: McGraw-Hill Book Company, 1978.

Diamond, Sara. *Roads to Dominion: Right-Wing Movements and Political Power in the United States*. New York: Guilford Press, 1995.

Diani, Mario. "Social Movement Networks Virtual and Real." *Information, Communication & Society* 3 (2000): 386–401.

Dobratz, Betty, and Stephanie Shanks-Meile. *White Power! White Pride! The White Separatist Movement in the United States*. New York: Cengage Gale, 1997.

Doheny-Farina, Stephen. *The Wired Neighborhood*. New Haven, CT: Yale University Press, 1996.

Durkheim, Emile. *The Elementary Forms of Religious Life*. New York: The Free Press, 1965 [1912].

Evans, Sara. *Personal Politics: The Roots of Women's Liberation in the Civil Rights Movement and the New Left*. London: Vintage, 1979.

Evans, Sara, and Harry Boyte. *Free Spaces*. Chicago: University of Chicago Press, 1992).

Eyeman, Ron, and Andrew Jamison. *Music and Social Movements: Mobilizing Traditions in the Twentieth Century*. Cambridge: Cambridge University Press, 1998.

Ezekiel, Raphael. *The Racist Mind: Portraits of American Neo-Nazis and Klansmen*. New York: Viking, 1995.

Feagin, Joe, and Hernan Vera. *White Racism: The Basics*. New York: Routledge, 1995.

Ferber, Abby. *White Man Falling: Race, Gender, and White Supremacy*. Lanham, MD: Rowman & Littlefield, 1998.

Flynn, Kevin, and Gary Gerhardt. *Silent Brotherhood: The Chilling Inside Story of America's Violent, Anti-Government Militia Movement*. New York: Signet, 1990.

Futrell, Robert, and Pete Simi. "Free Spaces, Collective Identity, and the Persistence of U.S. White Power Activism." *Social Problems* 51 (2004): 16–42.

Futrell, Robert, Pete Simi, and Simon Gottschalk. "Understanding Music in Movements: the U.S. White Power Music Scene." *The Sociological Quarterly* 47 (2006): 275–304.

Gardell, Mattias. *Gods of the Blood: The Pagan Revival and White Separatism*. Durham, NC: Duke University Press, 2003.

Glaser, Barney, and Anslem Strauss. *The Discovery of Grounded Theory*. Chicago: Aldine, 1967.

Goffman, Erving. *Stigma: Notes on the Management of Spoiled Identity*. Englewood Cliffs, NJ: Prentice Hall, 1963.

Goodrick-Clarke, Nicholas. *Black Sun: Aryan Cults, Esoteric Nazism and the Politics of Identity*. New York: New York University Press, 2002.

Hamm, Mark. *In Bad Company: America's Terrorist Underground*. Boston: Northeastern University Press, 2002.

Haraway, Donna. *Simians, Cyborgs, and Women: The Reinvention of Nature*. London: Free Association, 1991.

Jacobs, James, and Kimberly Potter. *Hate Crimes: Criminal Law and Identity Politics*. Oxford: Oxford University Press, 1990.

Jasper, James. "The Emotions of Protest: Affective and Reactive Emotions in and around Social Movements." *Sociological Forum* 13 (1998): 397–424.

Johnston, Hank. "New Social Movements and Old Regional Nationalisms." In *New Social Movements: From Ideology to Identity*, ed. Enrique Larana, Hank Johnston, and Joseph R. Gusfield, 267–86. Philadelphia: Temple University Press, 1994.

———. *Tales of Nationalism: Catalonia 1939–1979*. New Brunswick, NJ: Rutgers University Press, 1991.

Kaplan, Jeffrey, "Right-Wing Violence in North America." In *Terror from the Extreme Right*, ed. Tore Bjorgo. London: Frank Cass, 1995.

Kaplan, Jeffrey, and Leonard Weinberg. *The Emergence of a Euro-American Radical Right*. Piscataway, NJ: Rutgers University Press, 1998.

Langer, Elinor. *A Hundred Little Hitlers: The Death of a Black Man, the Trial of a White*

Racist, and the Rise of the Neo-Nazi Movement in America. New York: Metropolitan Books, 2003.

Lewis, Michael, and Jacqueline Serbu. "Kommerating the Ku Klux Klan." *Sociological Quarterly* 40 (1999): 139–57.

Loewen, James. *Sundown Towns: A Hidden Dimension of American Racism*. New York: New Press, 2005.

Lofland, John, and Lyn Lofland. *Analyzing Social Settings: A Guide to Qualitative Observation and Analysis*. Belmont, CA: Wadsworth, 1995.

McAdam, Douglas. *Freedom Summer*. Oxford: Oxford University Press, 1988.

McDonald, Andrew [William Pierce]. *The Turner Diaries*. Hillsboro, WV: National Vanguard Books, 1989.

McLean, Nancy. *Behind the Mask of Chivalry: The Making of the Second Ku Klux Klan*. New York: Oxford University Press, 1994.

McVeigh, Rory. *The Rise of the Ku Klux Klan: Right-Wing Movement and National Politics*. Minneapolis: University of Minnesota Press, 2009.

Melucci, Alberto. *Challenging Codes: Collective Action in the Information Age*. Cambridge: Cambridge University Press, 1996.

Miles, Mathew, and Michael Huberman. *Qualitative Data Analysis*. Thousand Oaks, CA: Sage, 1994.

Mitchell, Richard. *Dancing at Armageddon: Survivalism and Chaos in Modern Times*. Chicago: University of Chicago Press, 2001.

Moore, Leonard. *Citizen Klansmen*. Chapel Hill: University of North Carolina Press, 1991.

Newton, Michael, and Judy Ann Newton. *Racial and Religious Violence in America: A Chronology*. New York: Garland Publishers, 1991.

Noble, Kerry. *Tabernacle of Hate: Why They Bombed Oklahoma City*. Prescott, ON: Voyageur Publications, 1998.

Nunes, Mark. *Cyberspaces of Everyday Life*. Minneapolis: University of Minnesota Press, 2006.

O'Reily, Kenneth. *Racial Matters: The FBI's Secret File on Black America, 1960–1972*. New York: The Free Press, 1989.

Paxton, Robert. *The Anatomy of Fascism*. New York: Vintage, 2005.

Polletta, Francesca. "'Free Spaces' in Collective Action." *Theory and Society* 28 (1999): 1–38.

Rheingold, Howard. *The Virtual Community: Homesteading on the Electronic Frontier*. Reading, MA: Addison-Wesley Publishing Company, 1993.

Sax, Boria. *Animals in the Third Reich: Pets, Scapegoats, and the Holocaust*. New York: Continuum, 2000.

Scott, James. *Domination and the Arts of Resistance*. New Haven CT: Yale University Press, 1990.

———. *Weapons of the Weak: Everyday Forms of Peasant Resistance*. New Haven, CT: Yale University Press, 1985.

Shook, Summer, Wesley Delano, and Robert Balch. "Elohim City: A Participant-Observer Study of a Christian Identity Community." *Nova Religio* 2 (1999): 245–65.

Simi, Pete, and Robert Futrell. "Negotiating White Power Activist Stigma." *Social Problems* 56 (2009): 89–110.

————. "Cyberculture and the Endurance of Radical Racist Activism." *Journal of Political and Military Sociology* 34, no. 1 (Winter 2006): 115–42.

Simi, Pete, Lowell Smith, and Ann Stacey. "From Punk Kids to Public Enemy Number One." *Deviant Behavior: An Interdisciplinary Journal* 29 (2008): 753–74.

Simonelli, Frederick. *American Fuehrer: George Lincoln Rockwell and the American Nazi Party*. Urbana: University of Illinois Press, 1999.

Sims, Patsy. *The Klan*. Lexington: University of Kentucky Press, 1996.

Smith, Brent. *Terrorism in America: Pipe Bombs and Pipe Dreams*. Albany: State University of New York Press, 1994.

Street, John. "Fight the Power: The Politics of Music and the Music of Politics." *Government and Opposition* 38 (2001): 113–30.

Swain, Carol. *The New White Nationalism in America: Its Challenge to Integration*. Cambridge: Cambridge University Press, 2002.

Taylor, Verta. "Emotions and Identity in Women's Self-Help Movements." In *Self, Identity, and Social Movements*, ed. Sheldon Stryker, Timothy J. Owens, and Robert W. White, 271–99. Minneapolis: University of Minnesota Press, 2000.

————. "Social Movement Continuity." *American Sociological Review* 54 (1989): 761–75.

Thapar, Romila. "The Theory of Aryan Race and India: History and Politics." *Social Scientist* 24 (1996): 3–29.

Turkle, Sherry. "Cyberspace and Identity." *Contemporary Sociology* 28 (1999): 643–48.

————. *Life on the Screen: Identity in the Age of the Internet*. New York: Simon & Schuster, 1995.

Virnoche, Mary, and Gary Marx. "Only Connect—E. M. Forster in an Age of Electronic Communication: Computer-Mediated Association and Community Networks." *Sociological Inquiry* 67 (1997): 85–100.

Voss, Kim. "The Collapse of a Social Movement: The Interplay of Mobilizing Structures, Framing, and Political Opportunities in the Knights of Labor." In *Comparative Perspectives on Social Movements*, ed. Doug McAdam, John D. McCarthy, and Mayer N. Zald, 227–60. Cambridge: Cambridge University Press, 1996.

Ware, Vron, and Les Back. *Out of Whiteness: Color, Politics, and Culture*. Chicago: University of Chicago Press, 2002.

Wellman, Barry, and Milena Gulia. "Virtual Communities as Communities." In *Communities in Cyberspace*, ed. M. A. Smith and P. Kollock, 167–94. New York: Routledge, 1998.

Wellman, David. *Portraits of White Racism*. New York: Cambridge University Press, 1993.

West, Cornell. *Democracy Matters: Winning the Fight against Imperialism*. New York: Penguin, 2004.

————. *Race Matters*. New York: Vintage Books, 1994.

Wood, Elisabeth Jean. "The Emotional Benefits of Insurgency in El Salvador." In *Passionate Politics: Emotions and Social Movements*, ed. Jeff Goodwin, James Jasper, and Francesca Polletta. Chicago: University of Chicago Press, 2001.

Wright, Stuart. *Patriots, Politics, and the Oklahoma City Bombing*. Cambridge: Cambridge University Press, 2007.

Zeskind, Leonard, *Blood and Politics: The History of the White Nationalist Movement from the Margins to the Mainstream*. New York: Farrar, Straus and Giroux, 2009.

Index

About the Authors

Pete Simi is associate professor of criminology and criminal justice at the University of Nebraska, Omaha. He has published a number of articles on the white power movement and was awarded a grant from the Department of Justice to study recruitment strategies for white supremacist groups.

Robert Futrell is associate professor of sociology at the University of Nevada, Las Vegas. He has published widely on the white power movement as well as on issues of environmental sustainability in the West.